THE STORY
OF GREECE AND ROME

THE STORY
OF
GREECE AND ROME

Their Growth and Their Legacy to Our Western World

J.C. Robertson, M.A.
and
H.G. Robertson, Ph.D.
Victoria College, University of Toronto

Hillside Education

Copyright © 2016, Hillside Education

Originally published in 1928
by J.M. Dent & Sons Limited.

Cover image: Pompeo Batoni (1708-1787), *Aeneas fleeing Troy*. Galleria Sabauda, Turin, Italy.
Photo credit: Scala / Art Resource, NY

Cover design by Mary Jo Loboda

All images in the text are either from the original book or public domain, courtesy of Wikemedia, unless otherwise noted.

All rights reserved. No part of this publication may be
reproduced in whole or in part, stored in a retrieval system
or transmitted in any form or by any means, electronic,
mechanical, photocopying, recording, or otherwise, without
prior written permission of the publisher.

ISBN: 978-0-9976647-3-7

Hillside Education
475 Bidwell Hill Road
Lake Ariel, PA 18436
www.hillsideeducation.com

Preface

The one justification for producing still another history of Greece and Rome is that it essays to break new ground. It is neither new information, however, that is to be looked for in this book, nor novel theories and new interpretations; but there is an attempt at a new approach, or at least a new emphasis, of which a hint is given in the subtitle and of which more may be read in the Introductory Chapter. The writers have had in mind a reader who desires not merely a narrative that will set forth the leading events and movements in the national life of the Greeks and Romans, but one that will also enable him to understand the nature of the real contribution which these two nations are commonly credited with having made to our present-day western civilization. So treated, the history of the ancient world is seen to be linked with our modern life in a vital and significant unity.

Such a reader might be the average man or woman, attracted by the fame of Greece and Rome and desirous of learning why they have so great a name in the world; or the boy or girl, sufficiently advanced to be preparing for matriculation, for whom something more is desired than a mere textbook containing useful facts for an impending examination. The book is not written for the scholar already quite familiar with the subject; nor, on the other hand, is it written for those who must be entertained if their interest is to be captured and held, or for the "Tom Tullivers" who are devoid of historical imagination. And again the book is not meant for one part only, but equally for all parts of the English-speaking world, for all are equally indebted to Greece and Rome.

The legacy of Greece and Rome is not a new subject; but the books dealing with it are rather for readers of considerable maturity and scholarship, and do not aim at presenting at the same time a connected history of the Greco-Roman world. There are also many excellent school-manuals which are, in effect, condensations of the larger histories; but they tend to give disproportionate space to political and military affairs. They often leave serious gaps just where the national life, both of Greece and of Rome, is merging into the general current of world history; and their pages are often so filled with details that, as our proverb has it, one cannot see the wood for the trees. Instead of offering a 'reduced photograph' of the vast scene revealed by the larger histories, the present writers have sought to assume the selective attitude of an artist, who eliminates or emphasizes in harmony with his particular conception. They have thus omitted or passed lighly over many matters that may be indsputable facts of history, but that cannot be said to have noticeably affected the main course of events in ancient times or to have left any impression upon later ages. This has secured for some other topics more space than is usually given to them, but not more than they deserve, for instance, our enormous debt to the Greeks for science and mathematics; the personality and influence of Socrates; the distinctive qualities of Greek art; and the way in which conditions in the ancient world furthered the spread of Christianity and brought into being the kingdoms of western Europe which grew up out of the Roman empire.

It was a fruitless search for a book so planned that led the writers to undertake their task. They are much more convinced that there is a call for a book of this kind than that they in particular have been called to write it. They feel, however, that they may fairly claim the consideration given to the pioneers in the untried field; and they fortify themselves against misgivings as to their competence for so ambitious an undertaking by recalling the dictum of Dr. Johnson: "Great abilities [said he] are not requisite for an historian; for in historical composition all the greatest powers of the human mind are quiescent. He has facts ready to his hand; so there is no exercise of invention. Imagination is not required in any high degree; only about as much as in the lower kinds of poetry. Some penetration, accuracy, and coloring will fit a man for the task, if he can give the application which is necessary." All this is very reassuirng—provided that there is no flaw in the sagacious Doctor's theory.

Toronto 1927

Editor's Notes on New Edition

We have attempted a faithful reproduction of the original text but have taken advantage of the greater accessibility to images that was not available in the 1920s. Each chapter includes some comprehension questions, but a larger discussion about the events and their ramifications—as well as their relevance to our own times—would be appropriate. There are so many similarities to our own history in these stories. The authors intended to help students understand the foundation and the importance of our western civilization so that they might both better appreciate it as well as work to preserve it.

Since this text offers a broad survey of the history of the Ancient Greeks and the Romans, it would be advisable as well to stop along the way and do further research, filling in the details of any period that you are interested in. The teacher's companion book has suggestions for integrating this work with other sources for this time period, such as Plutarch's *Lives*, works of fiction, and various historical atlases.

Hillside Education, 2016

Contents

	Preface	v
	Editor's Notes on New Edition	vii
I	Introductory	1
II	The Older River-Valley Civilizations	5
III	The Sea Kings Of Crete	11
IV	The Lords of Golden Mycenae	17
V	The Heroic Age of Greece	25
VI	The Gods of Olympus	31
VII	The Dorian Invasion	35
VIII	The Poems of Homer	39
IX	The Expansion of Greece	45
X	The Greek City-State	51
XI	From Kings to Tyrants	59
XII	Sparta and Spartan Discipline	63
XIII	The Early History of Athens	69
XIV	Draco and the Causes of Discontent	73
XV	Solon, the Founder of Democracy	77
XVI	Pisistratus and Cleisthenes	81
XVII	Life in Sixth-Century Greece	85
XVIII	Croesus and Cyrus	95
XIX	The Revolt in Ionia	99
XX	Miltiades And Marathon	103
XXI	Ten Years' Breathing Space	111
XXII	Leonidas and Thermopylae	115
XXIII	Themistocles and Salamis	119
XXIV	The Final Repulse of Persia	125
XXV	The Delian League and the Athenian Empire	131
XXVI	Athens Under Pericles	137
XVII	Fifth-Century Culture	147
XVIII	The Peloponnesian War	159
XXIX	Socrates and His Circle	171
XXX	Epaminondas and Philip	177
XXXI	Alexander and Aristotle	183
XXXII	The Hellenized East	189
XXXIII	Rome and the Roman People	199
XXXIV	Rome under the Kings	203

XXXV	Patricians and Plebeians	209
XXXVI	The Conquest of Italy	215
XXXVII	The Romans of the Early Republic	221
XXXVIII	Rome and Carthage	229
XXXIX	Hannibal	235
XL	The Conquest of the Mediterranean World	241
XLI	The Roman People During the period of Conquest	245
XLII	The Gracchi and the Beginning of the Revolution	251
XLIII	Marius and Sulla	255
XLIV	Pompey and Cicero	261
XLV	Greco-Roman Culture	265
XLVI	Julius Caesar	269
XLVII	Octavian and Antony	275
XLVIII	Augustus and the Principate	279
XLIX	The Successors of Augustus	285
L	Arts and Letters Under the Empire	291
LI	Life in the Roman World	297
LII	Confusion and Reconstruction	309
LIII	The Dissolution of the Empire	315
LIV	Christianity and the Roman Empire	323
	Time-Chart of Greek History	327
	Time-Chart of Roman History	329
	Index	331

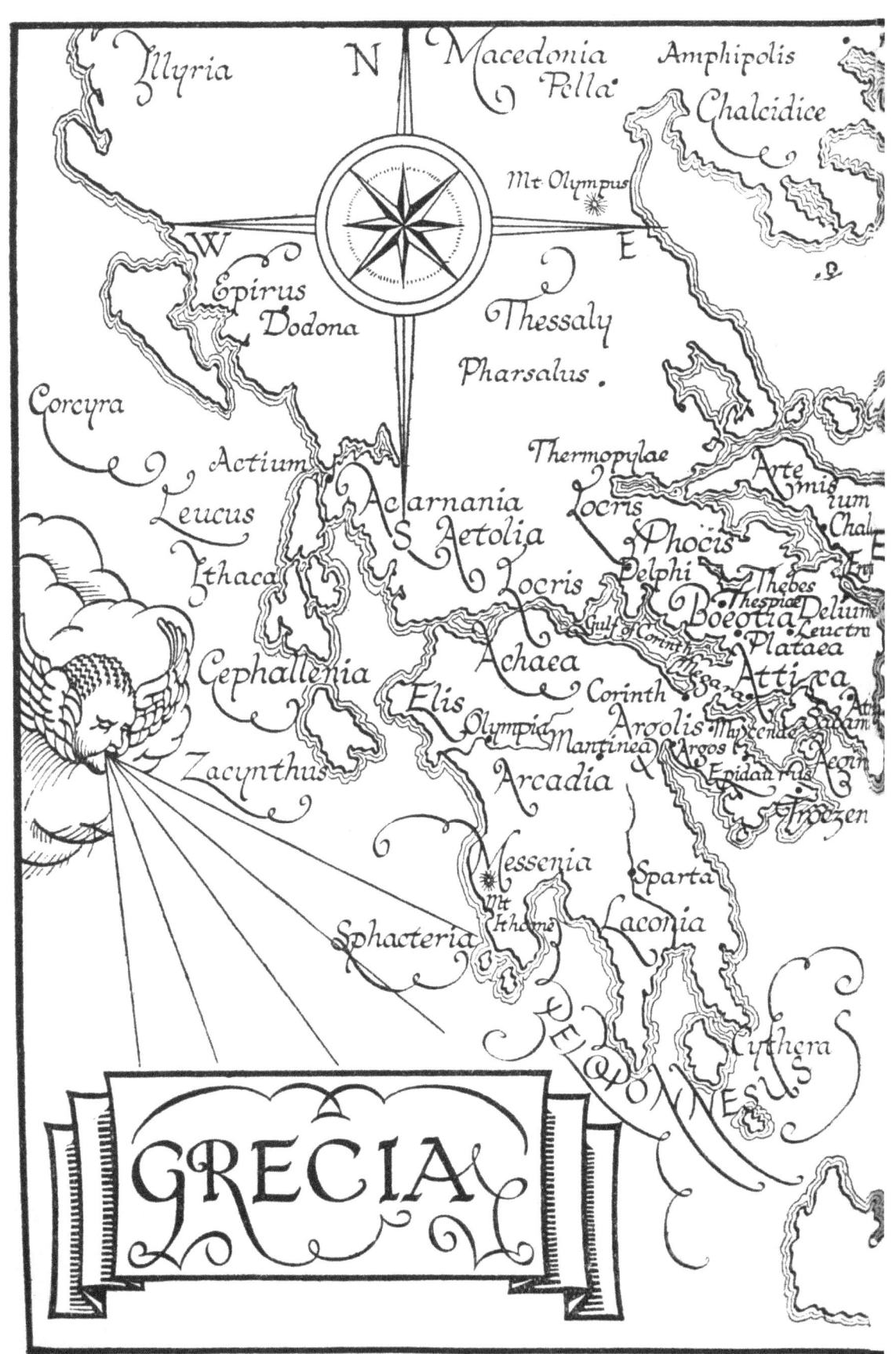

*Not to know
what happened
before you were born
is to remain always
but a child.
For what is man's life
if it is not linked
with the life of earlier generations
by the memory of the past?*

        Cicero.

Chapter I

Introductory

Why should one study the history of Greece and Rome? Why concern ourselves with nations so remote in time and place, and so unlike any people that we find in the world today? Why not study rather the origin and development of Japan or of the United States, with which our relations are, and will continue to be, so close and intimate? It can hardly be on the ground that the events of Greek and Roman history are themselves of transcendent interest; the history of France or of Holland would give us incidents quite as thrilling. And it is certainly not in order that we may model our conduct and our ideals on those of the ancient Greeks and Romans.

Our problem may suggest the still wider question: Why study any history? Why not let bygones be bygones, as some wit has advised, and confine our interest to the present? One reason undoubtedly that many would give for reading British history is that it is the story of the race to which they themselves belong, and that people are always interested in hearing about the doings of their forefathers.

But a little further thought will discover grounds for much more than this sentimental interest in the past. Our world is obviously what it is today because of what earlier generations have made of it and have bequeathed to us. And when we observe how much our own form of civilization differs from that of other races or countries, how we have ways and standards of our own, not merely in speech and appearance and dress, but also in ideals and customs and institutions, it is natural that we should seek to know how it has come about that we think and act and manage our affairs as we do.

And it is not only natural but desirable also. For it is only when we see how our civilization is the outcome of the struggles and aspirations of generation after generation, how it represents the accumulated experience of our race, how, like a coral island in the Pacific, it has been built up, age after age, by the labors and lives of innumerable individuals, that we really understand and appreciate it; and only by understanding our civilization can we be truly said to possess it for our own.

Now that is precisely the chief reason for studying the history of Greece and Rome. It enables us to understand ourselves and our civilization. For while we may have none of the blood of the ancient Greeks or Romans in our veins, yet there is an ancestry of the spirit no less than of the body; and the civilization of the English-speaking world has just as certainly come from the Greeks and Romans as it has from the Celts and Saxons and Normans of the British Isles. Just as the history of England under Elizabeth is our own history, whether we live in Great Britain or in North America or in Australia, so also the history of Rome under Augustus and of Athens under Pericles is our own history, at a still earlier stage.

For if we seek an answer to the question, *How did we get our liberty?*—whether we mean freedom from foreign domination or civil liberty or liberty of thought and speech or if we try to discover where we got our system of education, our law, our municipal government, our democratic institutions, our science, or our literature, we shall find that the search for the beginnings of all these, and of many more such things in our modern life, takes us back to the Greco-Roman civilization of 3000 years ago. We may compare our civilization to a house in which we are living while the house is still being built; a house to which each century makes its own contribution, so that its final appearance no one can predict; but a house of which the Greeks and Romans laid out the ground-plan and built the foundations, and so determined for all time some of its main features.

This, too, should be added: It is not merely the foundations and the beginnings that we owe to Greece and Rome. There are, of course, many things in which they were merely pioneers, and in which the world has long since improved upon their best endeavors. Yet even here they deserve all the credit that rightly goes to the first discoverer, as we honor the inventor of the steam-engine, for example, or the telephone, however much improvement may subsequently have been made. And when we come to know that ancient world, it is a constant source of wonder to realize in how many matters of the first importance they were the pioneers, and laid the enduring foundations on which we are still building. But there are other matters also, especially in the realms of literature and art, where far more was done than merely make a beginning, and where the achievements of those distant ages have remained to the world, ever since, an unchallenged standard of excellence, a perpetual incentive to emulation. Such achievements the greatest among the moderns may now and then hope to equal, but no one thinks of surpassing or superseding them, as no one would dream of our enjoying finer sunsets today than were those of ancient times. Of this sort of thing our great regret is that so much has been irrecoverably lost; that which remains the world counts among its greatest treasures. To be able to understand and appreciate and enjoy such things is itself a liberal education; while to be able to create something worthy of being placed by their side is to secure immortal fame.

Questions

1. What reason do the authors give for studying history in general? (Be sure to give their reason, not your own.)
2. According to the authors, what is so important about the study of Greece and Rome?
3. Explain how the analogy of building of a house is used by the authors to explain development of history. What role do Greece and Rome play in this analogy?

Vocabulary

transcendent
bequeath
aspirations

Relief painting from the tomb of Nakht, 18th Dynasty, Thebes by Norman de Garis Davies, Nina Davies (2-dimensional 1 to 1 Copy of an 15th century BC Picture)

Chapter II

The Older River-Valley Civilizations

When the Greeks and Romans are called the pioneers of our modern civilization, to whom we owe its first beginnings and its foundations, it is not to be understood that before their time mankind was in a purely savage and uncivilized condition. Beyond what we know of the history of even the earliest nations in the world lies a still earlier prehistoric period in which great progress was made, but of which no written record remains. We do not know in what way primitive man learned to domesticate animals and plants and to till the soil; to weave himself garments and build himself dwellings; to make pots of clay, and tools and ornaments of metal or wood; to build boats and to sail them. With varying degrees of proficiency, the discovery and development of these arts are common to the most diverse races of mankind. To that prehistoric period also belong the beginnings of trade and barter; the gathering of men together into villages, cities, and nations; the gradual formation of some kind of law and government. At the earliest period to which the records of any civilized nation take us, all these are already matters of familiar and established usage. We may exercise our imagination to conceive how these things may have come about; but we shall never know.

Moreover, the Greek race did not develop in isolation, uninfluenced by neighboring civilizations. In the valley of the Nile and in the lands watered by the Tigris and the Euphrates were nations that

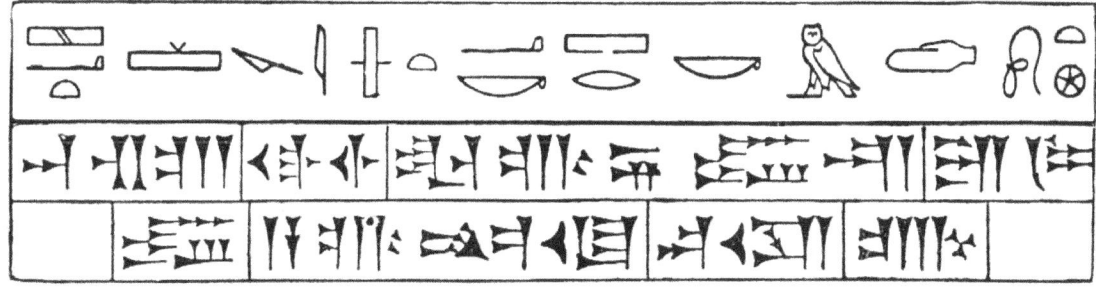

Egyptian Hieroglyphic and Babylonian Cuneiform Writing.

had already had a long history and were highly civilized societies when European history begins. In these two great regions, warm and fertile, easily irrigated, and protected from foreign invasion by great deserts and mountain ranges, the growth of a plenteous and settled way of living was very rapid. Long before 3000 BC, both Egypt and Babylonia were rich, populous, and civilized kingdoms. These great societies, with their highly organized civilization and the wonderful monuments of their progress and power, are among the most impressive examples of enduring stability in human affairs that this world has known. The deciphering of the inscriptions of Egypt and Babylonia in the last few centuries has revealed a continuous history in each of over 3000 years. It is no wonder that when the Greeks began to visit Egypt they were deeply impressed, not merely by its tremendous temples and pyramids, but quite as much by the antiquity of its ordered life; they long remembered the saying of the Egyptian priest to the traveler Solon: 'You Greeks are always children.'

With the history of these two countries, with the story of their wars and changing rulers, their manner of life, and the stages of their development, we have here no concern. It is more important to learn what contribution they made to the civilization of the western world, so that our own life today is in some measure what it is because of what the Egyptians or Babylonians did. There are two other great civilizations of the East, in India and China; civilizations of impressive antiquity and wonderful achievement; and the events of their history are of indisputable interest. But they have not made such an impression on our western world that we have any need to study their civilization in order to understand our own. With Egypt and Babylonia, however, it is different. The Greeks, at the beginning of their history, had among their nearest neighbors these two established civilizations, then fully 3000 years old; and because of what the Greeks learned from them and have passed on to our modern world, Egypt and Babylonia deserve some attention in this study of our origins.

The great Arabian Desert kept these two nations from direct intercourse. But a glance at the map will show that the upper Euphrates leads westwards towards the Mediterranean, and that there is a 'fertile crescent' of habitable lands connecting Egypt with Babylonia by way of Palestine, Syria, and the upper Euphrates highlands. This was the great highway between the two nations for royal couriers, peaceful traders, and hostile armies. It was because Palestine was on this route that the people of Israel became involved in the politics of Egypt and Babylonia, and more than once suffered invasion and conquest. At a point where the caravan route from the East through Damascus came near to the sea, was the country of the Phoenicians, who dwelt north of Palestine in their two cities of Tyre and Sidon. They were of the same great Semitic race to which both Israelites and Babylonians belonged; but they had become chiefly a trading and seafaring people. The forests of Lebanon gave them wood for building ships, and in these they not only carried far and wide their own products, including the famous Tyrian purple, but also served as the middlemen of that ancient world, exchanging Babylonian merchandise for the metals and other forms of wealth of the countries around the Mediterranean. The Egyptians had vessels of their own, and direct access to Egypt was always possible for the Greeks; but it was indirectly, and largely through the Phoenicians, that Greece was in touch with the civilization of Babylonia.

Even before the revelations of Tutankhamen's tomb, our great museums showed how expert the Egyptians were in making jewels, vases, and glass. In all the arts connected with working in gold, with enameling or inlaying, and with the engraving of gems, both Egypt and Babylonia excelled. Many objects of this sort were carried by traders to Greek lands overseas from a very early period, and doubtless helped to form the taste of men less advanced in artistic handiwork. But the most important contributions which these older lands made to the modern world through the medium of Greece were much less tangible and material than objects of art and adornment.

Both nations, but more especially the Babylonians, with their wide expanse of sky, very early became interested in star-gazing, and began to note carefully the positions and movements and changes of the heavenly bodies. Both nations again were conspicuous for the importance which they attached to their religious beliefs and their rites of worship; and as a consequence in both, the priests formed a well-organized class wielding enormous influence. These priests were in possession of the 'wisdom' of their day, and handed on from age to age their inherited knowledge and traditions. And so it came about that the priestly records contained not only the history of the successive sovereigns and dynasties of the past, but also the astronomical observations of many centuries.

The Egyptians used their observations chiefly to enable them to form a calendar and fix the recurring festivals of the year. But the Babylonians did more. They conceived the idea that the movements and changes in the heavens accompany or influence important events in men's lives. If their records showed that an eclipse of the moon occurred on the eve of some great defeat, or that a particular position of some conspicuous star coincided with a victory or with the death of a king, they believed that in the future similar results would follow. And so their study of the stars became a means of predicting the future, and Babylonian astronomy was largely astrology.

Their close scrutiny of the records, however, also revealed other facts that were more than fanciful grounds for superstitious hopes and fears. It was observed that there is a cycle of eighteen years

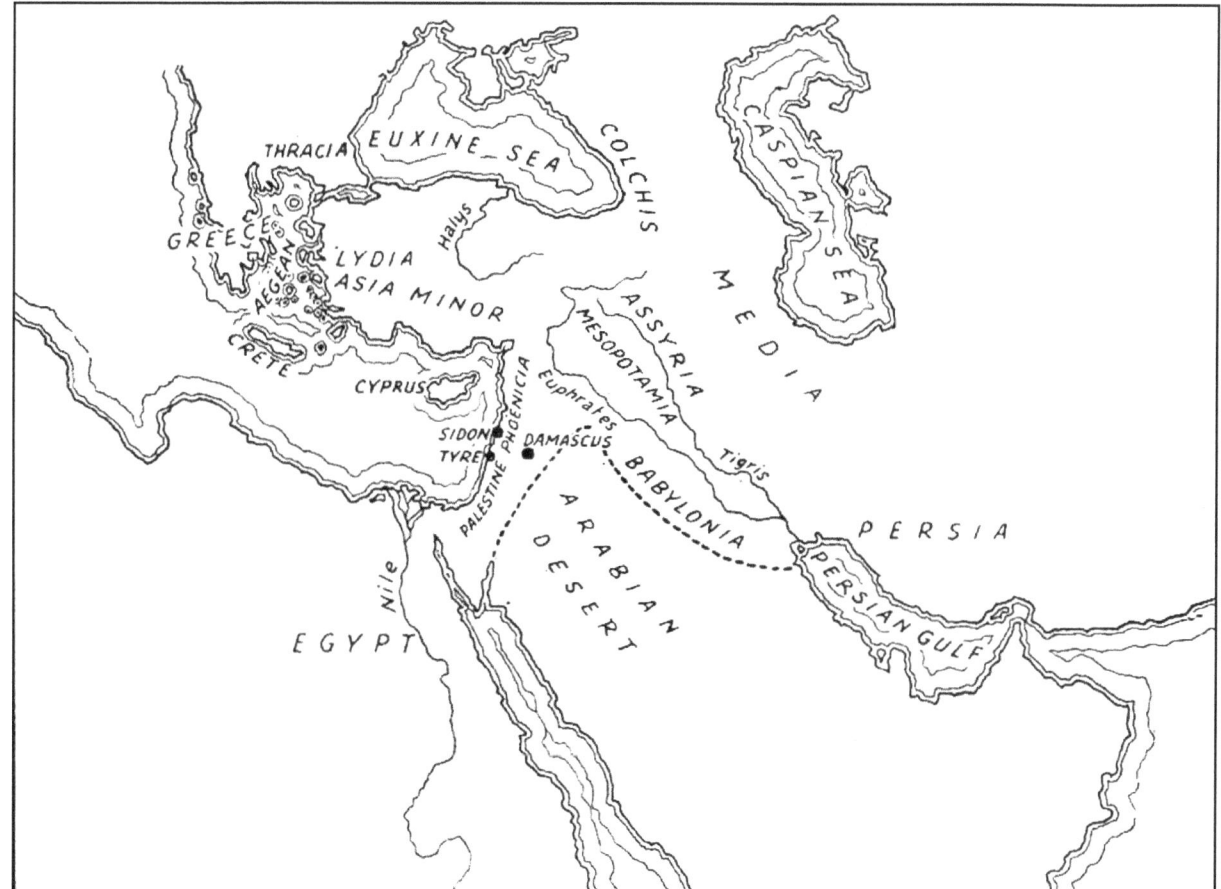

Greece and the Early Empires.

in which eclipses recur in the same order. We know now that this is due to the fact that, after that period of time, the sun, moon, and earth come back to the same relative position, so that the order of eclipses is repeated over and over with each recurring cycle. The Babylonian observers discovered the fact of this recurrence, but they had no idea of the cause, and apparently did not try to discover it. But this knowledge enabled them to predict eclipses with considerable accuracy. This, of course, is not science, but it might become a science, or the foundation of a science, if inquiring minds should begin to seek a reason and an explanation. This further step was left for the Greeks to take.

It is to these Babylonian observers that we owe the division of the stars into the groups we call constellations; in particular, they marked out the twelve signs of the zodiac, and also distinguished the five most conspicuous planets. The Egyptians established the year of 365 days, which they divided into twelve months. A certain proficiency in arithmetic was of course needed for these astronomical calculations and records. Both peoples counted by tens, the number natural to man with his ten fingers. The Babylonians also made considerable use of the unit 60 in their calculations, and hence comes the frequent use of 60 in our own measurement of time and degrees. It was the Babylonians, too, who established the custom of reckoning 360 degrees in a complete circle.

As the Babylonians by observing certain facts laid the foundation for the later Greek science of astronomy, so did the Egyptians for geometry, which as a science we owe to the Greeks. The word geometry means literally land-measuring; and with the Egyptians it was little more than this. Every year it was found that the inundations of the Nile disturbed the boundaries of their fields, and it was necessary to have some way of determining how the lines should run; and, for purposes of taxation also, there was need to be able to measure the area of fields of various shapes. Geometry, in the sense of land-measuring, first arose out of this practical need, and, like all the 'wisdom' of the Egyptians, went no further than a certain practical skill. They were quite satisfied with discovering some method that would yield the desired result and did not inquire into the reason why the method worked. They discovered, for example, that a triangle whose sides are as 3, 4, and 5 will give a right angle: this was something of which they could make practical use, and they were content. It was left for the Greeks to prove, by a process of reasoning, the general principle that in a right-angled triangle the square on the side opposite the right angle is always equal to the sum of the squares on the other two sides; and, further, to prove that the angle in a semicircle is always a right angle. The Egyptian rule can be applied without any particular exercise of the reason and, while useful in practice, has in itself no scientific value. The Greek rules are exact statements of relations that are universally true, and are so reasoned out that the mind can see that they must necessarily be true; in other words, they are scientific.

Practical skill, as a rule, must precede scientific reasoning. Men had to learn by practical experience how to erect buildings and how to till the ground and how to sail a boat, long before there could be a science of architecture or agriculture or navigation. But without scientific reasoning, practical skill soon reaches a limit at which progress ceases. The immense skill shown by the Egyptians in building their pyramids and temples did not appreciably advance between 3000 BC and 1000 BC. Similarly, the Chinese nation, equally expert but equally without science, has made but little progress in thousands of years. The world owes much to the practical knowledge of the Babylonians and Egyptians, which the Greeks acquired from them without the long labor of discovering it for themselves; but it owes much more to the inquiring minds of the Greeks, who, on becoming acquainted with the unscientific wisdom of the East, were not satisfied merely to use it and hand it down as a valuable tradition, but never rested in their effort to account for everything on rational principles, and thus created the scientific point of view.

Finally, the Greeks owed to their neighbors—in this case the Phoenicians—another and still more important debt, the alphabet. The earliest kind of writing among all nations is that wherein each idea is represented by a picture. These pictures may in time become so modified that it is not always easy to detect at a first glance what they represent. The first stage of more or less conventionalized picture-writing is represented by the Egyptian hieroglyphics and the Chinese characters. The next stage is where a picture is used to stand for the sound of the word it originally represented, wherever that sound occurs, as in a modern 'rebus' a picture of the *sea* and the *sun* may stand for *season*. As the number of separate syllables in any language is limited, a much smaller number of signs will suffice than in picture-writing. The Babylonians developed such a syllabary in their cuneiform writing. The third stage is when a sign, instead of being used for the whole syllable, is used for one sound only in that syllable. This still further reduces the number of signs that are required, and here at last we have a true alphabet. The Egyptians went through all three stages, and their inscriptions contain signs that are pictures, others that stand for syllables, and others that represent single sounds.

The Greeks got their alphabet from the Phoenicians, with whom they were continually mingling in trade. The Phoenician alphabet is practically identical with that used by the ancient Hebrews, of which the modern Hebrew letters are conventionalized forms. The order and names of this old Hebrew alphabet, which may be found printed in the 119th Psalm, so closely resemble the order and names of the Greek alphabet that no possible doubt can exist as to the relationship. The Phoenicians, like the Hebrews, wrote from right to left, and the earliest Greek inscriptions that have been found are in the same direction. Very soon the Greeks discovered the advantage of writing from left to right, and they proceeded to reverse their letters. The Roman alphabet, which we use to this day unchanged in our capital letters, and with modifications in our small letters and in our handwriting, was itself developed from a local variety of the Greek alphabet with some additional signs. The modern Russian alphabet is also a slightly modified form of the Greek alphabet.

Where the Phoenicians and the Hebrews got their alphabet is a disputed question. There are some reasons for believing that it may have resulted, from modifying and simplifying certain of the Egyptian signs, but there are also considerable difficulties in the way of this theory. In any case, the derivation of the Greek and other European alphabets from the Phoenician is certain, and in the alphabet we have a striking illustration of the long history that often lies behind some of the commonest things in our present-day civilization.

	A.	B.	E.	M.	P.	R.
Phoenician.	✗	⟨	⟨	⟨	⟩	⟨
Chalcidian Greek.	A	⟨	⟨	M	⟩	⟨
Attic Greek.	A a	B β	E ε	M μ	Π π	P ρ
Classic Roman.	A	B	E	M	P	R

Development of the Alphabet.

Questions

1. Why do the authors feel that we should not study the civilizations of China and India?
2. Name the three older civilizations that contributed to the history of Greece and Rome and describe the most important thing that each civilization contributed.
3. Describe the effects of geography on these civilizations and their ability to influence one another.

Vocabulary

proficiency
deciphering
indisputable
conspicuous

Chapter III

The Sea Kings Of Crete

One of the most famous of the Greek legends tells of the Athenian hero Theseus; how he was brought up by his mother far from Athens and in ignorance of his parentage; and how, on growing to the full strength of youthful manhood, he was sent by her to King Aegeus in Athens; how he met with many adventures on the way, from all of which he emerged triumphant; and how, on reaching Athens, he was discovered to be the king's own son, and was made heir to his throne.

Shortly after, Theseus observed a general sadness on the citizens' faces, and learned that the time was at hand when, to atone for some offence, the Athenians must send to Minos, the mighty king of Crete, the tribute of seven youths and seven maidens to be devoured by the Minotaur. This was a monster, half bull and half man, who fed upon human flesh and for whom a wonderful labyrinth had been constructed in Crete. The story goes on to tell how Theseus insisted on being made one of the doomed company, and how, when he came to Crete, he won the favor of the daughter of Minos, the princess Ariadne, and by her help slew the Minotaur and brought all his companions back in safety to Athens.

This story until very recently was regarded as pure myth; Minos and Theseus were deemed as fabulous almost as the Minotaur itself, mere legendary characters scarcely worth any historian's notice. But the excavations carried on in Crete since 1900 have shown that there is a substratum of truth beneath the legend. The island of Crete, it has been found, was once the seat of a mighty empire, and its civilization, though of shorter duration, was comparable with that of Babylonia or of Egypt, whether we look to the orderliness of its government and the extent of its power, or to the greatness of its resources and the refinement of its life. This civilization, which lasted from about 3000 BC to 1100 BC, is called by some writers Minoan, from the great ruler whom the later Greeks never wholly forgot; others call it the Aegean civilization, from the region over which it extended.

A reference to the map of Greece will show the Aegean Sea thickly studded with islands which are really the tops of the mountains of a submerged land, and closed towards the south by the long island of Crete. Two things are especially to be observed: First, the islands are so close together that it is not easy, in crossing the sea, to get wholly out of sight of land, a matter of great importance to

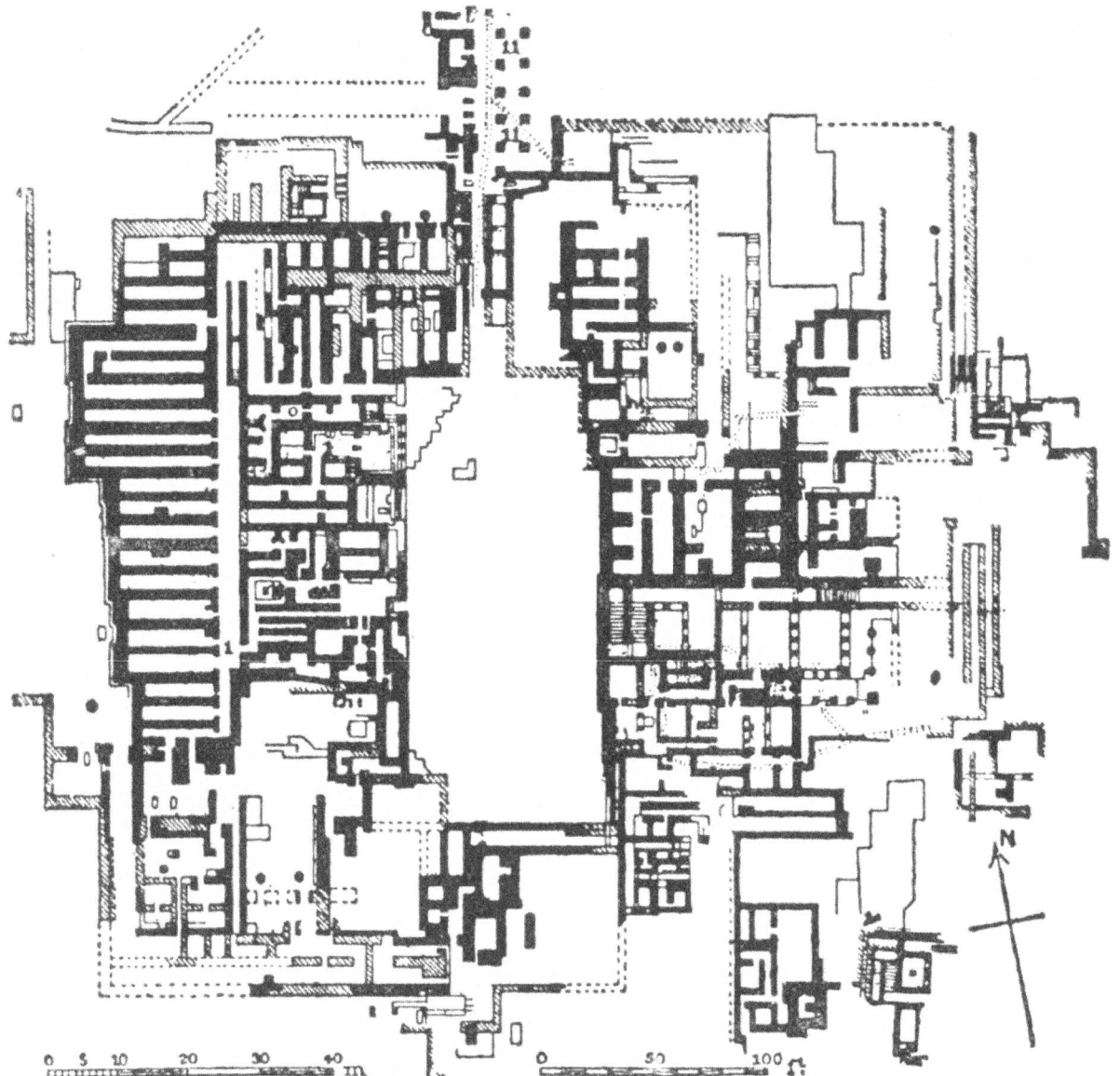

Plan of Palace at Knossus. University Press, Cambridge.

the simple navigators of early days. Secondly, this is the one region where Europe may be said to meet both Asia and Africa, and where we can readily believe that the first European civilization developed. It is a region sufficiently close to Egypt and western Asia for the exchange of wares and ideas, yet sufficiently distant to retain its independence.

The power of Crete was at its height about 1600 BC, when its rulers dwelt in Knossus in a great palace, the ruins of which show that it was the most magnificent royal dwelling that the ancient world knew before the days of the Roman emperors. It was built of blocks of stone, not of sun-dried bricks like the contemporary palaces of Egypt and the Euphrates valley, and in its adornment and its provision for comfort and sanitation it had few rivals until quite modern times. So vast was its extent (it covered five acres and was, in part, four stories high) and so intricate was its plan that we can easily see how the legend of the marvelous labyrinth arose. Vast storerooms or magazines bear witness to the immense revenues derived from trade and tribute. Other palaces existed in Crete,

Corridor at Knossus with Storage Jars. [Wasmuth: 'Altkreta.']

smaller and less magnificent, such as that at Phaestus on the south coast, whence commerce with Egypt was carried on. All the Cretan palaces, unlike the royal castles of medieval Europe, were undefended by walls: a significant fact, for it is evidence of a settled society and of mighty rulers whose fleets could be trusted to keep all enemies at a distance.

In that ancient Mediterranean world piracy was as prevalent as it was in the western seas in the days of the Northmen or the freebooters of the Spanish Main. Of the Norse Vikings Gibbon writes: 'Piracy was the exercise, the trade, the glory and the virtue of the Scandinavian youth. Impatient of a bleak climate and narrow limits, they started from the banquet, grasped their arms, sounded their horn, ascended their vessels and explored every coast that promised either spoil or settlement.' With the exception of the 'bleak climate,' all this was true of the Aegean world; and the suppression of piracy while the Cretan kings ruled the sea was an achievement remembered by

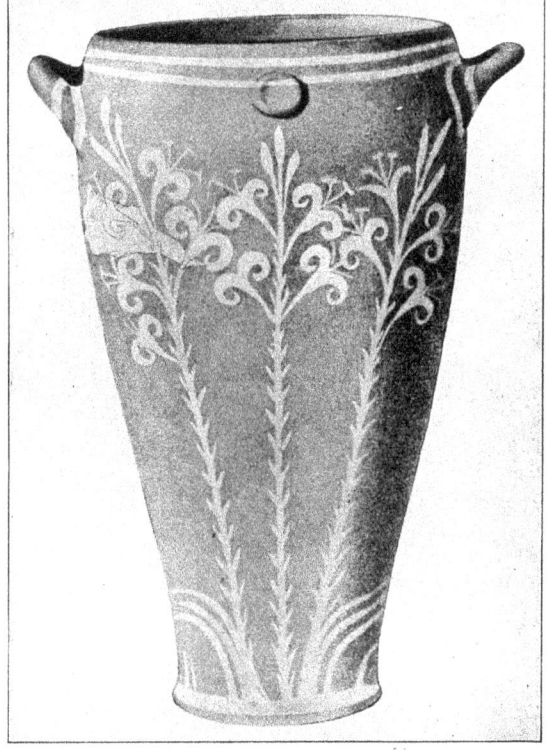

Minoan Vase with Lilies.

Cretan hieroglyphic script: the Disk of Phaistos

the later Greeks when all other record of Cretan history had been lost and piracy was again prevalent.

Of the events of history in this island-civilization even the archaeologists of today, with all their discoveries, can tell us nothing in detail. For, although many inscriptions have been found in the excavations, they are in a script of which no one has yet discovered the key. Thus it is not known even what language the Cretans spoke, but it is generally agreed that the Greek language had not yet been brought into that part of the world. One of the most striking features of this civilization was its development of art; and, even if the inscriptions cannot be read, yet the decorations on pottery and stone vases, the inlaid and engraved work in metal, and especially the remarkable frescoes (paintings on plaster) found on the various palace walls give a very vivid idea of what these Cretans looked like, how they dressed, and what were their amusements and ceremonies. Instead of the simple and graceful draperies of the Greek and Roman women, the dresses of these Cretan court ladies, with the gay patterns of the material and their abundant flounces and embroideries, appear extraordinarily modern, so that their first discovery was greeted with the remark: 'Why, these are Parisian dames!'

The Toreador Fresco, Minoan Crete artifact.

The skill with which, in the best period of Cretan art, the forms of animals and plants were reproduced is beyond all praise both for its truth to nature and for its beauty. In fact, all the art of this Aegean civilization was characterized by a naturalness and a vivacity that form a marked contrast to the stiff and conventional formalism of most Egyptian and Asiatic art. The same qualities are seen in all later Greek art, by which it is not unreasonable to suppose, they may well have been an inheritance from the Minoan period.

One subject that recurs on the frescoes again and again is the sport of 'bull-leaping' to which Crete was as much addicted as Spain is to the bullfight. In this exciting sport the charging bull was met by the athlete, who dodged, seized the bull by the horns, leaped to its neck, and then, gripping its flanks with his hands, turned a somersault and alighted safely on the ground behind the bull,. There is no doubt that the growth of the legend of the Minotaur was in some way connected with the prevalence of bull-leaping and also with the Cretan worship of the bull as a sacred animal, of which there are many evidences. Possibly the athletes were forcibly recruited from subject peoples; and it is also a very reasonable suggestion that the story of Theseus and the Minotaur is an echo of some ancient conflict between the people of Athens and the rulers of Crete, in which the former successfully rebelled against the domination of the latter.

Fresco of Minoan Woman. [Wasmuth: 'Altkreta.']

Questions

1. Name some of the distinctive features of the Minoan civilization.
2. Narrate the legend of the Minotaur and the Labyrinth.

Vocabulary

provision
vivacity
substratum

CHAPTER IV

THE LORDS OF GOLDEN MYCENAE

Thus far the Aegean civilization has been spoken of as belonging to Crete and the other islands where it had developed through long centuries. But by 1600 BC, when Knossus attained the height of its power, there is clear evidence that this civilization was also becoming established on the mainland of Greece, either by conquest or by the peaceful intercourse of trade. There are large bays opening to the south which would be the natural means of approach for Cretan ships, and nearly all the sites on the mainland where evidences have been found of the same art and civilization as flourished in Crete are precisely where we should expect them to be.

On the eastern coast, at the head of the gulf of Argolis, lay a considerable plain from which roads led through the mountain passes into the western interior and also northwards to Corinth, from which one can reach, either by land or by sea, the districts lying north of the gulf. At the junction of these roads was the hill fortress of Mycenae, and by their command of

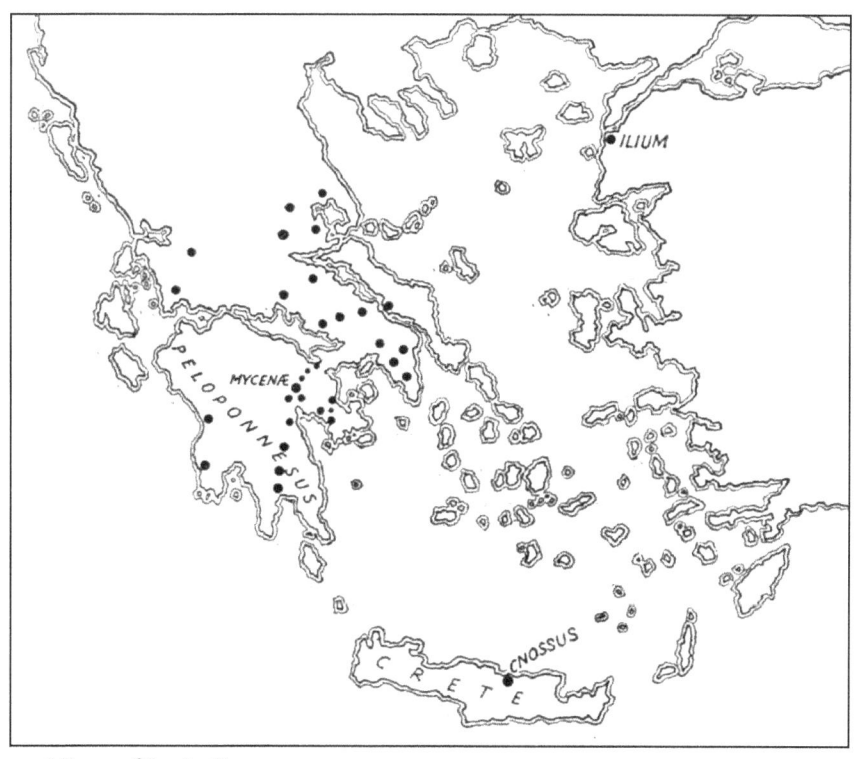

Minoan Sites in Greece.

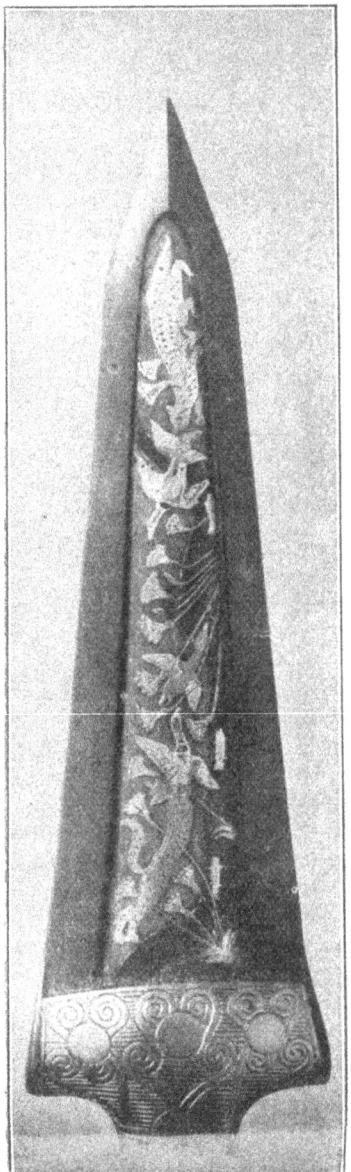 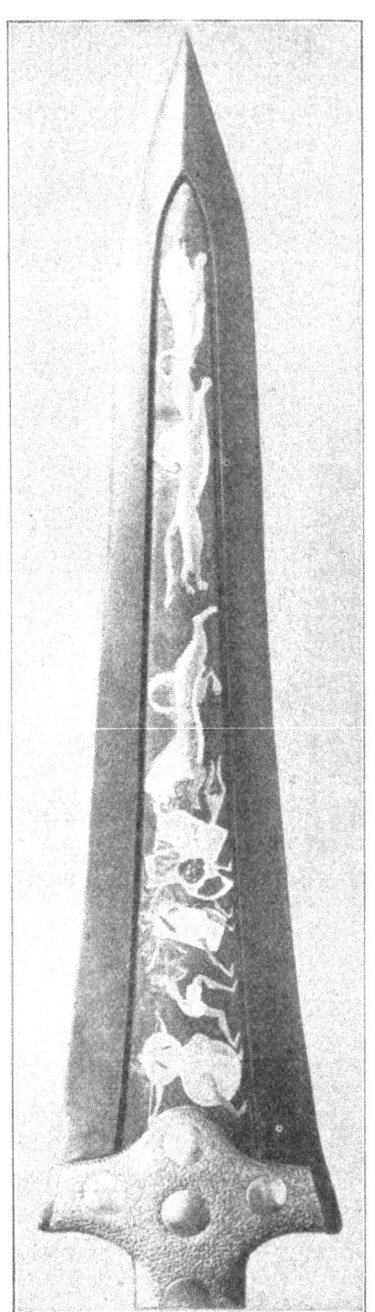

Daggers inlaid with gold from Mycenae. [Wasmuth: 'Altkreta.']

these important trade routes the rulers of Mycenae grew rich and powerful beyond all others on the mainland. In 1875 AD, the explorer Schliemann found six graves of the kings of a dynasty which ruled in Mycenae in the sixteenth century. The graves were rectangular shafts 10 to 30 feet long and nearly square, cut in the solid rock of the hillside. In these were found the undisturbed remains of nineteen royal personages, surrounded by such wealth of gold vessels, gold diadems, bracelets, and other ornaments as has never been discovered in any other ancient site. The faces of some of the kings were covered with portrait masks of beaten gold, and in one grave lay a queen with her baby, whose tiny form was wrapped about with thin sheets of gold. No wonder that 'rich in gold' was the traditional epithet of Mycenae in later ages.

Tiryns, Argolis, Greece: Entrance to a beehive tomb. [Photo credit: Schuppi]

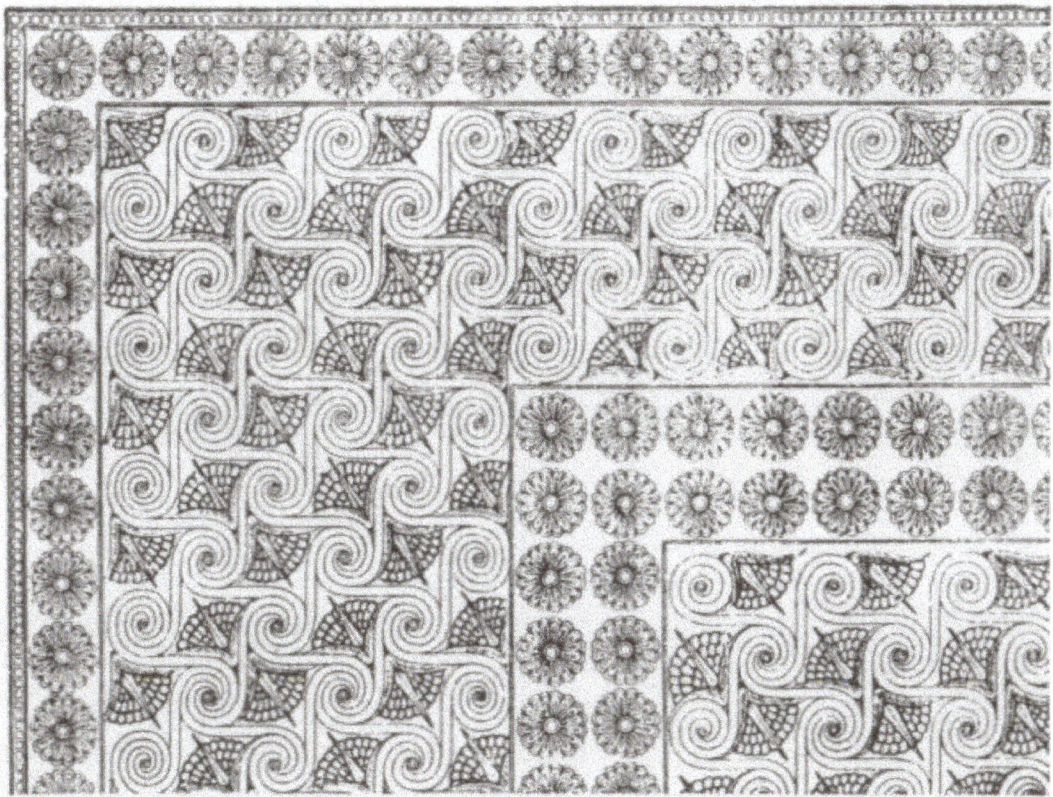

Portion of the Ceiling of a Tomb in Boeotia.

Tiryns fortress, remains of the wall. [Photo Credit Jean Housen]

The Grave Circle A, and the main entrance of the citadel (left), at Mycenae

The fifteenth century BC, however, saw a new dynasty reigning in Mycenae, which buried its dead not in shaft-graves but in beehive tombs. These were dome-like chambers hollowed in the side of a hill and lined with layers of hewn stones. Tombs of this sort have been found at various points both in the Peloponnesus and in Boeotia, showing the widespread influence of this new power.

At the close of this century, about 1400 BC, the palaces at Knossus and older Cretan cities were pillaged and burned, and though rebuilt in part, they never regained their former magnificence. What enemies or rebels worked this destruction is unknown; tradition is silent, and any records that exist cannot yet be deciphered. Cretan civilization was not destroyed, but after such a catastrophe it made no further progress, and henceforth the political supremacy of Knossus disappeared. For the next two centuries Mycenae became the dominating power, both on the mainland and in the Aegean.

The stronghold of Mycenae was now enlarged and defended by walls of immense strength. Apparently, in the more disturbed condition of the country, stronger defenses were necessary against actual or possible enemies, and, in any case, a mainland palace could not, like that at Knossus, rely solely on the protection of a fleet. In the rebuilding of the citadel, the shaft-graves of the earlier rulers were covered over, not to be seen again by the eye of man for more than 3000 years. In the side of a hill close by, one of the kings of Mycenae of this period built for himself a splendid domed tomb 50 feet high, which is still standing practically intact except for the bronze ornamentation of the interior walls.

On the plain a few miles away, near the head of the gulf, was a low eminence known as Tiryns. This had long been strongly fortified and was probably the dominant city of the plain prior to Mycenae. With the transfer of power to Mycenae, it now served as an outpost: to guard the approach from the sea. Enough of the walls of Tiryns still remain to amaze the visitor with their strength. They are from 30 to 40 feet thick, and were originally 50 feet in height; they were built of irregular blocks of roughly dressed stones of enormous size, with the interstices filled with smaller stones. The Greeks of a later day could so little believe that any human hands had built these walls that they called them 'Cyclopean,' from a fabled race of giants. On the walls of the living-rooms in the heart of this fortress, frescoes have been found, identical in style and subject with those which adorned the palace at Knossus, showing that, though the center of political power had shifted, the Mycenaeans preserved and carried on the civilization of Crete. Both at Mycenae and at Tiryns the fortified area is too small to contain a large population; evidently the great mass of the people lived outside the walls.

The power of Mycenae extended even farther than that of Crete, especially on the mainland of Greece; and commerce made Mycenaean products known on every coast of the Aegean and even beyond to Cyprus on the east and Sicily on the west. Of the history of the powerful dynasty that built the massive defenses of Tiryns and Mycenae nothing is known, and on the question of its probable origin and race the conjectures of the authorities are not agreed. But by the thirteenth century there is good reason to believe that the rulers in the cities of the Mycenaean dominion were a Greek-speaking people who had come from the north and whom the earliest Greek writings called Achaeans. Later tradition had many stories of the coming, about this time, of various strangers and adventurers to Greece. Among these was Pelops, from whom the southern peninsula came to be called the Peloponnesus or Pelops' island. The descendants of Pelops reigned in Mycenae and became the overlords of many other Achaean princes who ruled in the various strongholds of

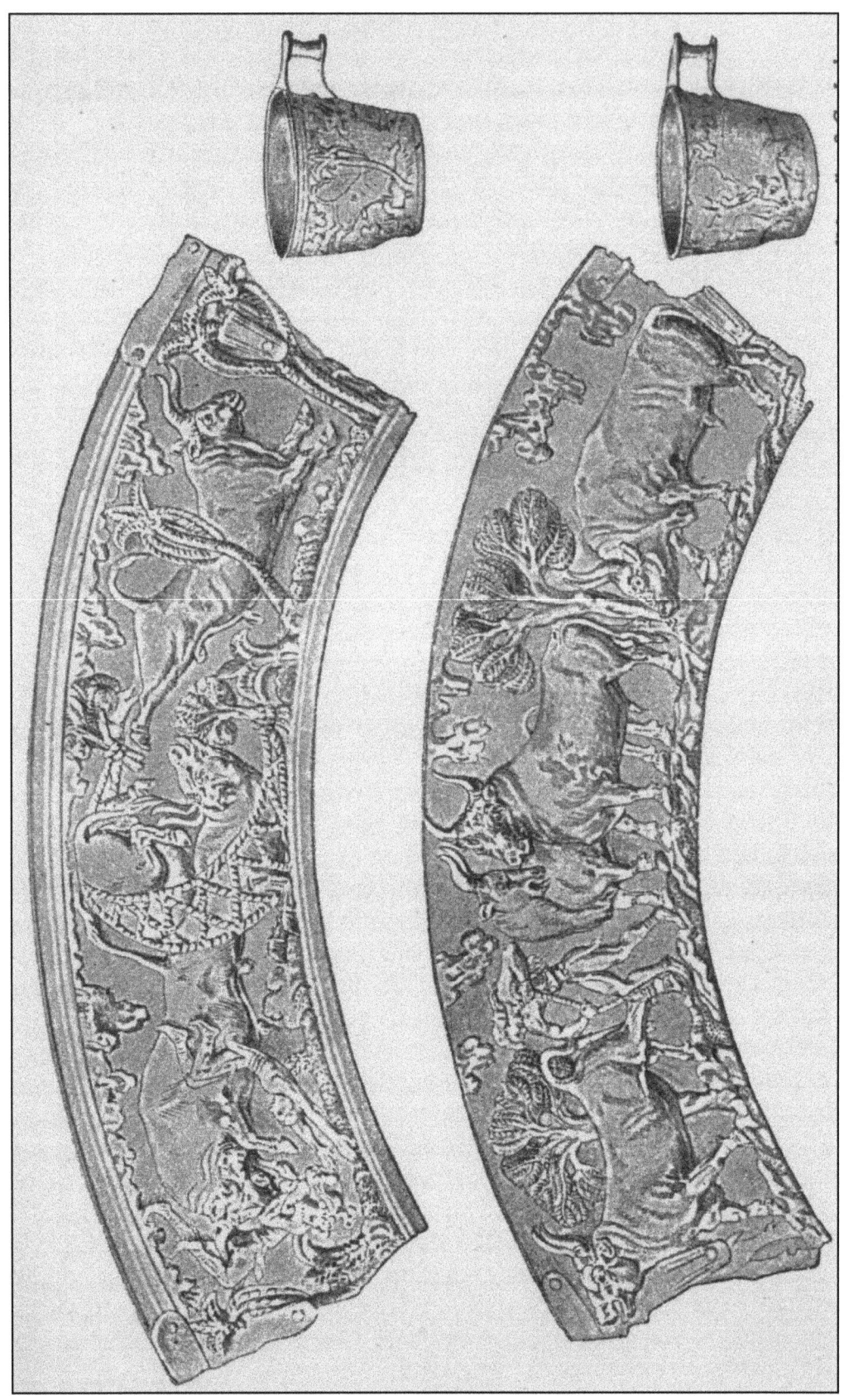

Gold Cups from a Beehive Tomb in Laconia. [Macmillan & Co. Ltd.]

Greece. The coming of these Achaeans was one, perhaps the first, of a series of waves of invasion and conquest by the people whom we know as Greeks, but who called themselves Hellenes.

Practically all the languages spoken in Europe are descended from the language spoken originally by a great white race which thousands of years ago dwelt somewhere in the central plains of eastern Europe. They were a pastoral people who had also made some progress in agricultural life. Groups of this race from time to time made their way southwards into more attractive districts, and not only penetrated the peninsulas of Greece and Italy and the countries of western Europe, but also crossed into Asia Minor and, still farther east, entered Persia and India. Into all these lands they brought their language, which is commonly known as Indo-European. This language was in many cases adopted by the various tribes with whom they came in contact, so that we must not assume that all the nations speaking the Indo-European languages are themselves akin. These migrations covered many centuries, and as the different migrating groups in time completely lost touch with one another, variations arose that have made the Indo-European languages seem so distinct that only within the last century have scholars learned to recognize and understand their relationship.

One division of this race made up of Greek-speaking tribes had long been resident in the central Balkan countries and westwards along the Adriatic. By the fourteenth century the Achaean vanguard had reached the Peloponnesus, and there came in contact with a more advanced civilization than their own, that of the Mycenaeans. They did not come in overwhelming numbers, apparently; it was rather by their superior military skill and their personal abilities that the Achaean chieftains established their supremacy in the chief Aegean centers, somewhat after the fashion of the Norman knights who crossed over into England. But so superior was the Mycenaean culture to anything the Achaeans had known, that they at once adopted it, and the coming of these new rulers, unlike that of the Normans into England, made no great difference in the art and customs of the land. The Mycenaean civilization seems to have had a continuous development from the sixteenth to the end of the twelfth century B.C., and then it abruptly ceases and completely disappears. The rule of the Achaeans comes to an end, and the excavators find that Mycenae and Tiryns with others of their strongholds were destroyed by fire.

Questions

1. Where was the Mycenae civilization located?
2. Describe the fortress at Tiryns.
3. What was the effect of the arrival of people from the north on the civilization of the Mycenae?

Vocabulary

citadel
eminence (see context)
pastoral

Chapter V

The Heroic Age of Greece

All nations seem to have tales and legends of their founders and early heroes. The Greek legends are unsurpassed for their number and their interest, and the Greek writers who tell these legends have had such an influence on all subsequent European literature that the Greek heroes, such as Achilles, Theseus, Odysseus, Perseus, Hercules, and Oedipus, have become part of the whole world's inheritance. The most famous of all these stories is that of the Trojan War, the conflict between the Achaean princes of Greece and the city of Troy in Asia Minor. But there are many others second only to this in interest and fame, most of them telling the exploits and adventures either of the heroes of the Trojan War or of the two or three generations immediately preceding. As the fall of Troy is placed shortly after 1200 BC, the thirteenth century may be called the heroic age of Greece, if we remember that we are dealing not with sober matter of fact, but with an imaginative record which has completely transfigured what may in many cases have been real events in the lives of real people.

One such story, for example, is that of Jason, prince of Iolcus in Thessaly, who conceived the project of sailing to the Far East into the unknown Euxine (or Black) Sea in search of a marvelous golden fleece. So he had built for himself a famous ship, the *Argo,* and collected a company of the noblest youth of the whole land to join him in his adventure. The Argonauts, as these young princes were called, came after many hazards to Colchis, the land of the Golden Fleece. How the fleece came to be there is another story; but, being there, it was guarded by a fire-breathing dragon, which Jason must first destroy, as well as pass certain other apparently impossible tests imposed by the king of Colchis. In all these he was successful, through the secret advice given by Medea, who was a sorceress as well as the daughter of the king; and thus finally he was able to carry off both the coveted treasure and the enamored princess. How they did *not* live happily ever after is also another story. Doubtless this legend with all its fairy-tale incidents rests upon some ancient memory of an early attempt by the Achaeans to penetrate hitherto unsailed seas in search of gold or other treasure. Many others of these legends are based upon the first seizure of power in Greece by the Achaean adventurers or upon their exploration of the Aegean world into which they were newly come.

The story of the Trojan War deserves a longer reference because of the unique place it has, not only in Greek and Roman writings but in modern literature as well. The city of Troy, according to tradition, was built on a hill near the entrance to the Hellespont (the Dardanelles), and here, some one-hundred years ago, its walls were laid bare by modern explorers. It was a strong citadel 600 feet in diameter, with well-built lofty walls strengthened by towers, a place so strong that one can understand how in the end it could be taken only by stratagem and not by force. The district around it was called the *Troad*, the land of the Trojans; the city itself bore the name *Ilios* (in Latin *Ilium)*, but it was also often called *Troia,* that is, the Trojan city. These Trojans were really a branch of the same Greek-speaking race as the Achaeans. They were part of certain tribes called Phrygian and Dardanian which had crossed over from Europe many years before and now held all the north-western portion of Asia Minor. Troy never formed part of the Cretan or the Mycenaean dominion, but it had commercial relations with the Aegean peoples.

According to the ancient story, the war was caused by a visit of Paris, the handsome son of Priam, king of Troy, to Lacedaemon in the land of the Achaeans. Here he induced the wife of King Menelaus, Helen, the loveliest woman in all Greece, to flee with him to Troy. Agamemnon, king of Mycenae, was the brother of Menelaus and espoused his quarrel. He called together the Achaean

Vase Painting. Achilles and Ajax playing draughts. [F. Bruchmann, Munich.]

The Walls of Troy, Hisarlik, Turkey. [Photo credit: Cherry X.]

chieftains from all parts of Greece, notably Achilles, the greatest warrior of them all, from Thessaly, and Odysseus (or Ulysses) from the island of Illiaca off the west coast, with Ajax and Diomedes and Nestor and many others. The expedition mustered at Aulis and then set sail in a thousand ships and more for Troy. Here they encamped on the plain, and many battles took place between the two armies. Priam in his turn had summoned to his aid his neighbors and kinsmen on both sides of the straits; his staunchest warrior was his own son Hector. The city was not regularly invested (the king of the city did not have vassals who were bound to render service in time of war); such was not the character of Greek warfare in those days. Yet, as in the feudal times of medieval Europe, the common soldier counted for little; the main interest and the real decision lay in the combats of individual warriors of noble blood, fully equipped with helmet, breastplate, and greaves, and armed, with spear or bow, and sword. These fought on foot or from chariots, never on horseback like the medieval knight.

For many years, so the story ran, the war lasted with neither side victorious. Hector was slain by Achilles, and Achilles himself afterwards met his death from an arrow shot by Paris. At last a stratagem, devised by Odysseus, accomplished what ten years of warring in the plain could not effect. A huge wooden horse was constructed and on some pretext was got into the city. At dead of night a few Greek warriors concealed within it issued forth and opened the gates to their comrades. The city was given to the flames, its defenders slain, and its women and children carried off captive into slavery.

The story did not end here. The return of the victors was the subject of many tales, especially the long wanderings and amazing adventures of Odysseus before he reached his island home and his faithful wife Penelope, and the tragic fate of Agamemnon, who returned triumphant, only to be slain by his faithless wife Clytemnestra.

Since the discovery on the traditional site of Troy of a walled city which had been destroyed by fire, and which, as the remains show, belonged to the same period as that of the Achaeans, few, if any, historians any longer doubt the reality of the siege of Troy. But there is lack of agreement as to the cause of the war. No doubt in that warlike age the abduction of a queen is credible enough, as is also the seeking of revenge by the aggrieved persons. But it would seem that something greater was at stake to account for so striking a feature as two strong confederacies confronting each other, one representing Achaean Greece and the other the coast of Asia Minor. The Greeks always regarded this as the first of the great conflicts in history between Europe and Asia. Two suggestions have been offered: one, that the war arose out of a commercial dispute over the control of the traffic between the Aegean and Euxine Seas. Troy was in a position to command this important trade route, and the Greeks may have been seeking to destroy its power of interference. The other explanation is that the war came about from a concerted attempt on the part of the Achaeans to extend their settlements to Asia Minor, a project naturally resisted by a combination of the tribes already in possession.

Questions

1. According to the stories, what was the cause of the Trojan war?
2. Where is Troy?
3. What race of people lived in Troy? How were they similar to the Achaens? How Different?
4. How was warfare conducted at this time?
5. Was the battle of Troy a real historical battle? How do we know this?

Vocabulary

citadel
stratagem
espoused
invested
conciliate

Athena, godess of wisdom and war. "Athena Mattéi" housed at the Louvre.

Chapter VI

The Gods of Olympus

One result of the coming of the Achaean Greeks into contact with the Aegean people was a blending of their religious beliefs. Most primitive races seek by rites and sacrifices to conciliate the powers of nature and the spirits of the dead, which they fear will, if unfriendly, do them harm. Many of these beliefs and superstitions persisted into historical times, and indeed have not wholly disappeared even yet in the Mediterranean countries. But in the Greek literature that has come down to us, they are much less in evidence than the worship of the Olympian gods, which in many ways is of a quite different character.

In the first place, these gods of the Greeks were not vague mysterious powers, but individuals with distinct characters, as vividly conceived as any human persons. They are more powerful than human beings and are immortal; but in other respects they are very human. They are subject to the feelings and passions of mortals; they are moved to anger and sorrow; they may be inspired by love or hate; they argue and quarrel; and they conspire among themselves or seek to thwart one another's purposes. These 'aristocrats of the universe' are too much like mankind to be perfect in goodness or purity of character, yet they are always on the side of right dealing and faithful performance of duty. Evil may come to man from their displeasure, but on the whole they are friendly and beneficent powers; there is no evil spirit among them, no Satanic power that leads man to sin and destruction.

The gods dwelt together in ease, enjoying not only the sweet savor of the sacrifices men offered to them but also 'ambrosia and nectar,' the especial food of the gods. Their home was in the unseen *aether* on the heights of Mount Olympus, whose snow-capped peaks were visible over most of northern Greece. The Achaeans continued to ascribe this local habitation to the gods when they brought their worship with them from their earlier northern home; but after they spread over all Greece and the Aegean, their gods gained a universality which the tribal gods of the ancient world generally lacked. The Olympian gods were the gods of the whole earth, whose power and interest were everywhere displayed, and not confined to the Greeks. No priests were necessary in the worship of these gods; any man might offer prayer and sacrifice to them, or, on behalf of the whole city or tribe, its king or chieftain.

Mt. Olympus, the legendary home of the ancient Greek Gods. It is the highest mountain in Greece and the second highest mountain in the Balkans. It is located in the Olympus Range on the border between Thessaly and Macedonia. Mount Olympus has 52 peaks, deep gorges, and exceptional biodiversity. The highest peak Mytikas, meaning "nose", rises to 2,918 metres (9,573 ft). [Photo credit: Athanasios Benisis]

Priests were always of secondary importance in Greece and were mainly concerned with the due observance of some local ritual. Soothsayers who could predict the future by various signs were held in more regard, than the priesthood.

The powers and prerogatives of the various Olympian gods were distinctly different. Foremost of all was Zeus, 'father of gods and men,' who ruled among the other gods as a patriarch over his household or an Achaean overlord among the other princes. He was the lord of the sky and the wielder of the thunderbolt, a conception which, like his name, was part of the Indo-European inheritance of the whole Greek race. To the Greeks, Zeus was also the god who protected the institutions of society and more particularly the right of the stranger to hospitality.

According to the Greek legend, Zeus and his two brothers divided amongst them the sovereignty of the world. Zeus took the sky and the upper world; Poseidon, 'the earth-shaker,' became lord of the sea; and Pluto, who was also called Hades (the unseen one), ruled over the underworld where are gathered all the dead. To Hera, as the consort of Zeus, belonged the safeguarding of the rites and sanctities of marriage.

Apollo was the god of prophecy and of music and also the god of healing and purification, the use of the chant or incantation being the connecting link. Artemis, his sister, 'queen and huntress chaste and fair,' was the goddess of the woodlands and of all wild things. It was a later development that regarded the former of these two as the god of the sun and the lord of light, and the latter as the moon-goddess.

Athena was preeminently the goddess of intelligence and prudent counsel, and therefore presided over skilled handicrafts. She was also a warrior goddess, but represented the courage of disciplined intelligence, defending the ordered ways of life, while Ares, the god of war, represented merely the fury of battle and delight in carnage, and therefore, except for an occasional appearance in poetry, was little regarded among the Greeks.

Hermes is best known as the messenger and herald of Zeus, the intermediary between gods and men, who also conducts the souls of the departed to the realm of Hades. He was the god not merely of heralds but of all wayfarers, and therefore especially of traders and merchants.

Demeter, or Mother Earth, the goddess of agriculture, had a beautiful daughter Persephone (Proserpine) who was carried off by Pluto, the god of the underworld. The mother after long wanderings found her daughter, who was thenceforward allowed to spend half the year with her mother in the upper world, while for the rest of the year she reigned as queen of the realm of Hades. The story is obviously an allegory of the alternate disappearance and rebirth of vegetation, the death of winter and the resurrection of the springtime, and is a good example of the way in which the Greek mythology dramatized and personified the operations and the aspects of nature.

Aphrodite, the goddess of love and beauty, had her chief seat of worship in the southern islands of Cyprus and Cythera, and, while always regarded by the Greeks as one of the Olympians and daughter of Zeus, seems to have been of Aegean or even ultimately of Asiatic origin.

Hephaestus, the lame god of fire, was the god of metal-working and the patron of all smiths. He, too, was not originally a Greek god, and he alone of all the Olympians had any physical deformity. The others were as superior to mortals in physical perfection as in power and length of life.

The names of some of the Olympians would seem to indicate that they were not brought by the Achaeans from their northern home, but were adopted by them from the people of the Aegean. Also the story that there was an earlier race of gods, and that before Zeus his father Cronus reigned until he was dethroned by Zeus, is very probably an echo of the change by which the Olympian deities of the Achaean newcomers displaced the gods of the earlier Aegean race.

Not all these gods were of equal importance. Zeus, Apollo, and Athena stand out as conspicuously the most important. But all twelve are found in the oldest Greek writings that we possess and in the literature of every succeeding period. [1]

When the Romans, centuries later, became acquainted with Greek literature, their writers proceeded to identify these Greek divinities with the nearest analogues among their own gods, and in retelling Greek stories or translating Greek poetry, would replace Zeus by Jupiter, Hera and Athena by Juno and Minerva, Ares by Mars, and so on, although the correspondence in character and attribute was often very inexact. It is these Roman names, as a rule, rather than the Greek, that our English writers have made familiar to us. But in dealing with Greek art or literature or religion it is better to retain the Greek names.

---

[1] Hestia, the goddess of the fireside and the home, is not mentioned in Homer, but is generally counted in later times as one of the twelve Olympian deities. Pluto, of course, was never thought of in connection with Olympus.

Questions

1. Describe the characteristics of the Greek gods.
2. What is lacking among the Olympian gods?
3. According to Greek mythology, where does evil come from?
4. What was the role of priests among the Greeks?
5. Name the twelve most important gods of the Greeks and, if possible, what they were in charge of.

Vocabulary

conciliate
incantation
analogues

Chapter VII

The Dorian Invasion

Whatever it was that the Achaeans had hoped to gain from the destruction of Troy, they did not long enjoy the fruits of their victory. Before the twelfth century was closed, they had been dispossessed of their sovereignty in Greece, and were fleeing before the superior strength of a new enemy. From the north country there came down in increasing numbers another portion of the Greek-speaking race, but with no feeling in its heart of kinship and sympathy. Taking several generations to occupy the land, they came like the Anglo-Saxons into Roman Britain, completely destroying the earlier civilization of the land they came in to possess, that Mycenaean civilization which the Achaeans had found glory and satisfaction in adopting. Why so strong an antagonism should exist between two branches of the same race is quite unknown. It will be seen in the sequel that the feeling was deep-seated and persistent, and was a factor in the downfall of the Greek nation.

The invaders are generally spoken of as the Dorians, but the Dorians were really only one of three divisions or tribes, more or less closely allied. Of these one division entered Thessaly, as it was afterwards called from their name, conquered it and made serfs of the earlier inhabitants. A portion of this group of invaders, after making their way into Thessaly, moved south into Boeotia and overwhelmed the Mycenaean civilization which had flourished there. The second division, the Aetolians, passed down the west coast and occupied it, while some of them crossed into the Peloponnesus and seized the district afterwards known as Elis. The third division, comprising the Dorians proper, took possession of Corinth, Argolis, and the whole eastern half of the Peloponnesus.

The superiority of the invaders was not due solely to their numbers or their greater military spirit. They had the advantage also of better weapons. The tools and weapons of the Achaeans and indeed of the whole Minoan and Mycenaean period had been made of bronze. Iron was beginning to be known, but was rare and costly, being much harder to extract from the ore and to work. But the Bronze Age was now passing into the Iron Age, as larger deposits were being discovered and worked, first in Asia Minor and afterwards in northern Greece. The Dorian invasion, which destroyed so much, may perhaps have one thing to its credit, the increased use of iron.

In the Peloponnesus, Mycenae and Tiryns were destroyed, and Argos became henceforward the chief city of Argolis. The conquering Dorians moved on into the plain of Laconia, overthrew the Achaean strongholds there and established the city afterwards to be known to fame as Sparta. As in Thessaly, so in Laconia, the great mass of the people were made serfs. Of the Achaean ruling class, some took refuge in the highlands of Arcadia, which the Dorians were never able to conquer; others crowded into Attica, which the invasion had left undisturbed. But Attica had little room for an increase of population, and large numbers went overseas and found new homes along the coast of Asia Minor and on the adjacent islands.

This was by no means the beginning of the Greek settlements on the eastern side of the Aegean. The same movement which had brought the Achaeans into the Peloponnesus and then to the Aegean islands, had led them naturally to the opposite coast, and even before the Dorian invasion. Lesbos and the most northerly section of the Asiatic coast had been taken possession of by settlers from Thessaly and Boeotia, while others were filtering into the cities lying along the coast farther south. But the Dorian invasion gave the movement new impetus, and before long, settlers from Attica and the Peloponnesus occupied the rich central portion of the coast, where afterwards flourished some of the most important cities of the Greek world (Ephesus, Miletus, Smyrna).

As the invaders were divided into three groups speaking closely allied dialects of Greek (Thessalian, Aetolian, and Dorian), so too the pre-Dorian Greeks, whom we have called by the common name of Achaeans, developed differences of dialect. These dialects were called Aeolic, spoken in Thessaly and Boeotia, Arcadian, and Ionic, which included Attic. This led to the coast of Asia Minor being called in its northern part Aeolis, and in its central part Ionia. Later some of the victorious Dorians in their turn crossed by way of Crete to the south-western corner of Asia Minor, which henceforth, bore the name Doris.

This process of invasion and overseas settlement was a long, slow, steady movement which it took many generations to complete. The final readjustment of population was not reached much before the end of the ninth century BC; but by that time the main divisions of the Greek world about the Aegean were fixed as they were to remain for centuries.

Virtually nothing is known of the history of any part of the Greek world at this period. This fact, combined with the confusion, of the times and the decline of civilization, has led to the term 'the Dark Age' being applied to these first centuries of the Iron Age. The opening of the new age must, indeed, have seemed, as the ancients believed, a change for the worse. Yet out of the troubled darkness which shrouded the transition from the age of Bronze to that of Iron, came at last the wonderful renaissance which produced the art and literature of classical Greece. All that had gone before was preparing the way for the brighter days to come.

Questions

1. What were the three groups that came southward and invaded and settled in Greece?
2. What factors gave them a superiority over the Achaeans?
3. What were the results of their invasion?
4. Why is this period called the Dark Ages?

Vocabulary

impetus
renaissance

Engraved frontispiece of a 1660 edition of Homer's The Iliad translated into English by John Ogilby.

Chapter VIII

The Poems of Homer

Besides preparing for a rebirth of civilization, the centuries of the Dark Age are marked by one actual achievement of the highest importance—the Homeric poems. In the palaces of the Achaean rulers of Greece a regular feature had been the presence of the bard, who recounted the deeds of the heroes of the race and sang the glories of the prince's ancestors. This practice was apparently continued in the new homes established in Aeolis and Ionia, in which fond memory kept alive for generations the story of the life lived in the palaces across the sea. Out of the many songs and poems so composed emerged the two epics that have come down to us under the name of Homer's *Iliad* and *Odyssey*. Neither poem attempts to tell the whole story of the Trojan War, but both have that war for their background. The *Iliad* tells of an incident which occupied a few days only in the tenth year of the war; the *Odyssey* deals with events which occurred many years after the war and far from Troy, but which were an outcome of the war.

The genius of Homer, whom all subsequent great poets of Europe ungrudgingly acknowledge to be their master, his ability

Bust of Homer, hellenistic period. Modern copy after an original in the National Archeological Museum of Naples

Priam begs Achilles for the body of Hector by Bertel Thorvaldsen, 1815.

to tell a thrilling story with equal simplicity and dignity, the appeal his characters and incidents make to the universal, human heart, together with the mingled beauty and naturalness of his diction and the glorious movement of his metre—all combine to make the first important production of western civilization also one of its greatest and most imperishable.

The *Iliad* has for its subject the wrath of Achilles—its origin and its outcome. Achilles, the swift of foot, the incomparable warrior, represents the ideal of a warlike age, just emerging, it may be, from savagery, but exhibiting, as many a high-minded savage has done, a noble spirit and a keen sense of honor. He is passionate and vindictive, intense both in his love and in his hate; yet he can be touched with pity and can show a noble generosity. In his youth he had been offered the choice of a long but inglorious life or an early death with glory, and had unhesitatingly chosen the latter. The story of the *Iliad* opens with a bitter quarrel between Agamemnon and Achilles arising out of the division of the captives taken in a raid by the Greeks. Stung to the quick by the slight done to his honor, Achilles withdrew to his tent, and swore an oath to take no further part in the fighting that the Greeks might rue their ill-treatment of him. In his absence the Trojans prevailed in the fighting on the plain and were able to press back the Grecian warriors to the line of their ships drawn up on the shore, and

Aias carrying the body of Achilles painted on a volute-krater (vase) 570-565 BC, Florence Archaelogical Museum. The inscription says "Ergotimos made me; Kleitias painted me."

finally were on the point of setting these on fire. In spite of the appeals of the Greek chieftains and Agamemnon's offer of full reparation, Achilles remained obdurate. At last he so far yielded to the urging of his bosom friend, Patroclus, as to lend him his armor in which to attack the Trojans. The reappearance, as they believed, of the dread Achilles struck terror into the Trojans' hearts and they fell back. But Patroclus disregarded Achilles' warning not to put his own life in danger, and in the combat he was slain by Priam's son Hector, the stoutest warrior among the Trojans.

When the news was brought, Achilles' wrath was kindled afresh and he roused himself to avenge his comrade's death. But though Patroclus' body had been rescued from the Trojans, the armor had been stripped from it. Thereupon Achilles appealed for help to his goddess mother, Thetis, who induced Hephaestus to provide a fresh and splendid suit of armor. Arrayed in this, Achilles sallies forth to seek out Hector. After fierce fighting, the Trojans take refuge within their walls, but Hector disdains to follow them. The combat between the two champions, fought out on the plain under the crowded walls of Troy, ends in the death of Hector, whose dead body is dragged back in vindictive triumph to the Grecian camp and Patroclus' funeral pyre. There follows a secret visit of Priam by night to Achilles' tent to beg from him the body of his son for burial. Achilles is moved to pity by the old man's sorrow and the story ends with the burial of Hector, while the Greeks, by Achilles' order, refrain from hostilities for the period of the funeral rites.

This summary of the main action takes no account of many digressions and minor incidents that are among the most moving in the story. The scene shifts time and again from the Grecian camp to the battlefield or to the city of Troy, and from earth to the courts of Olympus. For the gods are not merely sympathetic observers of the struggle, they are themselves active participants, some

Odysseus and Nausicaa by Joachim van Sandrart, Rijksmuseum Amsterdam. After being stranded because of a shipwreck, Odysseus is found by Nausicaa and her maids. [Photo credit: Vincent Steenberg]

Vase painting; A Boys' School. [Upper half: a signing and a writing lesson. Lower half: playing the lyre and reciting poetry.]

on the Trojan side, and others on the Grecian. Zeus himself is moved, like the reader, to admiration for the gallant but ill-fated Hector, and with reluctance at last allows his doom to fall.

The *Odyssey* deals not with war on land, but with adventure by sea in time of peace. Its hero, Odysseus, is not of the Achilles type; he represents, not ardent manliness and passionate feeling, but intelligence and resourcefulness, and appropriately is prompted and helped at critical moments by the goddess Athena. The war had been over for nearly ten years and Odysseus had not yet been able to reach his island home in Ithaca. We are first shown the condition of things in Ithaca, where Penelope is patiently waiting her lord's return and her son Telemachus is too young as yet to assert his authority against the many princes from the regions around, suitors for the hand of Penelope, who spend their time in her palace carousing and wasting her substance as they await her constantly deferred decision. Athena appears in disguise, and at her suggestion Telemachus sets out for the mainland to visit Nestor and Menelaus, who have long been borne from the war, to learn what tidings of his father they can give him.

The scene now shifts to the mythical island of Ogygia, where Odysseus was detained against his will by the nymph Calypso. To her, at Athena's urging, Zeus sent Hermes to command her to let Odysseus depart. So, by her directions, he built himself a raft and set off for the island of the seafaring Phaeacians who would take him back to his island home. But as he neared Phaeacia, his old enemy, the sea-god Poseidon, espied him and in wrath raised a storm which wrecked the raft and would have drowned Odysseus himself but for a sea-nymph's timely aid. Cast up on the shore of Phaeacia, he was rescued by the king's daughter, Nausicaa, who with her maidens was spending the day by the seashore, and following her directions he received shelter in the king's palace in the neighboring city. There he recounts to the king and his courtiers the tale of his wanderings since leaving Troy; the storm which drove his fleet to the land of the Lotus-eaters; his narrow escape from death when imprisoned in the cave of the giant Cyclops, Polyphemus; his sojourn in the palace of the sorceress Circe, whose magic he was able to circumvent; his visit to the underworld where he saw the spirits of former comrades before Troy and obtained from the shade of the seer Tiresias the directions which he sought for his safe return; the dangerous passage of Scylla and Charybdis and the device by which he escaped the fatal lure of the Sirens' song; and finally the storm in which all his comrades perished and he was cast ashore on Calypso's isle.

The Phaeacian king gave instructions to his mariners to carry Odysseus, with many rich gifts, to Ithaca. Here they landed him, in a deep sleep, in a harbor where their arrival would be unobserved. The rest of the story tells how Odysseus, awaking, learned where he was, and how, venturing in disguise to the palace, he discovered the state of affairs in his home. Disclosing himself to one or two faithful retainers and to his son Telemachus, he concerted measures for wreaking vengeance on the insolent suitors. This accomplished, he revealed himself to his wife, Penelope, who, at first incredulous, soon was convinced of his identity and gave him fitting welcome. The last book describes the visit of Odysseus to his aged father, Laertes, and his assertion of sovereignty over his kingdom once more.

Apart from its own superlative merits as a piece of literature, the Homeric poetry has a threefold value:

1. We get from Homer a most vivid picture of life among the Achaeans of the Bronze Age, so that this remote period is as intimately known to us as any other in ancient history. The nature of their dress and food, their palaces and their furnishings, the tools of the workers and the weapons of the warriors, their ships and many other aspects of their material civilization are clearly portrayed for us. We know their social organization, their trades and crafts, their religious ideas, their standards of conduct, their conceptions of the gods and the life hereafter. Especially to be noted are the freedom and the dignified position of women in the Homeric world, in strong contrast with the semi-Oriental seclusion and limitations which were customary later in Athenian life. Such noble and lovable characters as Nausicaa and Hector's wife, Andromache, would adorn any age and any literature, and the simplicity and homeliness of their manner of life add only further charm to the picture. The objects and life described by Homer are abundantly illustrated by the excavations of Mycenaean sites, and the correspondence is so exact throughout that no one any longer doubts that Homer gives us an essentially accurate picture of a world that really existed.

2. The education of Greek youth in classical times was largely an education in Homer. Their minds were fed on Homer, from the cradle up. Large portions were learned by heart, not merely that the literary taste might be cultivated, but that ideals of manliness might be formed and character molded. Homer has often been called the Bible of the Greeks; his poems were the most potent of all influences in fixing their conceptions of the gods and in shaping their religious beliefs and moral standards.

3. The poems have not only themselves been a 'possession forever' treasured, by every age and every nation, but they have also been the inspiration of much of the best poetry that European writers have since produced. The phrase used by a great Greek poet who said that his dramas were but 'crumbs from the banquet of Homer' might be applied to many other great works of literature, such as Virgil's *Aeneid* and Milton's *Paradise Lost*, and to innumerable shorter poems. Tributes to the magic exercised by Homer range all the way from the Frenchman's assertion that when he read Homer, he felt as if he were twenty feet tall, to the famous sonnet of Keats, 'On first Looking into Chapman's Homer.'

Questions

1. Give a brief synopsis of the story of the Iliad.
2. Give a brief synopsis of the story of the Odyssey.
3. What is the backdrop for both of Homer's great poems?
4. Describe the threefold merit of Homer apart from its literary merit.

Vocabulary

obdurate
circumvent
superlative

Chapter IX

The Expansion of Greece

If the mainland of Greece took a long time to recover from the shock of the Dorian invasion, on the other hand, in the oversea settlements in Asia Minor, the influx of new life into a region specially favored by nature and situation very quickly had its effect. Ionia by the eighth century had become the most prosperous and civilized portion of the Greek world. The new population was of a very mixed stock. The new settlers came from many parts of Greece, and not a few of them married wives from the peoples whom they found in Asia Minor. And even in Greece itself there had already been an intermixture of the Achaeans with the pre-Greek Aegean race. History has often witnessed an exceptional vigor and enterprise in a people of very composite origin, and the population of Ionia was in that respect very like the people of Tudor England or of the nations that have grown up in North America.

The newcomers found the coast of Asia Minor very similar to that which they had left, but with a richer soil and an even more temperate climate. A series of river-valleys are divided by mountain chains which run out into promontories so as to form deep bays; and the promontories are continued in islands. A coast like this was singularly well adapted to a seafaring people; and such the Greeks had become, although but a few generations before they had been an inland people without experience of the sea. Whether it was that their adventurous and enterprising spirit took naturally to the sea, or whether it was the pressure of economic necessity (for Greece is a bare mountainous land that can of itself maintain but a sparse population), or whether, as is most likely, it was due to both these causes, combined with their contact with the experienced mariners of Crete and the other islands, in any event, the Greeks by the eighth century had become a great seafaring and trading nation. The Phoenicians of Tyre and Sidon, who for centuries had done a thriving business as traders in the Aegean, were now driven to the far western end of the Mediterranean, where they established many trading centers, of which the chief were Carthage and Gades (Cadiz).

The Greek settlers in Ionia came to a land which already possessed a highly developed type of civilization, comparable with their own but quite different. The great interior highlands of Asia Minor had for a thousand years been the home of a series of empires, Hittite, Phrygian, and Lydian, the

Phoenician ship carved on the face of a sarcophagus. 2nd century AD.

last beginning in the seventh century. These kingdoms were rich and prosperous, as the names of Midas, the Phrygian, and Croesus, the Lydian, testify; and the caravan routes which ran along the rivers from the coast into Lydia and then on to the Euphrates valley brought the Greek settlers into such contact with other advanced civilizations as fostered a very rapid growth of their own culture, which was based on the traditions of the Mycenaean civilization that they had brought with them.

It deserves mention here that it was in Ionia, apparently, that the Greeks first became fully conscious of the distinction between the Greek-speaking tribes, however hostile to one another they might be, and the non-Greek races with whom they were now coming into close contact. Some of these, like the Lydians and the Medes and Persians of the interior, were recognized as civilized peoples; others, like the Carians on their own coast, were but half-civilized; and their mariners and traders, who were exploring the distant coasts of the Euxine and the Mediterranean, brought back many a traveler's tale of primitive tribes with all manner of outlandish customs. All these, however diverse, were alike in speaking unintelligible languages, while the Greek dialects, however different, were comprehensible, as we can understand broad Scotch or Cockney. To all these alien peoples they applied the common name *barbaroi,* which was about equivalent to 'the jabberers' and implied no reflection on their manners or customs, as the word barbarians does today. The name which, in contradistinction, the Greeks came to apply to themselves was *Hellenes,* of which the adjective is *Hellenic.* The term *Hellas* was used of the country of the Hellenes, including not merely the mainland of Greece with its adjacent islands, but the whole area inhabited by Greek-speaking peoples, wherever settled. [2]

In the next two centuries the Greek world was to become still more widely extended by a new movement to which, for the sake of distinction, the name of 'secondary colonization' is given. Many cities were concerned in this movement: some in Asia Minor, especially Miletus, which at this

---

[2] To explain the relation of the chief divisions of their race, the Greeks at a later date invented a myth. In the early ages of the world a certain hero named Hellen had three sons, Aeolus, Dorus, and Xuthus; and Xuthus in his turn had two sons, Ion and Achaeus. Through this ancestry they accounted for the common name Hellenes, for the threefold division of their own day, exemplified in the three districts of Asia Minor (Aeolis, Ionia, and Doris), and for the term Achaean used in Homer of a people whom their traditions stated to have been driven out along with the Ionians by the invading Dorians.

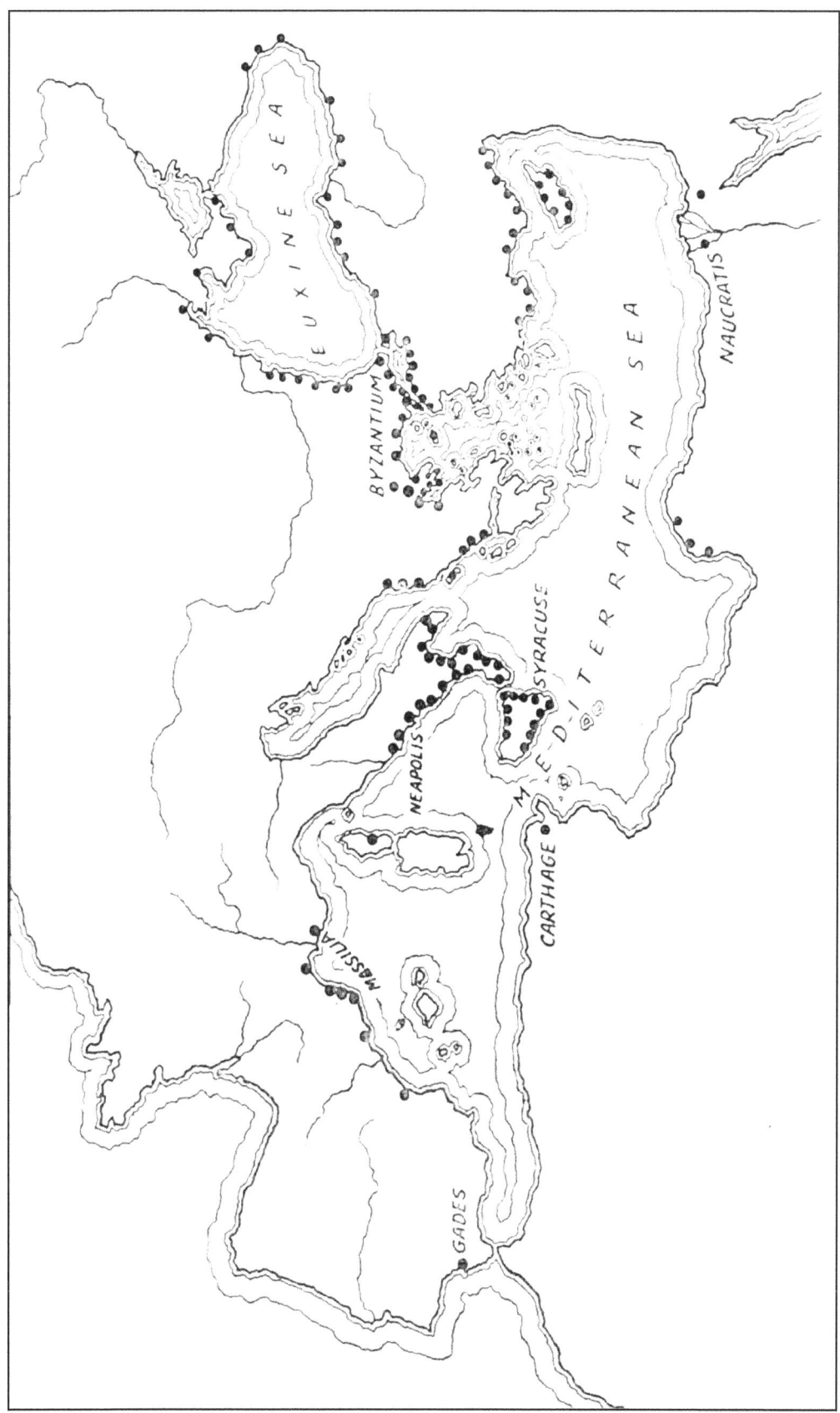

Greek secondary colonization.

period was the foremost city in the Greek, world; others on the western side of the Aegean which from their situation or for other reasons had early shared in the prosperity brought about by trading and commerce, such as Corinth and its neighbor Megara, or Chalcis and Eretria in Euboea. These cities now began to send out colonies of their citizens to settle on some advantageous site along the coast of the Euxine or the Mediterranean, and there build a new city and establish a new center for trade and barter with the tribes in the neighborhood. The moving force was in part the native Greek restlessness and love of adventure and novelty, and in part the impulse to find new markets for their fast-growing commerce. In a few cases, too, the formation of the colony was the result of political dissension, when a defeated or disaffected minority set out in search of a new home more to their liking. But in the great majority of instances colonization was the result of the population of a city expanding beyond the means of subsistence afforded in the narrow limits of the old home.

Many cities of great importance in the world were thus founded, the list including Byzantium or Constantinople, Syracuse, Neapolis or Naples, and Massilia or Marseilles. The wide extension given to the Greek language and civilization by this movement can best be judged by a reference to the map. These colonies were in one important respect unlike the settlements in Asia Minor made during the two or three preceding centuries. Each colony was definitely and carefully organized by its 'mother-city,' which is the proper meaning of the Greek word *metropolis;* the approval of the divine oracle at Delphi was sought; the religious rites and festivals of the mother-city were transferred to the colony, that its people might be under the protection of the same gods as of old; the fire of the public hearth was carried with them to be lit on the civic hearth of the new city; all this to bind the two cities by religious ties and common memories and to preserve the continuity of spirit and institutions. There was no bond of political dependence—the colony was entirely self-governing, but the religious bond was evidently, to the ancient Greek at least, as important as the political.

It might happen that in time a colony in its turn sent out another colony, as the city of Cumae, founded by settlers from Chalcis, afterwards colonized a site not many miles away, which was appropriately called *Neapolis,* the new town. In all such cases the sanction of the original mother-city was obtained and the new colony was founded under its auspices, not those of the daughter-city. This city of Cumae is noteworthy for another reason. It so happened that the colonists from Chalcis were associated in their enterprise with some members of a small neighboring tribe called the Graii. Now Cumae was the nearest Greek settlement to Rome, and in some way, the Romans came to apply the name *Graii* or *Graeci* not only to all the people of Cumae but also to all who spoke their language.

The Expansion of Greece

The acropolis of Cumae seen from the excavation of the lower city. [Photo credit Alexander Van Loon]

Questions

1. Describe the land in Asia Minor into which the Greeks moved. What advantages did it offer?
2. Generally describe the culture or civilization of the inhabitants of Asia Minor whom the Greeks encountered.
3. What did the Greek-speaking people become aware of through their contact with other cultures or peoples?
4. Describe the second wave of expansion known as the 'second colonization.' How and why did it take place?

Vocabulary

composite
enterprising
sanction

Chapter X

The Greek City-State

It is noteworthy that although the Greeks came down from the north as tribes and the tribal distinctions were always remembered, when the historical period is reached—in the course of the seventh century—we find them settled in very small self-centered communities, each independent of every other and jealously guarding its independence and separate individuality. The causes of this state of things were many. One of the most potent is disclosed by a study of the geography of Greece. The whole mainland is exceedingly mountainous, intersected everywhere by ranges of hills up to 8000 feet in height, which leave barely one-fifth of it level plain. The country is thereby cut up into innumerable districts, few of which extend more than ten or fifteen miles in any direction; the mountains which hedged them round were equally a defense against attack and a barrier to friendly intercourse. Of the innumerable islands, too, the largest contained but 300 square miles, and many of them held more than one independent community. Many a western ranch contains more cultivable land than most of these sovereign city-states of Greece, which made their own laws, waged war on one another, and have had a great name in the world. In some of the more backward inland parts, especially in the northwest and in Arcadia, the inhabitants still lived in villages scattered through the valleys and on the foothills. But usually the district held but one town or city, which the surrounding country supported with its produce. The site of this city, as a rule, was chosen because of its possessing an acropolis or rocky citadel convenient for retreat and defense. These isolated and exclusive communities are termed 'city-states.' The whole self-governing independent community was no larger than the city with its adjacent farmlands; the state and its capital were one and the same.

The keen rivalries of these small city-states were of the utmost importance in Greek history. All efforts to form some kind of union and make Greece a nation were defeated by the centrifugal tendencies of the separate units, by their reluctance to sacrifice their independence or to merge their individuality in any larger ideal. To form even a temporary union in the face of immediate danger was a difficult task. Had there been no other nations in the ancient world, this would have mattered

The Highway between Mycenae and Corinth.

little; but in the end Greece as a whole lost its independence because each part insisted on its own separate independence.³

Yet there was gain as well as loss from this division into many separate states. Each community was able to develop in its own way, and instead of the uniformity of type prevailing in the undivided expanses of the Asiatic nations or Egypt, there was to be found in Greece the utmost variety of customs and institutions, of experience and outlook and ideals. There was no standardization in Greek life or Greek character; within a radius of fifty miles might be found as great a variety of civilization as in the whole of North America. Nowhere in the ancient world had individuality such scope for its development as in Greece; nowhere was such rapid advance made through the opportunities afforded to explore every possibility and try every experiment.

But it was not all diversity and dispersion and disunion. For if the mountains kept men apart, the sea brought them together. The accessibility to the sea of practically every district in Greece is as striking a feature of its geography as its mountainous character. Not even England and Scotland have one-quarter as much sea-coast in proportion to their area; it would be hard to find a district from which, by climbing some nearby hill or mountain, the sea was not visible; and a strip of

---

³ Compare the spirit which long kept the various American states from accepting a federal government and the Canadian provinces from uniting. The insistence on state sovereignty had much to do with bringing about the great Civil War in the United States; as a witty American said: 'The war was really fought on a point of grammar: the North said "The United States *is*"; the South insisted on saying "The United States *are*."

Olympia in Ancient Greece [Pierers Universal-Lexikon, 1891]

sea-coast with a harbor of some sort was as regular a feature of a Greek city as its acropolis. Trade with one's neighbors was far more easily carried on by the small sailing ship than by pack-mules over the long, winding, ill-kept mountain trails; for to make good roads over the mountains would have been tremendously expensive and would only have opened a way to one's enemies. And so in Greece sea-borne commerce promoted intercourse and fostered interchange of ideas and experiences; and the discussions and criticism and comparisons that followed prevented the stagnation that might otherwise have been found in a small isolated community.

Two other features of Greek life also made strongly for unity: the great games, especially those held at Olympia, and the oracle of Apollo at Delphi. The prestige of Delphi and Olympia drew men from every part of Greece, and here the Greeks of every state met on an equal footing.

Tholos at the Sanctuary of Athena Pronaia in Delphi, Greece

All the great national games in Greece were instituted by and for the Dorian nobles, who set a high value on the training of the body which developed the manly warrior; but by the sixth century they were open to all Greek citizens of good character. The Olympic games were held in the autumn of every fourth year at Olympia in the plain of Elis, a more central position than would at first appear, for after the establishment of the Greek colonies no states took a keener interest in the games than the wealthy cities of Sicily and southern Italy. The contests included the footrace, boxing, wrestling, throwing the spear and the discus, and chariot races. The prize of victory was but a garland of wild-olive leaves; but so keen was the rivalry

Top view of the Temple of Apollo and surrounding landscape at Delphi, Greece. [Photo credit: Odysses]

and so highly was success esteemed that the victor was welcomed in his native state with civic rejoicings and was paid high honor there and often, given substantial rewards. Some of the finest poetry of Greece, too, like the odes of Pindar, was written to celebrate the victory of the scion of some noble house.

Gradually the sanctuary at Olympia was adorned with splendid buildings, pre-eminent among which is the temple of Olympian Zeus, and with votive statues and other memorials. For the month of the games a sacred truce was solemnly proclaimed throughout all Greece, and the cessation of all hostilities was scrupulously observed. The roads and adjoining harbors were filled with visitors from every quarter of Greece; poets and declaimers found here a distinguished audience; and traders and merchants doubtless reaped a good harvest. 'One thinks,' writes a modern scholar, 'of the time when those temples stood there in the glory of marble and gold and brilliant colors, when those statues were perfect, when that plain could show, besides, all living glories of the human form, when the line of those far-off snow-streaked heights in Arcadia met the eyes of the swift runner in the foot-race, and when as evening closed some day of brilliant rivalries, in Pindar's words, *the lovely light of the fail-faced moon beamed forth, and all the holy place resounded with festal Joy.*'

Although nothing definite is known of the Olympic games before the middle of the seventh century, the traditional date assigned for their institution was 776 BC, and from this the Greeks of later

Lycurgus consulting the Pythia as imagined by Eugene Delacroix, 1835/1845.

times used to date events, as happening, for example, in the first year of the seventy-fifth Olympiad (as the period of four years intervening between two celebrations was called).

In imitation of these games similar contests were instituted elsewhere; the Pythian games at Delphi, at which musical contests also were held in honor of Apollo, and the Isthmian and Nemean games, held in the neighborhood of Corinth and Argos respectively. These were all celebrated at fixed times, in such a way that there was no year in which a contest was not held.[4]

The Greeks, like most ancient peoples, believed in divination, that is, in ascertaining through various means (omens, dreams, seers, oracles) the judgment and the will of the gods. Chief among all the oracles in the Greek world was that of the Pythian Apollo at Delphi. It antedated the coming of the Dorians but was accepted and reverenced by them as fully as by the other Greek tribes. At Dodona, in central Epirus, there was another famous oracle, that of Zeus, equally revered and of even greater antiquity, but too remote and inaccessible to be frequented as Delphi was. Delphi is

---

[4] The word *stadium* (in Greek 'stadion') was properly a measure of length, 600 feet. This was the length of the course for the foot-race at Olympia, and in time the word was transferred to the racecourse itself. Both at Olympia and at Athens the race was run on the level ground at the foot of a sloping hill, on which the spectators stood or sat. The building of tiers of seats for the comfort of the spectators belonged to a later and more luxurious age.

situated but a few miles from the Corinthian gulf, but high up in wild mountain scenery, in a setting of incomparable grandeur that must have increased the awe with which the worshipper approached the shrine of the god. In the center of the sacred precinct stood the temple of Apollo, where the Pythian priestess, going into a trance, uttered the responses of the god to the questions asked. The advice of the oracle was sought on all manner of questions involving religion, or matters of state policy, or the advisability of undertakings, private or public. The inquirer might be some private person, or the official representative of some Greek state, or even the envoy of some king of a land quite outside the Greek world, so famous was the oracle.

Besides the intimate knowledge of affairs which they gained from being consulted so widely on the important issues of the day, the Delphic priesthood must also have had secret sources of information that enabled them to give what the inquirer accepted as inspired pronouncements. The answers were sometimes judiciously obscure and enigmatic. The oracle usually 'played safe' and favored moderate, conservative policies, though occasionally taking strong ground on behalf of some weak but deserving cause. But on the whole it exercised a steadying influence in Greece, and worked for uprightness and sound public policy.

This widespread reverence for their great oracle, the general worship of Zeus and the other Olympian gods, their common participation in the same festivals and games, the common possession of the Homeric poems, with their tradition of a great national enterprise, and the growing consciousness of a difference between the Greek-speaking race and the rest of the world—all these things tended to produce a feeling of unity and solidarity which was none the less real for resolutely stopping short of political union or any kind of federation.

Questions

1. What is a city-state?
2. List some of the positive and negative effects that arise from the fierce independence of these Greek city-states.
3. Describe the effect of geography on Greek life.
4. What factors contributed to the unity of the Greeks?
5. Describe the early Olympics.
   a. events-
   b. purpose-
   c. rewards-
   d. effects-
6. What was the oracle at Delphi? For what purpose did the people go there?

Vocabulary

centrifugal
sovereign
scion
enigmatic

Chapter XI

From Kings to Tyrants

In Homer we find each tribe of warriors and each community under the rule of a king who is at once leader in war, dispenser of justice, and high priest for his people. His sovereignty, whether hereditary or bestowed on him by common consent, is based on his personal prowess and superior capacity. With him are closely associated other warriors, also of noble birth, who form his council both in war and in peace. In one sense this manner of rule could as properly be called an aristocracy as a monarchy, for the king and his council of nobles, of whom he is simply the noblest, possess all the power, and the common people have neither authority nor rights. There is, indeed, an assembly of the whole people; but it is only that proclamation may be made of what the king and his council have decided. There is discussion and free expression of opinion in the council but not in the assembly.

This organization of the state was not only a very natural one in a primitive and warlike age, but it was also the one which, apparently, existed in all branches of the Indo-European peoples at an early stage of their development. And so we find the same three elements—king, council of nobles, and assembly of the people—not only among the Achaeans but also among the Dorians, and not only among the Greeks but also among the Romans and the Teutonic tribes. Out of these three elements and the modifications of their respective rights and powers have grown monarchy, aristocracy, and democracy, and all the other forms of government that we meet in later Greek history and indeed generally in European history to the present day.

Before the seventh century in Greece the king had disappeared from nearly all Greek communities. But the abolition of the monarchy did not mean that the common people had increased powers or enlarged rights. The authority of the king now belonged to the nobles, and in many cases the commons may have been worse off under the rule of a group of self-seeking high-born families than under that of a powerful and just-minded king. The change from monarchy to aristocracy followed naturally when the country became more settled and competent leaders in war were no longer necessary as in the days of the Achaean lords and the Dorian invasion. Moreover the very conditions of city life would foster criticism and conspiracy on the part of men who, in their pride of birth, might not unnaturally resent being subject to any one man's authority.

But a privileged class easily tends to become selfish and exclusive, instead of regarding its advantages as a trust for the benefit of all. Throughout Greece generally, when the curtain rises on the seventh century, we find a growing dissatisfaction with the unequal conditions created by the privileges of the ruling nobles. The unprivileged masses were beginning to question the right of the hereditary classes to monopolize political power, the possession of the land, and the administration of the law. It was not the poorer citizens only who were debarred from political rights. There were also many unprivileged rich people. For as commerce began to prosper in Greece, in many centers able and enterprising men who did not belong to the noble families acquired wealth by trade and manufacture, and these discontented rich merchants were apt to be even more dangerous critics of privilege than the discontented peasants and artisans.

In many of the important states of Greece, these conditions led to the rise of the so-called 'tyrants' to power during the seventh and sixth centuries. Some able and ambitious citizen—a wealthy merchant perhaps, or at times even a noble, more rarely some vigorous member of the common people—would take advantage of the prevailing discontent, and, coming forward as the champion of the popular rights, would wrest power from the nobles and establish himself as ruler in their place.

The name 'tyrant' did not at that time imply, as now, the exercise of cruelty and oppression. Many of the tyrants were in fact enlightened and progressive rulers, 'benevolent despots,' whose aim it was to make the people contented and prosperous. The term originally meant simply an absolute ruler whose position was not regularly provided for in the constitution of the state. It indicated a particular manner of *acquiring* power, not the manner of *using* it. But the tyrants' irresponsibility to any authority seemed objectionable and shocking to the Greeks of a later generation, who had a strong belief in constitutional government as a bulwark against oppression. If the absolute ruler was subject to no law, how, they argued, could he resist the temptation to be lawless, rapacious, oppressive? This reasoning was often, but by no means always justified by the actual facts; and it is from this conviction, rather than from the facts of history, that the later use of the term 'tyrant' has arisen.

These tyrannies began to appear in the Greek world before the middle of the seventh century; they had passed away nearly everywhere, except in Sicily, before the close of the sixth century. They reappeared again in the fourth century, and, in fact, all through history there has been a tendency for some dictator to appear when discontent has attained a dangerous strength. Sooner or later in Greece the rule of the tyrant was overthrown. The successors of the original tyrant seldom proved as able and acceptable rulers as he had been; the wealthier and more influential citizens resented their exclusion from power; or the people generally rebelled against oppression. At the next stage we find the chief cities of Greece under either oligarchical or democratic government; under the rule of the few who were rich, or of the many who were not.

The general tendency in the Ionian states was towards democracy. The Dorian states as a rule were oligarchical; but the ruling few were no longer merely those who had noble descent and birth. Henceforth the qualification was rather the possession of wealth, with the implied belief that the wealthier citizens were better educated and more intelligent, had a greater stake in the country, and were more likely to give continuously efficient government.

Questions

1. Describe the form of government by which most Greek communities were ruled during the time of Homer.
2. What three 'elements' arose in Greek society? What three forms of government came about from these elements?
3. Why did the rule of kings gradually disappear from most Greek societies? Who took over the ruling authority in many cities?
4. What universal statement does the author make regarding the privileged class?
5. What was the cause of unrest in many Greek city-states? Who was unhappy?
6. At this time in Greece what did the term 'tyrant' mean? How did many tyrants rule their cities?
7. What happened to the rule of tyrants in Greece by the close of the 6th century BC? Why?
8. What universal claim does the author make about tyrants and dictators?
9. After the rule of tyrants passed by what form of government were the Ionian states ruled? The Dorian?

Cleombrotus II ordered into banishment by Leonidas II king of Sparta, Pelagio Palagi (1775-1860).

Chapter XII

Sparta and Spartan Discipline

When the Dorians, after conquering Argolis, crossed the mountains and made themselves masters of the cities and the fertile plain of Laconia, they found that, while most of the survivors of consequence and enterprise fled the country, there remained large numbers of the earlier inhabitants, chiefly composed of the common folk and peasants. It was like the Norman king with his knights and barons and their armed retainers on the one hand, and the conquered Saxons on the other. The Dorians proceeded to make serfs of the conquered pre-Dorian folk, and always henceforth there were in Laconia two great divisions of the population, the free Lacedaemonians and the *Helots*, as, for some obscure reason, the serfs were called. The latter were practically slaves, belonging to the state but attached to the lands of individual masters, who might not sell them or set them free, and to whom they were under obligation to render a fixed amount of farm produce annually. They did all kinds of menial work, and in war were called on to act as light-armed skirmishers attached to the fully armed troops composed of the free Lacedaemonians.

These latter in their turn were not all of equal status. A new capital city, named Sparta, had been built, supplanting the chief of the earlier strongholds which they had destroyed, and the free citizens of Sparta, called *Spartiates*, alone controlled the government of the country. Throughout the rest of Laconia round about Sparta were planted numerous settlements which served both to guard the frontiers from foreign invasion and to keep the Helots from escaping or combining to make trouble. The residents of these outlying towns were called *Perioeci* (literally 'dwellers round about'). They were free and had full control of their local affairs; they formed part of the heavy-armed troops in war, and in most other respects were like the burghers of Sparta; but they had no share, not even their nobles, in the government of the state. This does not seem to have been due to any inferiority of origin, as in the case of the Helots, but largely to the fact that at that very early date no one had conceived any way by which people living at a distance could be given a real share in the conduct of affairs and could be not only free but also citizens.[5]

Across the mountains immediately west of Sparta lay the district called Messenia, with a plain even richer than that of Laconia. Messenia had so far escaped invasion either by the Aetolians from the west or by the Dorians from the east. Towards the end of the eighth century, however, the Spartans invaded Messenia, and after twenty years' fierce fighting they annexed it. The accession of this fertile territory close at hand explains why Sparta took no such active part in the colonizing movement of that era as did many of the neighboring Dorian states; there was no need to send any surplus population overseas. Nor was Sparta touched by the contemporary impulse to engage in distant commercial ventures and to seek increase of wealth by trade as well as by tilling the soil. The Spartans remained a conservative land-owning aristocracy, regarding themselves as a chosen people, born to rule others.

But there were other results of the conquest of Messenia. Sparta had not merely doubled her territory; she had also doubled the number of her Helots, for to this condition she had reduced the defeated Messenians. In the latter part of the seventh century, a serious rebellion broke out among the oppressed Messenians. For a time the Spartans lost ground steadily, but finally, inspired, so tradition says, by the stirring war-songs of Tyrtaeus, a Spartan, poet of the day, they crushed the rebellion, ruthlessly and completely. Up to this time there is evidence that the Spartans were sharing in the advances in culture that were spreading from Ionia over Greece, and that life among these privileged aristocrats was gay and brilliant and full of ease. Alcman, one of the great lyric poets of that age, was a Spartan; and besides making progress in sculpture and pottery and architecture, Sparta excelled particularly in the field of music. But now came a great change. The Messenian rebellion, so nearly successful, made them realize their danger.

It is calculated that out of a total population of 300,000, the Spartiates numbered but one-tenth and the Perioeci another tenth. For every Spartan there were eight Helots, enslaved 'like asses bent beneath intolerable burdens,' as Tyrtaeus described them, but, unlike the patient ass, deeply resentful. Sparta alone of all the Greek states had enslaved and humiliated another Greek state, and the Spartans realized that they were living, and would always live, upon a volcano.

They saw but one sure way to be always ready to meet the danger, and they steeled themselves to pay the heavy cost of their mastery. Sparta became an armed camp; all the citizens, boys and girls, men and women, were subjected to a stern discipline that was to last from the cradle to the grave; any natural impulse, any ambition, that might stand in the way of military efficiency was ruthlessly repressed. Only those children were allowed to live in whom officers of the state discovered at birth no physical weakness. Till the age of seven the boys were carefully and rigorously reared at home under state supervision. Then they were taken from home, and till the age of twenty remained under the care of state drill-masters, who trained them to endure pain and hardship and to become expert in athletic exercises and military drill. They slept on rushes without bedclothes; they had no more clothing in winter than in summer; they were given insufficient food that they might learn to forage for themselves; they were encouraged to fight with one another in any fashion, however vicious, that would bring victory, for this would be useful training for war, and for the same reason they were encouraged to steal so expertly as to escape detection; if caught, they were severely

---

[5] This was in essence like the problem the British Commonwealth had devising a means by which the citizens of the oversea dominions can fully share in the determination of imperial international policy.

punished, not to cure them of stealing, but to teach them to mend their clumsiness. And once a year, at a great festival, each boy got a sound thrashing that would test how much pain he could endure without a murmur. They were taught also to bear themselves modestly and silently, especially in the presence of their elders, and to be obedient to those in authority.

At twenty they might be called on to serve in war; and they were now allowed to marry, but must still continue to live, eat, and sleep in their military barracks. At thirty their training was deemed to be complete, and they now became full citizens. This did not mean that they were now free to engage in business or to travel or to indulge a taste for art or literature. They remained professional soldiers to the end, engaged in regular drill and military exercises, dining daily in the barracks on simple fare in small groups of lifelong messmates, enjoying no homelife, but accepting through all the years of peace such privations as other men have to undergo only in a hard campaign. The girls also were carefully trained to be athletic and hardy, that they might grow up to be fit mothers of warriors; other accomplishments had no place or value.

By such means the Spartans attained efficiency in war; for the next two centuries they were wellnigh invincible in the field. And to many there has seemed something attractive in the severe simplicity of their lives, the stability of their character, and the spirit of self-sacrifice for the welfare of the state. But the discipline was too one-sided, the life too narrow, to be admirable or wholesome; too much was disregarded that is noble in human nature, and in civilization; individuality was repressed and family life made impossible; nor should it be forgotten that hardy courage and disciplined self-restraint were valued not simply for their own sakes, but because through them the Spartan aristocrat could best maintain his lordship over the unhappy Helot.

The ever-present danger of the Helot explains why the Spartans, though always ready for war, were not aggressive and did not lightly make war on other states. Indeed they were extremely reluctant, as will be seen, to send their armies out of their own territories even when the very existence of Greece was at stake. No state in Greece was more self-contained, and they were as chary of admitting strangers into Laconia as they were themselves averse to foreign travel. They sought only to save themselves and to preserve their own institutions intact; they made no contribution to Greek civilization, nor are any of the great gifts of Greece to the modern world associated with the name of any Spartan.

The threefold division of the citizens into king, nobles, and commons, while persisting, fades into insignificance beside the all-important distinction between the free citizens and the Helots. It is one indication of the conservatism of the Spartans that although among them, as elsewhere, the time came when the nobles wrested control of the government from the kings, yet the kingship was not abolished; the office was merely shorn of its former absolute authority. In Sparta there was the curious variation of two kings, the heads of two different royal families, reigning simultaneously. This was probably the result of some unrecorded amalgamation, on an equal footing, of two divisions of the Dorians in Laconia. The council consisted of the two kings and twenty-eight others chosen for life from among the elders of the noble families.

At some period, however, conflict must have arisen between the nobles and the general body of Spartiates or warrior citizens, as a result of which the general assembly each year elected five ephors (the word means literally 'overseers') who served as a check upon the absolute power of the kings and the nobles alike and, in many ways, seem to have been the real heads of the state. They carried on all negotiations with foreign states, presided over the council and the assembly, and conducted much of the judicial business of the state. In time of war one of the two kings was appointed to be leader of the army, but two of the ephors were always sent out with him.

The Spartans[6] attributed their institutions, including both the organization of their government and their rigid discipline, to a great and ancient lawgiver, called Lycurgus. It is extremely doubtful whether any such lawgiver ever existed, and, in any case, the Spartan form of government was the result of a gradual modification of the original constitution common to all the Greek tribes, while their peculiar social institutions, as we have seen, are little earlier than 600 BC.

Lycurgus of Sparta by Merry-Joseph Blondel, 1828, Musee de Picardie

---

[6] The term Spartan is generally used today as the national name, in contrast with Athenian, Corinthian, etc. The customary Greek term was Lacedaemonian, from Lacedaemon, an ancient name of the city, Sparta, going back to Homeric times. The term Spartiates is used only in contrast with Helots and Perioeci.

Questions

1. After the Dorian invasion of Laconia, what was the major division of the people in Laconia?
2. What were the responsibilities of the Helots?
3. How were the Dorians in Laconia divided? (By what criteria? What were their names?)
4. What did Sparta gain as a result of the Spartan conquest of Messenia?
5. What danger did the Spartans face after the conquest of Messenia? How did they decide to meet that danger?
6. Describe the Spartan culture before the conquest of Messenia? How did the conquest affect Spartan culture?
7. Describe the education of Spartan youths.
8. Give a brief explanation of the Spartan government.
9. To whom do the Spartans attribute their system of laws?

Vocabulary

obscure
menial
forage
chary

Agora of Ancient Athens

Chapter XIII

The Early History of Athens

The map of Greece shows Attica as a triangular district about the size of one of our counties, projecting well into the sea at the extreme east of the mainland. Like the rest of Greece, it is intersected in every direction by mountain ranges, leaving three or four well-marked plains. The largest of these, that surrounding Athens, is scarcely more than ten miles wide and twenty miles long. Even in these plains the soil is poor, and the inhabitants of Attica were never able to take life easily. But, as a recompense, nowhere in Greece was the air purer and more invigorating, and in time also it was discovered that the soil was especially adapted to the cultivation of the olive tree and the manufacture of earthenware vessels. By the export of pottery and of olive oil, Attica was able to buy in return the grain of which her own soil did not yield nearly enough for her population.

Partly because there was nothing particularly tempting in its rocky soil and partly because it lay in a corner off the main routes of travel, Attica had not been invaded in the period of the great Dorian migration. As a result, the population, which was of Ionian stock, was unusually homogeneous; we do not find here, as we do in so many other districts, a superior race of conquerors and a subject race. This is undoubtedly one reason why democracy, with its ideals of equality and fraternity, first came to birth in Attica.

By the beginning of the seventh century, when something like authentic history begins in Greece, we find that Attica, instead of consisting of several small independent states, has become united in one political community, with Athens for its capital. The choice of Athens is easily explained. It had a central position; it had an unsurpassed place of defense in the Acropolis, with its broad, level surface and its precipitous sides; it was surrounded by the largest of the Attic plains, and close at hand was an excellent harbor. When or by whom this union was brought about is not known, but clearly it was not by conquest or compulsion, but with the full assent of all the uniting communities, and all free inhabitants of Attica, wherever dwelling, were alike citizens of Athens. The Athenians themselves attributed the change to their legendary hero Theseus, who, after slaying the Minotaur in Crete, returned to Athens to succeed his father on the throne.

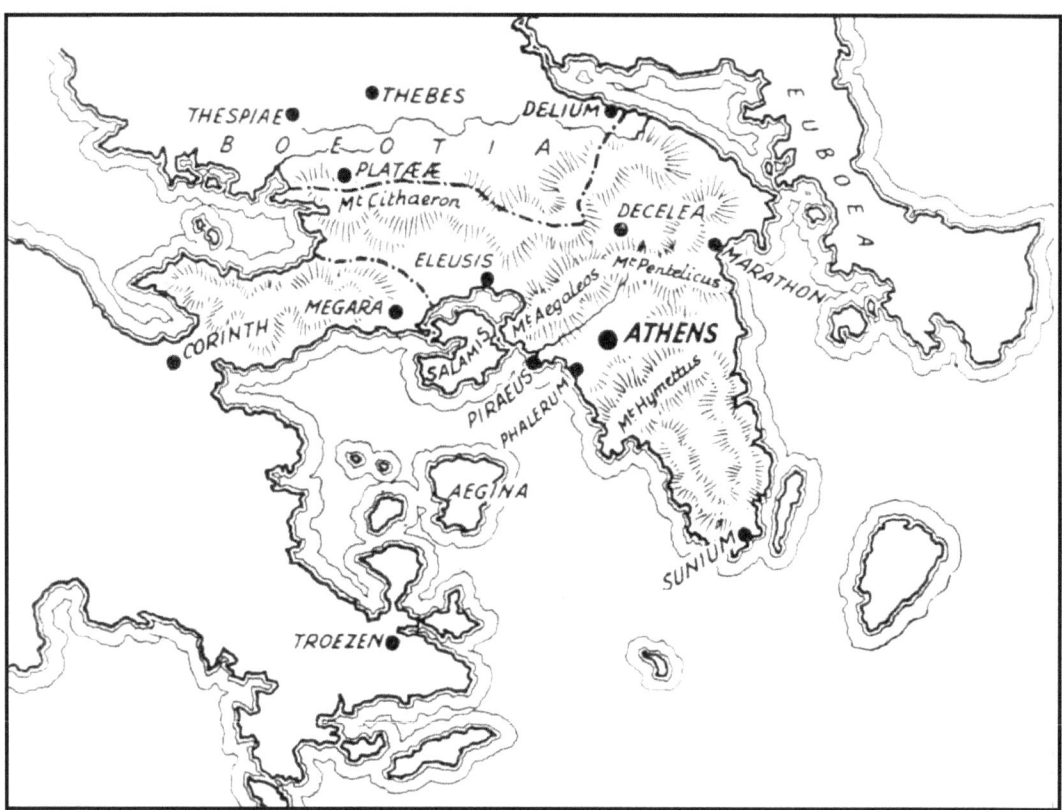

Map of Attica.

Thus Athens early in her history became the center of the largest united community in Greece, and the strength and preeminence which this gave her were among the causes contributing to her future greatness. The other states which in size and strength were to be her greatest rivals were in a different position. In Laconia, Sparta was sovereign over a large conquered population held in subjection by force; in Boeotia, Thebes presided over a league of cities which retained their independence and autonomy.

In Athens, as generally in Greece, the monarchy had disappeared by the beginning of the seventh century; the government was in the hands of the nobles, or, as they were called at Athens, the *eupatridae* (the 'well-born'). The change had doubtless been a very gradual one, but the Athenians themselves believed that as early as the eleventh century Athens had had its last king in the person of Codrus.

According to the legend, the Dorians were at war with Athens, and an oracle foretold that they could not be victorious if they slew the Athenian king. Learning of this, Codrus resolved to sacrifice himself for his country's preservation. Going out in disguise, he provoked a quarrel with some Dorian soldiers, who killed him, mistaking him for some poor peasant. When they discovered what had been done, the Dorians despaired of victory and withdrew their forces. In gratitude for this patriotic devotion, the Athenians abolished the kingship, for no one, they believed, could ever be worthy of the title which Codrus had borne.

Under the rule of the *eupatridae,* the actual conduct of affairs in the seventh century was in the hands of nine officials known as archons (rulers). One of these, who was often called *the* archon, was the chief magistrate, and events in Attica were dated as occurring in his archonship; a second, the polemarch, acted as commander-in-chief. These archons held office for one year, and were chosen from among the nobles only; for those alone who possessed birth and wealth also enjoyed full civil rights. Attica was at this time still very largely an agricultural district. There were, of course, artisans and small traders and fishermen, but the time had not yet come for the extensive oversea commerce of later centuries. The large holdings in the richer plains belonged chiefly to the well-born nobles; in the more hilly regions were shepherds and herdsmen and woodcutters. All these humbler classes were freemen and members of the citizen body; they were not serfs or dependents of the nobles. But they had as yet no part in the government of the country, not as a result of any deliberate policy of oppression, but because no one had yet conceived the idea of a democratic society, where all citizens should have equal political rights.

We are apt to forget that democracy was an unknown, untried, unimagined thing in the world until it was developed in Athens during the next two centuries. If we look back over the course of its development, we shall realize that government by the nobles was, in fact, a most useful stepping-stone to democracy, a half-way house between obedience to the authority of a single monarch and the equal participation of all citizens in the government. When these *eupatridae* were learning gradually how to deliberate about the welfare of the state, how to organize a system by which to carry on the business of the community, and how to take turns in command and obedience, they were in reality making discoveries in the art of government that were invaluable a little later, when the whole body of the citizens undertook control of the state.

There were many things that at the time would make the dominance of the well-born seem reasonable. As the heads of families of long descent, they were naturally looked up to by the common folk as their leaders. As the chief possessors of wealth, the chief burden of expense in maintaining the state fell upon them, and in war they bore the brunt of the fighting, for they alone could equip themselves with heavy armor and horses, the latter always rare and expensive in mountainous Greece.

Acropolic of Athens [Photo credit Arian Zwegers]

Questions

1. Describe the geography and climate surrounding Athens.
2. How did the geographic location of Athens affect its history?
3. How did its climate and soil affect its history?
4. What people made up the population of Athens? What difference did this make?
5. *How* and *why* did Athens become the capital of Attica?
6. How did Athens differ from Sparta and Thebes in her early history (i.e. the 700s)?
7. Who was the last king of Athens? Describe the circumstances of his death.
8. Describe the government of early Athens.

Vocabulary

homogeneous
compulsion
magistrate

Chapter XIV

Draco and the Causes of Discontent

The first clear indication of dissatisfaction in Attica with the rule of the nobles is the appointment of Draco to draw up a code of laws for the Athenian people. No state can exist without laws, but laws arise out of custom and usage, and may for ages remain unwritten. In early communities, when disputes arose about property or bargains, or when evildoers were to be punished, trusted men who knew the traditional usage gave judgment and settled disputes. In Attica the judges, like the other magistrates, were chosen from and by the ruling nobles, and in time their good faith began to be questioned. The only men who knew the law and could declare and interpret it belonged to the very class which too often used its exclusive privileges for its own selfish advantage; and it was natural to suspect that in the law-courts the privileged gained unduly, and the unprivileged suffered, from this exclusive knowledge. Hence, as a security against inequality and injustice, there arose a demand that the laws should be written down and published.

One striking thing about the code of laws published by Draco was the severity of the penalties. For nearly all crimes there was the same penalty of death. Those convicted of idleness and those who stole vegetables or fruit received the same punishment as those guilty of sacrilege or murder. We may compare the severity of the English law as late as a few hundred years ago, when theft, forgery, and scores of other offences were punishable by death. This rigor led to the Greek saying of a later and humaner age, that Draco's laws were written in blood; hence, too, our epithet 'Draconian.' Draco, of course, was not himself the author of these severe laws; his duty was to edit and publish the laws as he found them. Such severity did not long commend itself to the Athenian people. Draco's laws were repealed by Solon in the next generation, with the exception of those relating to homicide, in which Draco had drawn certain useful distinctions between murder and accidental or justifiable manslaughter.

The publishing of the laws by Draco had done something, but the popular discontent was too deep-seated to be so easily removed; the real source of the evil had not yet been reached. The common people were at that time suffering great distress from poverty and indebtedness, in addition

The olive tree at Acropolis of Athens, Greece, which, according to the myth, was Athena's gift to the city and earned her the right to name it, being more useful than Neptune's water.

to being without political power. The latter disability might not have greatly troubled them, had they been completely free from the miseries of poverty and debt. It is the combination of economic distress with political inferiority that breeds revolution. While from the nature of the soil Attica was ill adapted to farming, it was still largely an agricultural country. But the many small farmers were being driven by poverty to mortgage their holdings to the rich nobles who already had large estates. With the high rate of interest prevailing (ten percent at the very least), they found it impossible to repay the loans, and so, parting with the ownership of their little farms, they became laborers where formerly they had been freeholders. Then, further, the tenant farmers, who leased small holdings at a heavy rental from the nobles, and the free laborers on the land also became heavily involved in debt. The severe laws of those days made the insolvent debtor a slave, to be used on his owner's estate or even sold away from his native home. As a result the rich were growing richer and the poor growing poorer. The whole country was coming to be owned by a few persons; the small proprietors were becoming landless, and the landless freemen were becoming slaves.

But what brought about this state of things? Why was there so much dire poverty and distress at this particular period? In part it was due to a succession of bad harvests in a land where it was at the best of times hard to wrest more than a bare living from the soil, and in part it was due to a long war with Megara for the possession of Salamis. This island lies in such a position that it might be claimed by both Athens and Megara, and its possession was vital to the safety of each. The war, which ended in Salamis becoming a permanent possession of Athens, withdrew men from the work of farming, and this interruption, which of course affected the small farmer more than the rich landholder with many slaves, left many a man poorer at the end of the year than at the beginning.

Ancient coin of Athens

There was another cause, however, which was even more potent, although at first it may not seem to have much relation to the poverty of the Athenian farmer. This was the invention of coined money, an invention which, like the introduction of new machinery into industry in the 1800s, made great changes in the life of the people, and for a time, in spite of all its advantages, caused widespread distress and discontent.

In early ages men paid in kind by barter, or, in the case of large transactions, by bars of metal of unfixed weight. The kings of Lydia in the seventh century were the first to adopt the practice of issuing small pieces of metal stamped as having a fixed weight, and therefore a guaranteed value. Like the plow and the printing press, it was one of those simple inventions which, once discovered, humanity cannot imagine itself without. It spread rapidly to Greece. In the course of one or two generations, all the leading Greek states were coining their own money, and every creditor was asking to be paid his debts in gold and silver. It seems a simple change. But its effect upon the villager was as disastrous as the invention of the steam engine. It created an economic revolution in the Mediterranean communities. Consider what the change meant in the life of a peasant, who is living from hand to mouth on his yearly harvests. He used to take his produce to market and exchange it for the goods he needed—wool for his wife to spin, children's shoes for the winter, or tiles to mend the roof—or he would pay the smith and the joiner in wine for repairing his plough and his cart. But now most of them will not accept his corn and wine until he has turned it into money. How much is his produce worth? He has not the least idea, for it depends on factors outside his range which he has no means of controlling. He takes what the middleman gives him, and the middleman makes a living on his commission. At the end of the year he is alarmed to find he has not as much margin as usual. When the inevitable lean year comes he has no margin at all. In fact he cannot see his way through the winter without help. His only resource is to borrow. The interest charged was high, for coined money was a new thing and was scarce; the only security he could give was his land and his labor; and when his mortgaged land was lost, the next stage was to pledge his own person and his family for his increasing debt.

Questions

1. Why did the Athenians ask Draco to write down the laws of Athens?
2. What were these laws like? Describe them.
3. What two problems persisted after Draco wrote down the laws?
4. What was the regular punishment for an Athenian who could not repay his debts?
5. What factors helped "the rich get richer and the poor get poorer?"
6. How did the invention and use of money cause a great disparity (difference) in the wealth of the Athenian citizens?

Vocabulary

insolvent
margin
mortgage

Chapter XV

Solon, the Founder of Democracy

The situation was so alarming that the eupatrids recognized that something must be done to allay popular excitement. Fortunately Athens had a man worthy of being entrusted with the difficult task of reform, and fortunately all classes were agreed upon asking him to undertake it. Solon was a member of a eupatrid family which claimed descent from King Codrus. His father having met with reverses, the son had turned to a commercial career, and both his early adversity and his extensive travels broadened his mind and enlarged his sympathies. He was a man singularly reasonable and fair-minded; a man of high principle and unselfish devotion to the public good; and a man of great intelligence and sound judgment, so that the Greeks always included him among their 'Seven Wise Men.' He had some years before played a distinguished part in the final conquest of Salamis, and certain vigorous writings of his on the problems of the times, of which considerable portions remain, further commended him to his countrymen. Solon was chosen archon and given extraordinary powers as mediator and reformer.

To remedy the prevailing economic evils Solon proposed (1) to set free all who had been enslaved for debt; (2) to cancel all existing debts for which the land or the person of the debtor was pledged as security; (3) to make it illegal in future to loan money on similar security; (4) to set a fixed limit to the amount of land any one man might own. The first two righted existing wrongs, while the other two safeguarded the future. The poor welcomed the 'shaking off of burdens,' as this legislation was called, and the rich were not dissatisfied, for they had been afraid of a demand for a general redistribution of land. The remedy was severe but effectual; Attica was never troubled again with an agitation about land and wealth.

But Solon saw clearly that the best safeguard against a recurrence of trouble was to effect some change in the form of government. On the one hand, the poor must be guarded against possible oppression by the rich, and the ruling classes should not be in a position to use their powers and privileges for their own selfish ends. On the other hand, he was convinced that the general masses of the people had not sufficient judgment or experience to be entrusted as yet with the actual conduct of the state's affairs. Therefore he did not establish what we know as democratic government, for he believed that 'the few' were better fitted to hold office; but he gave 'the many' as much power as in his judgment they could make good use of. We have his principle of mediation or balance recorded in his own words:

> *'To the commons such honor I gave as their need would demand; no power they lost, nor was power thrust into their hand. While for those who through wealth were exalted, whose rank gave them weight, I contrived that naught should their honor degrade or abate. And I stood over both with the shield outstretched of my might, nor suffered that either should triumph apart from the right.'*

In general terms this object was accomplished by the following means:

(1) He established four classes of citizens, arranged in a graded scale according to income. The three highest were of people possessing property; the fourth class was made up of free laborers and artisans and others who had little or no property.

(2) The archons were to be chosen only from the highest of the four classes, and the other officers and magistrates of the state only from the three propertied classes. The fourth class was not eligible for office.

(3) So far there was little or no change; but henceforth all four classes were to form the general 'assembly' of the state (the *Ecclesia*), by which the archons and the other magistrates were elected, and in which every citizen had an equal vote.

(4) Furthermore, all four classes were to form the general 'court' of the state (the *Heliaea*), which not only heard appeals in judicial cases, but also reviewed the work of every magistrate at the end of his year of office and could inflict punishment if the scrutiny was adverse.

This is not democratic government, which was as yet unknown in the Greek world, but the Athenians always and rightly considered Solon to be the real founder of their democracy. For in the power to elect the magistrates and even more in the power to hold them responsible for their conduct of affairs, and in the control of justice through the right of appeal to the general court of the people, democratic control of the constitution was established in fact, if not in theory.

Although at the time there was criticism of these political proposals, the prestige of Solon was such that he might easily have made himself tyrant. Indeed some of his friends suggested to him that he should do so. He was too high-minded a patriot to take their advice. When his work was done, he retired from office and left Athens to travel abroad for ten years, while the citizens in his absence should have a chance to try how his constitution would work.

A story of Solon from Herodotus

On this account, as well as to see the world, Solon set out upon his travels, in the course of which he went to Egypt to the court of Amasis, and also came on a visit to Croesus at Sardis. Croesus received him as his guest, and lodged him in the royal palace. On the third or fourth day after, he bade his servants conduct Solon. over his treasuries, and show him all their greatness and magnificence. When he had seen them all, and, so far as time allowed, inspected them, Croesus addressed this question to him. "Stranger of Athens, we have heard much of thy wisdom and of thy travels through many lands, from love of knowledge and a wish to see the world. I am curious therefore to inquire of thee, whom, of all the men that thou hast seen, thou deemest the most happy?" This he asked because he thought himself the happiest of mortals, but Solon answered him without flattery, according to his true sentiments: "Tellus of Athens, sire." Full of astonishment at what he heard, Croesus demanded sharply, "And wherefore dost thou deem Tellus happiest?" To which the other replied, "First, because his country was flourishing in his days, and he himself had sons both beautiful and good, and he lived to see children born to each of them, and these children all grew up; and further because, after a life spent in what our people look upon as comfort, his end was surpassingly glorious. In a battle between the Athenians and their neighbours near Eleusis, he came to the assistance of his countrymen, routed the foe, and died upon the field most gallantly. The Athenians gave him a public funeral on the spot where he fell, and paid him the highest honours."

When he had ended, Croesus inquired a second time, who after Tellus seemed to him the happiest, expecting that at any rate, he would be given the second place. "Cleobis and Bito," Solon answered; "they were of Argive race; their fortune was enough for their wants, and they were besides endowed with so much bodily strength that they had both gained prizes at the Games. Also this tale is told of them: There was a great festival in honour of the goddess Juno at Argos, to which their mother must needs be taken in a car. Now the oxen did not come home from the field in time, so the youths, fearful of being too late, put the yoke on their own necks, and themselves drew the car in which their mother rode. Five and forty furlongs did they draw her, and stopped before the temple. This deed of theirs was witnessed by the whole assembly of worshippers, and then their life closed in the best possible way. Herein, too, God showed forth most evidently, how much better a thing for man death is than life. For the Argive men, who stood around the car, extolled the vast strength of the youths; and the Argive women extolled the mother who was blessed with such a pair of sons; and the mother herself, overjoyed at the deed and at the praises it had won, standing straight before the image, besought the goddess to bestow on Cleobis and Bito, the sons who had so mightily honoured her, the highest blessing to which mortals can attain. Her prayer ended, they offered sacrifice and partook of the holy banquet, after which the two youths fell asleep in the temple. They never woke more, but so passed from the earth. The Argives, looking on them as among the best of men, caused statues of them to be made, which they gave to the shrine at Delphi."

When Solon had thus assigned these youths the second place, Croesus broke in angrily, "What, stranger of Athens, is my happiness, then, so utterly set at nought by thee, that thou dost not even put me on a level with private men?"

"Oh! Croesus," replied the other, "I see that thou art wonderfully rich, and art the lord of many nations; but with respect to that whereon thou questionest me, I have no answer to give, until I hear that thou hast closed thy life happily. For assuredly he who possesses great store of riches is no nearer happiness than he who has what suffices for his daily needs, unless it so hap that luck attend upon him, and so he continue in the enjoyment of all his good things to the end of life . . . There is no country which contains within it all that it needs, but each, while it possesses some things, lacks others, and the best country is that which contains the most; so no single human being is complete in every respect—something is always lacking. He who unites the greatest number of advantages, and retaining them to the day of his death, then dies peaceably, that man alone, sire, is, in my judgment, entitled to bear the name of 'happy.' But in every matter it behoves us to mark well the end: for oftentimes God gives men a gleam of happiness, and then plunges them into ruin."

Such was the speech which Solon addressed to Croesus, a speech which brought him neither largess nor honour. The king saw him depart with much indifference, since he thought that a man must be an arrant fool who made no account of present good, but bade men always wait and mark the end.

Croesus Shows Solon his Treasure by Frans Francken the Younger, 17th century [Photo credit: dorotheum.com].

Questions

1. Give three reasons why all Greeks were willing to accept the laws of Solon.
2. Describe the changes that Solon first made in Athens. How were these changes received by the poor?
3. What did Solon think about the common man? The noble man?
4. Describe the government set up by Solon.
5. When Solon left Athens, was it a democracy?

Vocabulary

mediation
abate

Chapter XVI

Pisistratus and Cleisthenes

The establishment by Solon of something like democratic government did not free Attica from all faction and dissension. As in Canada under a more complete democracy there is plenty of party strife, due in part to the divergent interests of the maritime, central, and western provinces, or again of the farming, industrial, and commercial classes, so in Attica there were three parties representing different districts with widely different interests and policies. The 'Men of the Plains' included the great, landholders of noble descent, who disliked Solon's political reforms. The 'Men of the Hills' were mainly herdsmen and woodcutters and the poorer farmers, who would have liked Solon to go still further in equalizing rich and poor. The 'Men of the Shore' included not only the population of the coast and those interested in the increasing sea traffic, but also most of the artisans and the middle classes generally, who were well-satisfied with the changes of Solon.

The strife between these parties continued for a generation to agitate Athenian politics. Then Pisistratus, an ambitious Eupatrid of a younger generation than his kinsman Solon, and like Solon distinguished for his leadership in a later war with Megara, determined to make himself tyrant. He allied himself with the radical and discontented hillsmen, and in twenty years made three attempts to seize the reins of power. On the last occasion, after spending several years in securing influential support abroad, he returned with a strong force to aid him, landed at Marathon, and defeated those who offered opposition. For the next thirteen years he remained tyrant of Athens, and on his death, was succeeded by his son Hippias, who retained power for seventeen years more.

Under the weight of Pisistratus' authority the strife of opposing factions ceased. Many of the more conspicuous of the nobles who had opposed him left the country. Their property was confiscated, and their large estates divided among the landless farm-laborers and poor men from the city, who, had they remained in Athens, would have been idle and discontented. He did much to promote agriculture, advancing money to the new landholders where necessary; in particular, he fostered the extensive planting of olive groves, and thus enriched Attica with a new and important source of revenue. Unlike most tyrants, he did not suspend the existing constitution. He and Solon had been friends, though not agreeing in their political views. The constitution of Solon remained in force throughout his reign; he merely took care that some member of his family should be among the archons. Thus, while even under the most moderate tyranny there cannot be true self-government, yet the Athenians were able, for practically the whole of the sixth century, to accustom themselves to the working of a limited form of democracy and to the practice of open discussion and voting with a citizen-wide franchise. They were thus well-prepared when the time came for the more complete democracy of the next century.

The two greatest names in Athenian history prior to 500 BC are Solon and Pisistratus. Solon's chief importance is in connection with the social and political development of Athens. To Pisistratus, Athens owed the beginnings of her greatness as a rich and powerful imperial state and the home of art and literature.

Pisistratus established a fortress at the entrance to the Helespont to safeguard the Athenian trade with Thrace and the countries on the Euxine (or Black Sea). With his approval and support, also, an eminent Athenian named Miltiades went to Thrace and succeeded in making himself master of the Thracian Chersonese (the Gallipoli peninsula). This extension of Athenian influence may be regarded as the first step taken towards the great Athenian empire of the next century.

Like many absolute rulers, Pisistratus sought to make his capital preeminent for its culture and the splendor of its appearance. This was partly to make the citizens forget their loss of liberty, but it was also because he himself possessed a cultured taste. He built temples, not so grand as the masterpieces built a century later, but for that day most beautiful and impressive, and he brought eminent sculptors to Athens that their works might adorn the temples and the public places. Pisistratus also encouraged the worship of the god Dionysus and instituted a great new yearly festival in the city. At this festival there were choral dances and songs celebrating the adventures and exploits of the god.

Cleisthenes

During the tyranny of Pisistratus, Thespis introduced into his performance a separate recital by the chorus-leader, and from this beginning, in a very few years the Attic drama was developed, one of the greatest gifts of the Greek genius to the world.

At this same period began a great festival and pageant held every four years in honor of Athena, the guardian goddess of Athens. At this 'Panathenaic' festival there were athletic and musical contests, a great procession of the citizens to the temple of Athena on the Acropolis, and recitations of Homer by professional minstrels. In order to improve and dignify this last feature, Pisistratus brought scholars to Athens to determine and publish a proper text of these poems, and this became the standard text of Homer thenceforward for the Greek world.

After the death of Pisistratus, Hippias continued his father's policy for the greater part of his reign. But when his brother Hipparchus was slain by two young Athenians, as the outcome of a purely personal, and not a political, quarrel, he became embittered and suspicious. After a few years of oppression, Hippias was driven from Athens by a force gathered by some of the exiled nobles and supported by Spartan troops. But in spite of the expulsion of the tyrant and the recovery of self-government, there were many of the peasants and common folk who long looked back to the reign of Pisistratus as to a golden age.

As soon as the strong hand of a tyrant was removed, party strife sprang up again in Attica. But the masses of the people were by this time strong enough to assert their power; and when one of the ablest of the exiled nobles, Cleisthenes, allied himself with the commons, they had no difficulty in winning the day from those who, assisted by Sparta, wished to set up an oligarchical government. The struggle lasted only two years, although the Spartans a few years later made one more effort to destroy the democracy. This, too, failed completely, and the Athenian people were now masters in their own house.

Immediately after the earlier victory Cleisthenes was appointed by the citizens to effect such changes in the constitution of Solon as experience showed to be desirable. He did not seek to make the constitution any more democratic than it had been before. It still remained a restricted or moderate democracy; large numbers of citizens were still excluded from public office, and especially from the archonship. Most of the changes he introduced were to remove local conditions that tended to create friction and thus interfered with the working of Solon's constitution.[7] In this effort he was eminently successful. The type of constitution devised by Solon, when assured a fair chance by Cleisthenes, enabled the Athenians in a few years to achieve the completest civic life known to the ancient world.

It was obviously impossible to administer the public business of Athens through so large a body as the *Ecclesia* or general assembly—a parliament in which every citizen of Attica was a member. (It was centuries before the idea was conceived of a sovereign assembly made up of elected representatives.) In order to expedite the conduct of business, Cleisthenes gave increased powers to the council (or *Boule),* which had always had a place in the Attic state. This council prepared the business for the assembly, and drew up the measures that it was to discuss and vote upon. It saw that the assembly's decrees were carried out, and exercised supervision over all officials and magistrates. It prepared the financial estimates, and received foreign embassies. In fact, it was the executive committee of the state, through whose hands all public business passed.

The council held office for a year and consisted of five hundred members, fifty being chosen from each of the ten Attic tribes. But even five hundred is an impossible body for practical administration. So Cleisthenes had each tribal group of fifty take turns, for thirty-five days or so, in the actual daily conduct of affairs, reporting to the whole council from time to time. In this way a large number of men gained practical acquaintance with the business of the state, and the election to this council was regarded as the most important of the year.

Thus through her development in the sixth century, under Solon, Pisistratus, and Cleisthenes, Athens was preparing, though she knew it not, for the great crisis and the great future that were awaiting her in the fifth century.

---

[7] For example, he grouped the parishes or 'demes' into ten electoral divisions called 'tribes' in such a way that each tribe was made up of demes situated in different parts of Attica. In this way he broke up the personal influence of the noble families, which would be strong in their own neighborhood, but not elsewhere.

Questions

1. After Solon left Athens, how were the people of Attica, the region surrounding the city, divided?
2. How did Pisistratus come to power in 560 BC?
3. How did many nobles react to his becoming a tyrant? What difference did this make?
4. What happened to the laws of Solon during the reign of Pisistratus? What effect did this have?
5. How did Pisistratus, a tyrant, prepare Athenians for democracy?
6. Describe the ways that Pisistratus caused Athens to develop into a great city.
7. How did Cleisthenes change or improve the work of Solon? How did he set up the government?

Vocabulary

oligarchy
dissension
eminent

Chapter XVII

Life in Sixth-Century Greece

In the Greece described by Homer we find something very similar to the patriarchal life described in the Old Testament. The people lived a very simple life; their cities were little more than country villages, and each community, and even each household, was practically self-supporting. Wealth consisted in flocks and herds and in ornaments or vessels of gold and silver. The very highest in the land shared in the ordinary tasks of life. The queen, like other matrons, sat among her handmaidens busy with spinning and weaving; the king might be found building a house or constructing a bed for himself; a prince, shepherding his flock or attending to his horses; and a princess, taking the household linen to wash by the riverside. There were slaves, some taken in war or in a piratical raid, some born in the household; but they lived on terms of intimacy with the freeborn members of the household and were not regarded as menials. A scale of social gradation existed, but it had no relation to the performance of useful labor. All the ordinary needs of the family—clothing, food, furniture, implements, buildings, boats—were supplied by the handiwork of its own members. There were no manufactories and no artisan or trading class. One man might be more skilled at this or that than his fellows, but he did not depend for his living on his special skill. Still less was his position in the community determined by his handicraft.

By the sixth century conditions had changed in many ways, although life was still extremely simple as compared with present-day standards. The distinction between town life and country life was clearly marked, and communities were no longer self-supporting. The practice had grown up of importing food supplies and in return exporting some product of one's own country which was in demand elsewhere. The colonies on the Euxine, for example, were in lands where the olive tree and the vine would not grow, but where there were great wheatfields and rich fisheries. From these, Athens, like other cities in Greece, obtained grain and dried fish in return for oil and wine, and they found it advantageous to do so, for an acre in Attica planted in olives would bring in five times as much grain as that same acre could have itself produced. Manufactories also were springing up where there were special facilities for production. In these manufactories slaves were employed, as also in the mines which were now being worked here and there, and such slaves bore a much less intimate relation to their owner. In all the towns, further, men were now to be found engaged in special callings—the shoemaker, the smith, the potter, the builder, as well as the sailor and the trader—and making their livelihood thereby. Simultaneously, too, the man who was sufficiently well-to-do to possess slaves and lands, or who was making money in commerce, had now begun to look down on manual labor and the handicrafts. Not that there were as great disparities then as now between rich and poor. Greece was too small and too barren a land for large fortunes to be made. Asia Minor, on the east, and Italy and Sicily, on the west, were far richer in natural resources. Large estates in Greece were almost unknown, and a landed proprietor in Attica who owned forty acres was counted rich. Manufactories were small, most with with no more than twenty slaves engaged at work.

There was less change in the activities of the women than of the men. They still remained as of old busied in the duties of the home, and the matron still superintended her maidens as they spun and wove or baked. In Athens a custom was coming into adoption which was probably borrowed from Ionia and was ultimately of Oriental origin, whereby women of respectable families were seldom seen abroad, and the care of their children and their houses was their sole sphere of activity and interest. In other parts of Greece women did not live so secluded a life, and this sixth century is notable for the number of cultured and brilliant women whose names have come down to us as writers of poetry. Chief of these was Sappho, of Lesbos, the surviving fragments of whose lyric verses show how great is our loss through their disappearance. No century since in European history, until the last two hundred years, has had so many women writers of high rank. In other ages women may have inspired great poetry, but they seldom, if ever, have written any.

If one went into the market-place of a Greek town (the *agora* or gathering place, as it was called), it would not be found filled with market-women and housewives engaged in lively bargaining. The Greek agora was the meeting place of the men. There they did the marketing for the household and transacted other business. There was held the assembly of the citizens to settle public affairs, to vote on peace or war, to enact some new law, to elect magistrates, or to conduct a trial, and there again they met for ordinary gossip and discussion such as the Greek has always loved.

Another common place of resort, especially for the well-to-do and their sons, was the gymnasium. One must not think of a modern building with its special apparatus and its shower baths and swimming pool. The Greek was content with an open space of beaten earth or sand, where he could practice wrestling, leaping, discus throwing, and other athletic exercises, with some simple covered place adjoining where he could rest out of the sun and where others could watch and talk. Before engaging in exercise, the athlete rubbed himself down with olive oil, to make his body supple; after he was through, he took a curved instrument to scrape off the mingled oil and sweat and dust from the arena, after which he might have a jar of water thrown over him to complete the cleansing. The object of the athlete was all-round excellence and general bodily agility and grace, rather than distinction in one particular line. He did not seek to make records by unduly developing one set of muscles at the expense of another; his object was to attain manly vigor and beauty, and graceful bearing was as important as muscular strength. One reason for the exceptional excellence of Greek sculpture and figure painting was the unique opportunity afforded the artist in the gymnasia for observing closely and constantly the human frame in action and repose, as these well-formed Greeks, exercising naked as they usually did, displayed the body in every conceivable attitude.

Greek statue Discus-thrower, Roman bronze reduction of Myron's Discobolos, 2nd century AD.

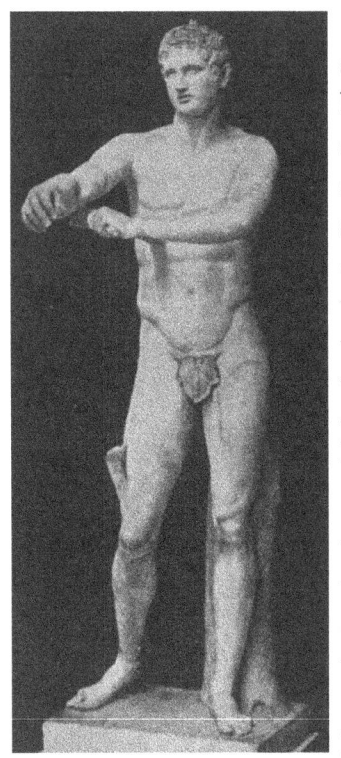
Apoxyomenos. (Athlete using a Scraper.)

These same citizens might at other times be seen practicing in full armor in preparation for the wars that were so frequent between neighboring states. The Homeric style of warfare, where heroes engaged in single combat, had passed away. All through Greece the custom had spread of fighting in close ranks which were trained to move together as one body and to stand fast against the most violent attack. As every citizen who had means to purchase armor and weapons could serve in the 'phalanx' the city's fighting strength was increased, and at the same time, in harmony with the political tendency of the age, the change put the noble and the ordinary citizen on a level in war. There were as yet no professional armies—the citizen and the soldier were identical, and in time of war all the men of military age were called out.

There had been a change in shipbuilding also. The Homeric ship was a simple affair, perhaps forty feet long and eight or ten feet wide, with a small raised deck at either end. In the center on thwarts sat the oarsmen, ten to twenty on each side. A mast with a simple square sail was provided for use when the wind was favorable. The warship of the sixth century, the trireme, was a recent invention of the Phoenicians. It had the oarsmen arranged on each side in three banks or tiers, so that greatly increased power and speed were obtained without lengthening the boat. These vessels were made more formidable also by the addition, at the prow, of a beak shod with bronze and projecting just beneath the

Early Greek Merchant Ship (British Museum, London).

waterline, with which to ram an enemy's vessel and sink it. For carrying merchandise the sailing vessel was still in use, slower of movement but more spacious. No Greek ship could tack against the wind, and in case of adverse winds the sailing vessel, unlike the war-galley with its oarsmen, held to 'lie to' in such shelter as it could find. At all times the ancient mariner, who had no compass to steer by, avoided getting out of sight of land. Thus the ordinary course to Italy and Sicily was to sail north to Corcyra (now Corfu), from which the passage to Italy is shortest. So too the Phoenicians crept along the African shore to reach their cities in the western Mediterranean.

To walk through the streets of the ancient Greek cities would be like walking between monotonous walls of rubble or of sunbaked brick on a stone foundation, with here and there a plain doorway, for there was no attempt to make the exterior of a house attractive. No windows broke the line of the wall, on the ground floor at least. The only buildings, as a rule, to attract attention or to make any claim to architectural beauty would be an occasional temple in some open space. The ancient Greek temple was not built for a congregation to worship in; it was the abode of the god, developed from some simple covered shrine. A very small building therefore might, and usually did, suffice. Small groups of worshippers might at times enter the temple shrine, where stood the statue of the god. But on any festal day, when a large procession of citizens came to offer sacrifice, they would remain without, and, the doors of the temple having been thrown wide open, would see their offering placed on the altar before the god.

By the sixth century the Greeks had developed a normal type of temple building, which varied only within certain definite limits. The building was rectangular, and was often divided by a cross-partition into two rooms, of which the second, contained the treasure of the god and the appurtenances of his worship. In the simplest structure two pillars stood between the projecting ends of

Early Greek Warship (British Museum, London).

Temple of Hephaestus in Athens, Greece, the best preserved of the ancient temples (449 BC) [Photo credit: Sailko].

the side walls to mark the doorway. Or a whole row of pillars might be placed in front of the door, and this feature might be repeated in the rear of the building. If further adornment were desired, an additional row or rows of pillars might extend round the whole structure. These pillars were of two kinds, known as Doric and Ionic; the former, sturdier in its proportions and plainer in its details; the latter, more slender and graceful, with a base and a more elaborate capital. The only other differences of importance are to be found in the treatment of the space intervening between the pillars and the roof. In each type of temple there were certain spaces which the Greeks from very early times were accustomed to fill with sculptured figures, often telling in stone or marble some legend connected with the divinity who dwelt within. These places were the pediment and the metopes in the Doric temple, the pediment and the frieze in the Ionic temple (see illustration p.92).

As represented by Homer, the worship of the gods was an occasion for rejoicing and feasting, not for fasting or humiliation. The Greeks had no deep sense of sin, and their conscience did not greatly trouble them for any evil they may have done. If they have displeased a god, he is kindly and is easily entreated, and his passing wrath may be appeased by a fitting sacrifice—a sacrifice, be it noted, which is itself an occasion for merry-making rather than for sorrow, for the worshippers do not present whole burnt-offerings, but themselves feast on the victims, of which only a negligible portion has been the god's share. In the sixth century, however, some influence, perhaps from Semitic or other Eastern sources, had deepened in the Greek consciousness the sense of the enormity of man's sinfulness, and the need of purification if one was to win happiness here, and, what was more important, hereafter. And so we find at this period certain new rituals coming into vogue which professed to give to those who participated in them purity of living here and a good hope for the life to come. These were especially the Orphic rites and the Eleusinian mysteries. The former, supposed to have been handed down from the great Thracian singer Orpheus, were connected with the worship of Dionysus, the Thracian god of wine and fertility, whose cult, recently introduced, had gained a strong hold upon the Greek imagination. The mysteries celebrated at Eleusis, near Athens, were connected, with the worship of Demeter (see page 33). The myth of the death and rebirth of nature wa spiritualized into a belief in another life after death, and the solemn initiation of the worshipper into the secret ritual of Eleusis was believed to ensure his welfare in that after-life. These new beliefs and ceremonies never displaced the joyous worship of the Olympian deities, but they did create a more serious view of life in the minds of many, and they deepened the moral sense and quickened the spiritual imagination of some of the greatest poets and thinkers of Greece in the next two centuries.

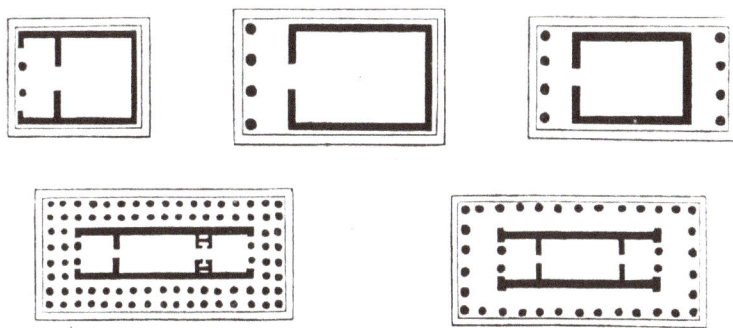

Plans of Greek Temples.

Another movement of the time deserves closer study, not so much because at the time it was at all conspicuous, but because in its outcome, it profoundly affected the development of human thought. There was something in the Greek mind that drew it naturally to a love of orderliness and symmetry and a dislike of caprice and lawlessness. One sees this clearly in all the products of the

Doric Temple of Poseidon at Paestum.

Greek genius, notably in its sculpture, its architecture, and its poetry. The time was now come when it occurred to certain Greeks to ask of themselves the question: Is it possible that there is some order in the constantly changing and apparently chaotic world of nature about us? Is this infinitely varied universe constructed according to some definite plan that human reason can discover and comprehend?

Some such question was first asked by Thales, a prominent citizen of Miletus in Ionia, and other citizens of Miletus after him carried on his inquiry. The particular explanations which they gave of this unity and ordered law of nature were quite erroneous and need not detain us. The important thing is that this question had begun to be asked—that this new point of view was beginning to occupy men's minds. For as a result of these questionings, we can clearly trace in the course of the next century the rise of natural science, and the first beginnings of geology and astronomy and

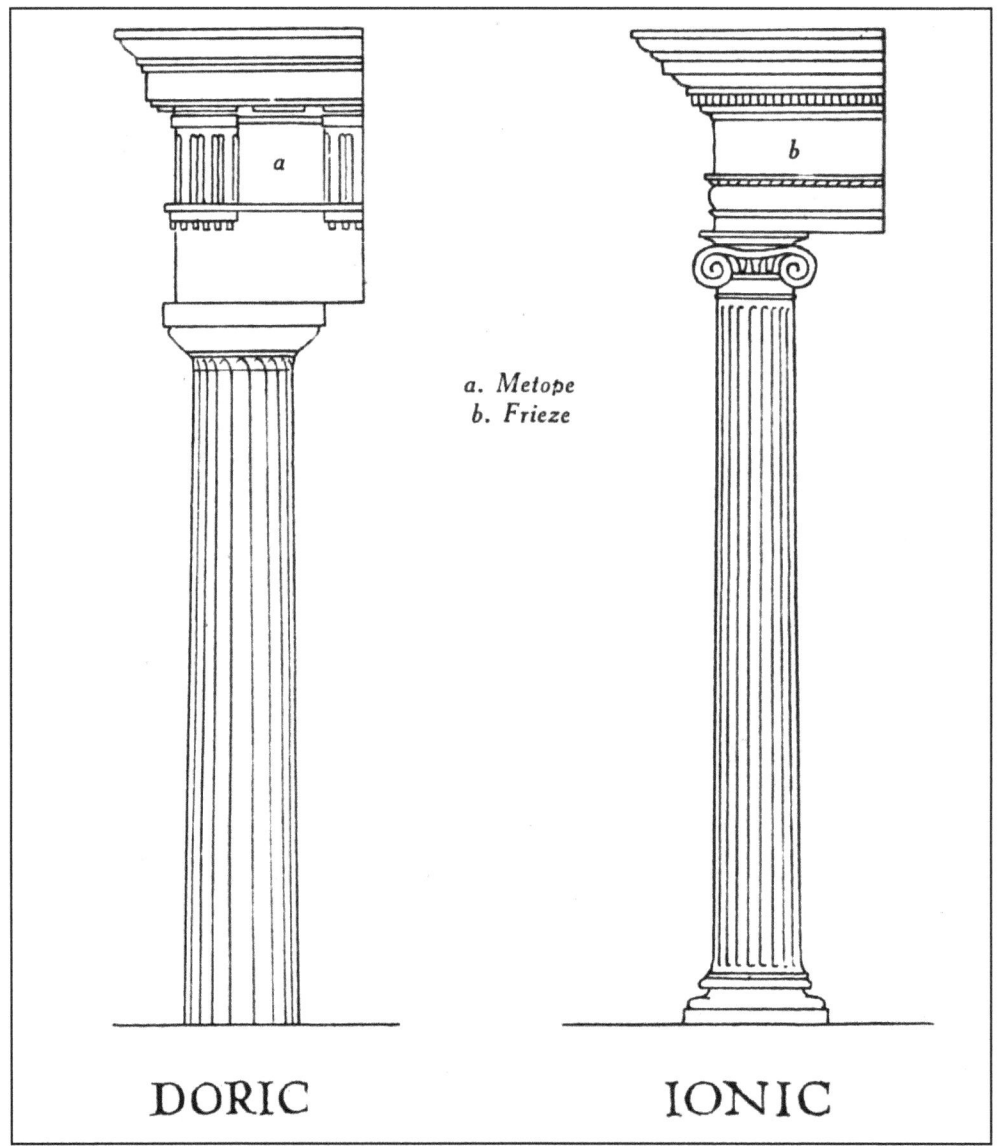

Doric and Ionic columns compared. (Common to both Doric and Ionic temples was the pediment, or triangular space under the cabled roof).

physics and biology and physiology. It was natural enough that Miletus should be the scene of these first attempts at scientific reasoning. The city was rich and men had leisure for indulging the native Greek spirit of inquiry and thirst for knowledge. It was connected with Babylonia by the overland trade routes, and also with Egypt through its colony of Naucratis, on one of the branches of the Nile. Thales is said to have been well acquainted with the astronomical and mathematical lore of these older countries, and to have been the first in the western world to predict an eclipse of the sun (that of 585 BC). It was also citizens of this same Miletus, with its many colonies overseas, who made the first attempt to construct a map and to write a description of the known world. Absurd mistakes may have abounded, but again the important thing is that a beginning of scientific geography had been made.

Finally, mention should be made of the literature produced in this century. Instead of the epic, we find a new type of poetry prevailing which turned from the past to the present, and from the great deeds of heroes to the personal feelings and experiences of the writer and his criticism of life. These personal and reflective poems were naturally much briefer than the epic, and for them the Greek, with his instinctive sense of the appropriate, devised new types of metre and rhythm and stanza to replace the majestic roll of Homer's verse. According to its subject matter these poems are called lyric, elegiac, or gnomic. The lyric, which was ordinarily meant to be sung to music, told of joy or sorrow, love or hate, whether real or imagined, or celebrated some special occasion such as a marriage, a banquet, or a victory. One important variety was the choral lyric, which was written for a large number to sing and was accompanied by dancing and rhythmic action, so that trained bands of professional performers were required to give a proper rendering. Elegiac verse included the many inscriptions, written with marvelous terseness and charm, on the occasion of someone's death or as an epitaph on the fallen in battle. For these a special metre was used. Gnomic poetry, which also was written in the elegiac metre, expressed the poet's judgments on life or on politics and gave counsel in the conduct of private or public affairs. The gnomic poets often summed up in a neat, concise fashion, perhaps in a single line, the accumulated experience of the past, and these, terse, pithy utterances were much quoted among the Greeks, so that the gnomic poets ranked second only to Homer as the molders of the national character and beliefs.[8] The chief lyric poets during the seventh and sixth centuries were Alcaeus and Sappho. The most famous of the writers of elegiac and gnomic verse were Sinionides and Theognis. The greater part of the poetry of this age has perished, partly because of its early date and partly because of the very multitude of short poems of which few were conspicuous above the others.

---

[8] *The* Greek word gnome meant first a judgment and secondly a maxim or proverb.

Questions

1. Describe the major differences between the Greek way of life in Homeric times versus life in sixth century Greece. Include differences in agriculture, trades, slavery, warfare, etc
2. What kind of activities took place in the market place?
3. Describe the Greek gymnasium and the activities that took place there.
4. What were Greek men hoping to achieve through their athletic activities?
5. What changes had taken place in Greek shipbuilding?
6. Describe how Greeks adorned or decorated the exterior of their homes.
7. What purpose did Greek temples serve?

Vocabulary

piratical
appurtenances
pediment
metopes
frieze

Chapter XVIII

CROESUS AND CYRUS

The growth of Greece had so far been unhampered by her neighbors, but now, 600 years after the Trojan war, the time was at hand when the Greeks were again to come into conflict with Asiatic powers. Great changes had been going on in the eastern world during these centuries. Great empires had arisen and had fallen; but the Greek world had not been affected, and knew little, even by rumor, of what was happening outside the Mediterranean area.

In the seventh century, after the Greek cities on the coast of Asia Minor had been long established, the neighboring kingdom of Lydia, under a new dynasty of kings, began to increase in power and wealth, and soon adopted a policy of aggression towards the coast cities. During several reigns no actual conquest was achieved or perhaps even attempted, but the Greek territories were raided and plundered incessantly. One city, Smyrna, was captured and destroyed. Finally Croesus came to the throne and definitely set himself to extend his rule to the Aegean Sea. The Greek cities were doubtless weakened in man-power by the numerous colonies they had sent out. Their wealth and prosperity had made the population more effeminate than the Greeks usually were. They were separated from one another by deep inlets of the sea and mountainous promontories; and such united action as might have been concerted they failed to take, in this displaying the common defect of the Greek city-states at all periods. One by one they were attacked and reduced to submission.

While the Asiatic Greeks were now for the first time subjects of an oriental monarch, there was much to compensate them for the loss of their independence. Croesus, so far from proving an oppressive ruler, was himself an admirer of the culture of the Greeks and assiduously courted their friendship. Lydia seemed more likely to become Hellenized than the Greek cities were to become orientalized. Their commercial prosperity suffered no abatement, and probably the fixed tribute which they now had to pay appeared a welcome exchange for incessant raids and harryings. The splendor of Croesus and his court made a profound impression on the Greeks. To them he was a darling figure at the head of a great empire, the nearest and the first they had known of those oriental kingdoms which impressed the Greeks by their size and magnificence as compared with the small poor states of their own homeland.

Meanwhile, in the far east, a thousand miles away, another power was rising which was destined to overthrow Croesus and absorb all his dominions. One of the main divisions of the Indo-European family, called the Iranian, had come down into Asia through the Caucasus, and had established itself on the high plateau between the Caspian Sea and the Persian Gulf, east of the empires in the valley of the two rivers. This vigorous race was composed of two branches, the Medes and the Persians, as closely related as the Angles and the Saxons who invaded Britain. The Medes, who occupied the northern portion, were at first the more prominent of the two. The powerful kings of Assyria for a time made vassals of the Medes as they did of Babylonia and Egypt and all the lands between. But towards the end of the seventh century Media and Babylonia rebelled; Nineveh, the Assyrian capital, was captured and destroyed, and the vast and cruel empire which had lasted for seven hundred years vanished for ever.

The Median kings succeeded to the northern part of the Assyrian empire, which extended westwards into Asia Minor, till at the river Halys it touched the eastern borders of Lydia. So things remained until, about the middle of the sixth century, a prince of the Persian line seized the kingship of the Medes and inaugurated a vigorous and successful policy of conquest. This was Cyrus, called the Great, one of the mightiest conquerors and empire-builders in the world's history, who not without reason styled himself 'king of kings' and 'king of the world.' In an incredibly short time Lydia was invaded, its capital city Sardis was taken, and Croesus made a captive. If the Greeks were impressed with the wealth and magnificence of Croesus, they were even more impressed by his sudden and complete downfall when at the very height of his greatness. A later generation moralized his fate in the following story, which was long current among the Greeks, but of which it is unlikely that any of the details are true to fact. Croesus, bound in chains, was about to be burned

Tomb of Cyrus the Great (Photo credit: Persian Dutch Network).

alive by order of Cyrus, on a great funeral pyre, and in this extremity was overheard to call three times the name of Solon. Cyrus was curious to know the reason for this. He was told by Croesus how once upon a time this wisest of the Athenians had visited Lydia and, after being shown all his treasures, was asked by Croesus whom he counted the happiest and most enviable of mankind. Solon, far from giving the expected answer, made reply: 'Call no man happy until he has died. One should in all things look to the end. For to many a man God gives happiness for a while, then casts him down in utter ruin.' Cyrus was so struck with this warning that he spared Croesus and ever after treated him as a friend.

The Greek cities sought to make terms with the conqueror of Croesus, but Cyrus refused. Being recalled to the far east by conditions there, he entrusted the subjugation of the coast to his general, Harpagus. The residents of Phocaea and of Teos, rather than submit, abandoned their cities and sailed away in a body to found new homes, the one in the western Mediterranean, the other on the north coast of the Aegean. The other cities were conquered and all became part of the Persian empire. Cyrus on returning to the east subdued Babylonia and then pushed his conquests eastwards to the river Indus. Far in the heart of Asia beyond the Caspian Sea he was killed in battle, leaving an empire which extended from the Aegean to the borders of India, and from the Caucasus to the Arabian gulf.

His son and successor, Cambyses, in his short reign added Egypt to the empire and was succeeded by Darius, who became the great organizer and administrator of the empire which Cyrus had conquered and founded. The empire, apart from Persia itself, was divided into twenty provinces, over each of which was placed a 'satrap,' who ruled it virtually as a king, responsible only to the 'Great King' who had appointed him. Susa, the king's capital near Babylon, where he had his winter palace, was linked with these provinces by a system of military roads, chief among which was the 'royal road' from Susa to Sardis in Lydia, a distance of 1500 miles. It was divided into stages, each of them provided with a station where reliefs of horses and couriers were always ready to carry the king's messages. A common system of gold and silver coinage for the whole empire greatly facilitated commerce. Each province, according to its resources, had to send annually to the king a fixed amount of tribute, and each was under obligation to furnish its appropriate contingent to the king's army and navy. And so a strong fleet had been created in the Mediterranean, composed of ships from Phoenicia, Egypt, and the Greek cities. No such extensive or well-organized empire had ever appeared in the world before.

Letter from Darius the Great to Gadatas, satrap in Ionia, about his management of a paradise (royal garden). Greek copy made during the Roman Era, found near Magnesia ad Mæandrum.

Questions

1. Who was Croesus? What did he do to the Greek city-states?
2. What factors led to the defeat of the Greek city-states?
3. What "common defect" or shortcoming led to the defeat of the Greek city-states?
4. How did Croesus treat the Greeks under his rule?
5. In what ways was life under Croesus better for the Greeks?
6. How did Cyrus treat Croesus? Why?
7. How did the Greeks respond to the Persian conquest?
8. How did Darius improve the administration of the Persian empire?
9. What is a satrap? How did the establishment of satrapy help govern the Persian empire?

Vocabulary

assiduously
contingent
satrap

Chapter XIX

The Revolt in Ionia

For the next forty years little is known of conditions or events among the Greeks of Asia Minor. During that period Darius, having set his empire in order, aspired in his turn to extend its borders as Cyrus and Cambyses had done. He organized an expedition which crossed to Europe near Byzantium by a bridge of boats, and annexed all Thrace as far as the Danube on the north and the Strymon on the west. This involved the conquest of numerous Greek colonies scattered along these northern shores; and naval and military contingents from the Greek cities in Asia Minor were compelled to take an unenviable part in enslaving their own kinsmen.

Ionia, which had been joined with Lydia in one satrapy, with Sardis for its capital, finally rose in revolt, led by Miletus. The Greeks, as time went on, had become more and more restive under the despotism of Persia. Their new masters were much less sympathetic to Greek ideals than Croesus and the Lydians. After having a ruler so approachable (in more senses than one) as Croesus had been, it was a great change to realize how insignificant they were in the eyes of the mighty potentate at Susa, two or three months' journey distant. The contrast also between their own subjection and the freedom of the European Greeks must continually have galled them. In addition to all this, at a time when the rest of the Greek world had outgrown the rule of tyrants, the Persians had set up in each city on the coast a tyrant or despot, who was really an agent of the Persian government and who was much less anxious to please the citizens than the king and satrap by whose support and at whose pleasure he ruled.

And so the first step taken by the rebels was to depose these tyrants and set up democratic government in their cities. Appeal was then made to Sparta and Athens for help. Sparta declined to embark on so distant and uncertain an enterprise; but Athens sent twenty ships to aid her fellow Ionians, and to these Eretria, in Euboea, added five, in gratitude for help once received from Miletus. An Ionian army, including the Athenian and Eretrian forces, made an attack on Sardis in the first year of the revolt. The citadel was not taken, but the town was sacked and burned. On its way back to Ephesus the Greek force was attacked by the Persians and defeated, and shortly afterwards some change of political feeling in Athens led to the recall of the Athenian fleet. But the burning of

Sardis roused the other Greeks in Asia Minor, and the revolt spread to the Hellespont on the north and to Cyprus on the south. Persia now massed all her forces in the west to crush the rebellion. Yet, in spite of the tremendous odds against them, the Greeks fought bravely for several years, and it was not till 493 BC that the rebellion was at an end. It culminated in the siege of Miletus by the concentrated land power of Persia, aided by a strong Phoenician fleet, which blockaded the harbor. Finally, off the island of Lade close by, an inferior Greek fleet was badly defeated. Miletus was then taken by storm; its men were all put to death and the women and children carried off into captivity.

Such was the lamentable fate of Miletus, which had for centuries been the foremost city in Greek lands, eminent for its commercial and colonizing activities and memorable for its contributions to the refinement of life and to human thought. The torch of Greek civilization, hitherto borne by Miletus, was henceforth to be carried by Athens. Not long afterwards the poet Phrynichus composed a drama called *The Taking of Miletus,* which so harrowed the feelings of the Athenian audience that they all fell to weeping, and Phrynichus was heavily fined for so vividly recalling to the Athenians their own misfortunes. Perhaps, besides the poignant grief that they felt, there was also some remorse for not having given stronger support to their kinsmen in their revolt.

The Capture of Miletus by Andre Castaigne, 1898

Questions

1. Look on the map at the beginning of the book and locate Ionia?
2. Why did the Greeks become "restive" or unhappy under the rule of Persia?
3. To whom did the Ionians appeal for help? Who came to their aid?
4. How did the Persians respond?
5. How did the destruction of Miletus affect Athens?

Vocabulary:

harrowed
poignant

Cynaegirus grabbing a Persian ship at the Battle of Marathon (19th century illustration). Despite their numerical superiority, the Persians were routed and fled to their ships. The Athenians pursued them, and Cynegeirus in his attempt to hold on the stern of a Persian ship with his bare hands had his hand cut off with an axe and died (Herodotus, Book 6)

Chapter XX

Miltiades And Marathon

When he was told of the burning of Sardis, Darius is said to have given orders that three times each day one of his slaves should say to him: 'My lord, remember the Athenians.' So when the revolt was quelled at last, he made no delay in preparing to exact punishment from the two cities, Athens and Eretria, which had dared to aid his rebellious subjects and to attack his satrap's capital. His son-in-law, Mardonius, was sent with an army into Thrace to march along the coast to Greece, while the fleet accompanied its progress. One reason for choosing this route was to re-establish Persian power in Europe, for during the Ionian revolt Thrace had resumed its independence. But when the great triple promontory of Chalcidice was reached, a violent storm overtook the fleet as it was founding the rocky headland of Mount Athos, and so many ships were wrecked and so many men lost that Mardonius had to return with the king's desire for vengeance unappeased.

There were, of course, other things in the mind of Darius than mere revenge. It was highly desirable to put an end to the disturbing contrast between the freedom of the Greeks in Europe and the subjection of those in Asia; and the ambition also must have been present to add to his empire the one important portion of the civilized world yet unconquered. Moreover, for some years Hippias, the exiled son of Pisistratus, had been at the Persian court, urging that he be restored to his tyranny in Athens, on the understanding that he should hold it as vassal of the king of Persia.

Two years later an entirely different route was taken. A great army was gathered and embarked on a fleet of 600 vessels which, under the command of Datis and Artaphernes, was to sail direct to Greece across the Aegean sea through the islands. Heralds had previously been sent to the chief cities of Greece to demand 'earth and water,' which, according to Persian usage, were the tokens of submission. Many cities complied with the demand: the might of Persia appeared to them irresistible. The greatest powers that they knew, Lydia and Egypt, had been quickly forced to yield, and the fate of Miletus was fresh in the memories of all. Having also had no experience of the rule of an alien despotic power, they perhaps scarcely realized the value of their freedom. But Sparta and Athens brusquely refused. At Sparta the king's messengers were thrown into a muddy well and bidden to find there the earth and water their master desired. Sparta with most of the Peloponnesian states had formed a league, to which Athens also had lately been admitted; but there is no indication that any common measures of defense were being planned. In the usual Greek fashion, each state acted by itself. We may be sure, however, that at Athens there was much discussion of the question what should be done, as news kept coming of the gradual approach of the Persian fleet.

It was fortunate for Athens that she had now had twenty years of self-government, during which her chief men had grown wise in council through the responsibilities of leadership laid upon them, while her citizen soldiers had gained a new military spirit born of freedom. Herodotus, the Greek historian of the war with Persia, tells how the Athenians, as long as they were under a tyranny, were no better than their neighbors, but, when rid of the tyrants, they became the best of soldiers. As he explains, men working for a master never do their best as they will when achieving something for themselves. Especially was Athens fortunate in having the services of Miltiades, an exceptionally able Greek who had lately arrived in Athens. He was the nephew of that Miltiades who, in the time of Pisistratus, had gone out to rule the settlement founded by Athenians in the Thracian Chersonese (now the Gallipoli peninsula), and on his uncle's death he had succeeded to his power. Besides being a man of great ability and well versed in the management of men and affairs, he had personal knowledge of the Persians. He had been with the Persian army during the campaign in Thrace twenty years before and knew their methods of warfare, their strength, and their weaknesses. Now, though he had taken no open part in the Ionian revolt, he deemed it politic to leave the country when the revolt was crushed and to make his residence in Athens. Here he was allowed to resume his citizenship, and his ability and experience were recognized by his being made one of the ten generals who led the various tribal divisions of the Athenian army, under the polemarch (or commander-in-chief) Callimachus.

To the anxious citizens of Athens and their leaders trading vessels and fugitives brought frequent word of the enemy's movements. They heard thus, late in the summer, that the Persian fleet had at last set sail from Samos; that Naxos, an island hitherto free, had been visited, the town with its temples burned to the ground, and such of its inhabitants as had not escaped to the hills made slaves; that Delos, the birthplace of Apollo, had been spared, though its people had fled from it in terror of the Persians. After Delos the route to Athens and that to Eretria diverged; which city would the Persians attack first? Then came word that they had turned north to Euboea and had landed at Carystus, at its southern extremity. The Carystians at first rejected the Persian terms, but were soon forced into submission. Then came the turn of Eretria, and day after day news came of the disembarking of the enemy, of the Eretrians retreating within their walls, because they felt themselves too weak to oppose the Persians in the field, and of their stout resistance for six long, anxious days. Finally the news came which they were dreading to hear. On the seventh day, by an act of treachery from within, the city was taken, plundered, and burned, and all its inhabitants were placed on transports to be taken back as slaves to Darius as he had commanded. And now the Athenians knew that their turn would come next, and the council of war had to decide what plan to adopt. Miltiades strongly urged that they go forth boldly to meet the enemy when he landed, and Callimachus had the good sense to take his advice.

The rocky coast of Attica does not permit the landing of an army from a fleet at many points, and the Athenians may have suspected that Hippias, who was returning with Datis and Artaphernes, would advise them to follow the plan that had proved so successful years before, when his father

Plain of Marathon from the top of the Tomb of the Athenians (Photo credit: Tomisti]).

Pisistratus, also coming from Euboea, had landed quietly at Marathon and had then marched on the city, only twenty-five miles distant. So when word came that the Persians were disembarking in the bay of Marathon, the Athenians were not taken by surprise, and their force of 9,000 or 10,000 men at once marched out and took up a position which experts today agree was most admirably chosen. Looking on Marathon one sees a curving shore and a small plain shut in by hills on every side. Two roads from Athens enter the plain, the main road at the south end, along the narrow space between the mountains and the sea, the other a path coming in from the south-west over the hills.

The Athenians came by the latter route and, without descending to the plain, encamped on the high ground where they would have the protection of the hills from any flank attack, and at the same time could watch every movement of the Persians.

They had, meanwhile, sent their swiftest runner to Sparta, one hundred and forty miles away, to tell them that the Persians were landing, and to urge them to send a force to their aid. The Spartans readily promised help, but said that certain religious rules forbade their setting out before the full moon, and this meant a week's delay. On the other hand, the Athenians were encouraged by a force of 1,000 heavy-armed men marching in from the town of Plataea just over the border in Boeotia. This little state had many years before had trouble with Thebes, which sought to force it to enter the Boeotian league. The Plataeans, who were probably of pre-Dorian stock, like the people of Attica, had objected, and Athens had given them her support and protection, never dreaming that she would ever find reinforcements from little Plataea so welcome.

The Persians were in some perplexity; they had counted on approaching Athens with their whole force of infantry and cavalry marshalled in an invincible array; but now if they attempted to march out by the road along the shore, they were in danger of a flank attack upon their long line of march. There was a delay of several days, which well suited the Athenians, for every day brought

The Treasury of the Athenians at Delphi. (Erected after Marathon. The inscription is still legible: 'The Athenians to Apollo the spoils of the Medes from the battle at Marathon.')

nearer the full moon when the Spartans would march to reinforce them. At last the Persians made their decision; they set about re-embarking part of their troops, which were to be sent round by sea to land opposite Athens. At the same time the rest of their army, considerably more numerous than the Athenians, was drawn up in battle array at a short distance from the shore. It was a shrewd plan. If the Athenians remained in their camp, they must leave their city without defense; and if, alarmed for the safety of Athens, they should withdraw, the Persian army could march unmolested to join the others when they landed.

The Athenians did not do either. They had now the opportunity for which Miltiades had been waiting, and they at once made ready to attack. But they were inferior in numbers, and if they made their line of uniform depth, it would be shorter than the Persian line, and when they reached the plain might easily be enveloped from the wings. Callimachus therefore lengthened his line by weakening the center, while the two wings were left at full strength. The plan of attack was thoroughly understood; nothing was left to chance, and everything happened as the Greek leaders had expected. The Greek equipment was quite different from the Persian. The Greeks were armed with long spears and protected by breastplates, greaves, and stout shields. As they advanced, the first line or two would have their spears lowered for the attack, while those behind, with their spears aloft all ready to be lowered when needed, would give impetus to the shock when the actual moment of onset came. The Persians had bows and arrows, with which they were very expert, and short swords for close fighting if it came to that. Their defensive armor was very slight consisting mainly of wicker shields.

The Greeks raised their battle-song and advanced over the plain towards the Persian line, which had its best troops in the center. When they came within range of the Persian archers they were met with a shower of arrows, but immediately they quickened their pace to a run so as to lose as few men as possible before getting to close quarters. As had been foreseen, the weak center was able to make no impression on the Persian line and was driven back; but the two wings, charging with tremendous force, swept aside the troops opposed to them. Then, instead of exultantly pursuing them

Helmet of Miltiades given as an offering by Miltiades to the temple of Zeus at Olympia. Inscription on the helmet: MILTIAΔES dedicates this helmet to Zeus (Archaeological Museum of Olympia. Photo credit: Oren Rozen).

Soldier of Marathon announcing the Victory, by Jean-Pierre Cortot, 1822, Louvre Museum. [Photo credit Stephane Magnenat] See footnote on opposite page.

as would ordinarily have happened, they kept their heads and, following the plan agreed upon, wheeled inwards towards the center and made a quite unexpected attack from either flank upon the Persians, who were doubtless somewhat disorganized in their repulse of the Greek center.

The Persian center was completely crushed, and the Greeks, pursuing them to the shore, cut down many as they were taking refuge on their ships. The fighting at the shore was even fiercer than in the plain, and it was here that the chief Athenian loss was sustained. But altogether only 193 of the Greeks perished, while the Persians lost over 6,000. All the Persian ships except seven got clear away, and the whole fleet sailed off to the south, hoping to find the city unguarded. But the Greeks started back at once, and had time to reach the city before the enemy could land. Their arrival prevented any landing being attempted, and the Persian fleet was soon seen disappearing in the distance on its way back to Asia. The Persians had still a much stronger force than Athens could oppose to them; but they knew now the fighting qualities of the Athenians, and they also very probably knew all about the impending reinforcement from Sparta. The Spartan force was sent, as promised, and arrived soon after the battle, but too late to be of any service. They marched on to Marathon, however, viewed the battlefield and the spoil and the bodies of the Persian dead, and then with words of high praise for the Athenians they returned home.

Marathon has always been counted one of the most important battles in the world's history. It did not actually decide finally whether European Greece should be free or become subject to an eastern despot; for Persia had immense resources which had by no means been fully used in this expedition, and, so far from the defeat disheartening the Persian king, it but added one more to the offences for which that proud monarch had resolved to obtain vengeance and satisfaction. But what the victory did accomplish was to put fresh courage into the hearts of the freedom-loving Greeks, so that when the Persians should come again they would find a stouter resistance. Especially it also kindled the pride and roused the spirit of the Athenians, who now felt that their city was indeed second to none in Greece. For all time, the Athenians looked back upon Marathon as their most glorious exploit, as the English look back upon the defeat of the Armada or the Scots upon Bannockburn; and the memory was cherished all the more because, except for the Plataean aid, the strategy and the victory were all their own. So the epitaph composed for the great poet Aeschylus made no reference to the dramas which have made his name immortal, but proudly told that he had been one of those who beat back the Persians at Marathon. To those who fell at Marathon a signal honor was paid. The usual custom was to bring back the bodies of those slain in battle for burial, at home; but these were buried on the field of their glory, and the mound raised over them stands conspicuous on the plain of Marathon to this day and is known as the Tomb of the Athenians.[9]

---

[9] The story is told how the messenger sent from Marathon to Athens to bring word of the victory so exerted himself to his very utmost that on arrival he could but gasp out his glorious news and then fell dead among the throng of citizens. When, in 1896, the Olympic games were revived, the first celebration was appropriately held at Athens, and it was decided to have a race run over the road from the battlefield to the city, a distance of about 25 miles. This distance has been retained in all succeeding Marathon races wherever the games have been held. On this first occasion, to the very natural delight of the Greeks, the first runner to reach the goal in Athens was one of their own countrymen.

Burial Mound of the Plataeans, Marathon, Greece [Photo credit: Alun Salt].

Questions

1. Why did Darius hate Athens so much?
2. What happened to the first attempt to invade Greece by the Persians under Mardonius?
3. How did Sparta and Athens react to the Persian request to surrender?
4. How had the 20 years of self-government affected the Athenian people?
5. According to Herodotus, why did democracy make the Athenians better soldiers?
6. Describe the strengths of Miltiades.
7. What did the Persians do to Eretria? How did this influence Athen's plans?
8. Draw a diagram of the battle at Marathon and describe the Athenian strategy.
9. What did this battle fail to accomplish?
10. Why, according to the authors, has the battle at Marathon always been counted as …one of the most important battles in the world's history?

Vocabulary

despot
epitaph
stouter

Chapter XXI

Ten Years' Breathing Space

Deeply incensed at the failure of Marathon, Darius set about making sure of his revenge in a new invasion. But a serious revolt in Egypt broke out, and, while engaged in suppressing it, he himself died. His son, Xerxes, who succeeded him, put down the Egyptian rebellion and then began most elaborate preparations for completing his father's unfinished task. Thus the third attempt to conquer Greece was delayed until 480 BC. Xerxes determined to follow the route taken by Mardonius in 493 BC, but to have both army and navy vastly stronger. To prevent a recurrence of the disaster off Mount Athos, he had a canal dug through the isthmus north of this stormy headland. This work took three years, during which ships were being built and a double bridge of boats thrown across the strong current of the Hellespont. Thus was Xerxes to 'march over the sea and sail through the land.' The fleet was not only to act as a naval force but also to transport provisions for the land army. For in so mountainous and sparsely populated a land, the army could not possibly live off the country. In Thrace, therefore, depots of provisions were established along the line of march, while after these were left behind the fleet would serve as a base of supplies.

Even though the Greeks may have known little of these extensive preparations, it would seem mere elementary prudence, after the danger they had just escaped, for the states of Greece to take counsel with one another how to meet the impending invasion. But some were afraid to resist, and others hated their neighbors more than they feared Persia. Many also believed, or affected to believe, that revenge on Athens alone was intended; and even if all had been convinced that their own freedom was menaced, the ingrained habit of generations would have made impossible a really effective league for common defense. Indeed, bitter warfare between neighbors did not cease, in spite of their common danger. Thus Argos and Sparta were at war in 494 BC, as were Athens and the large neighboring island of Aegina for several years after 487 BC. Two things saved Greece and European civilization: the fact that Sparta, which was the predominant power in the Peloponnesus and had the strongest army in Greece, was under no illusion but saw clearly that the Persian king contemplated the subjugation of all Greece; and the fact that at this time Athens had, in Themistocles, one of the ablest statesmen that ever lived.

Themistocles was not of noble birth, and before the time of Cleisthenes would have had no chance of political preeminence in Athens. He was distinguished for two qualities: his gift of farsighted vision, and his ability to decide rapidly on the best course in an emergency. The former alone might have left him an ineffective visionary; with only the latter he would have been but an adroit politician and opportunist. He saw more clearly than any of his contemporaries the value of a strong navy in meeting a foe so dependent on their fleet as the Persian invaders; and, looking beyond the immediate present, he realized that a strong navy would give Athens predominance in Greek affairs such as even Sparta's incomparable army could not secure for her. It was by virtue of this insight that, as a modern historian writes, 'he contributed more than any other single man to the making of Athens into a great state.' But he had to meet strong opposition in getting his policy adopted. The influence of sea-power was a new idea; the army of heavy-armed foot-soldiers, such as had fought so well at Marathon, was the traditional dependence of every Greek state.

He had begun to urge his revolutionary policy even before Marathon. His first success was in getting the Piraeus, instead of Phalerum, made the harbor for the Athenian war-vessels. Phalerum is but a stretch of open beach, convenient enough for hauling the light Greek vessels up on shore and in full view from Athens. The bay of Piraeus is hidden from the city by rising ground between, but it is a fine natural harbor and could easily be made impregnable by fortifications; and these fortifications Themistocles persuaded the Athenians to sanction. Experience has ever since confirmed his judgment. Today the Piraeus is one of the great sea-ports of the Mediterranean, while Phalerum is but the summer bathing resort of Athens. His second success was more striking. The silver mines at Laurium in south-eastern Attica belonged to the state, and the revenue had greatly increased of late because of some newly discovered veins. The usual practice would have been to divide wealth thus accruing among the citizens; but Themistocles was able to persuade them to forgo their immediate pleasure and devote the whole sum to adding vessels to the fleet, an increase which made it far the strongest Greek fleet in the Aegean.

During all this time Athens was becoming steadily more democratic. Of the two great parties which now divided the state, one party, consisting of the farmers and landholders, was conservative in its views. The other, made up of the artisans and traders and sailors of Athens and the Piraeus, tended to be more radical. But neither party favored a return to a tyranny or to an oligarchy. Aristides, commonly called 'the Just,' a scrupulously honest patriot, was leader of the conservative democrats and opposed the new policies advocated by

Bust of Themistocles the Museo Ostiense (Ostia Antica). [Photo credit: Sailko].

Themistocles, but unsuccessfully. In adopting these policies, Athens was really deciding that she was to become a naval and commercial, instead of an agricultural, state, and that her democracy was to tend in the direction of radicalism. One change that was made at this time is worth noting. The nine archons, it was decided, should no longer be chosen by ballot, but by lot from a large selected list of citizens. This was considered a more democratic method, for every man's chance of the honor was now more nearly equal. The real outcome was that this office ceased to be of much importance, as the lot would usually fall on very average people, and an archon, moreover, could not be re-elected. On the other hand, the board of ten generals gained what importance the archons lost; for it was obviously absurd to choose a general by lot, and an able and popular man might be elected general year after year and thus exert great influence in the state's affairs.

Port of Piraeus today - Panoramic view of the western part of the city and the port of Piraeus (periphery of Attica) in Greece [Photo credit: Nikolaos Diakidis].

Questions

1. What preparations did Xerxes make for the invasion of Greece?
2. How did the Greek city-states act toward each other after Marathon while the Persians prepared to invade again?
3. What two things during this period saved Greece and European civilization from the impending invasion of the Persians?
4. Describe Themistocles. What two qualities did he possess that made him a great leader?
5. Describe the policies that Themistocles convinced Athens to adopt that prepared them for an invasion by Persia.
6. Changes were taking place within the government of Athens during this time. Describe both the general changes and the particular changes in the government and what diffence these changes made to Athens.
   a. General (overall) changes:
   b. Particular changes:

Vocabulary

subjugation
adroit
impregnable

Chapter XXII

Leonidas and Thermopylae

If Xerxes' army was made up, as we are told, of contingents from forty-six nations comprising his vast empire, many thousands of his troops must have been more picturesque than useful. But, like many other details given in the ancient accounts (such as the prodigious number of 5,000,000 men in the army and fleet combined, the seven days and seven nights required to march across the Hellespont, and the rivers drunk dry by the immense host on the march), this statement would seem to be an artistic exaggeration intended to heighten the contrast between the elaborate preparations and the ultimate failure. A fair estimate of the strength of the expedition would give about 300,000 infantry, with a considerable number of cavalry and camp-followers, and a fleet of perhaps 1,000 vessels, of which two-thirds would be war-vessels. But even with this huge reduction, the numbers were far beyond any land force that the Greeks could assemble. Thanks to Themistocles' foresight, the disparity in ships was not so great.

Xerxes in person led his army, which marched through Thrace and Macedonia, without encountering any opposition. North of the Isthmus there was but one place where the Persian advance might possibly be checked. No position could be imagined more suited to the strategy of the Greeks than the pass of Thermopylae, by which any army advancing out of Thessaly must enter southern Greece. A mountain range crossed the country without a practicable opening, and ended in a steep cliff overlooking the sea and leaving only a few yards of roadway between. Here a small force could hold back a multitude. But could not the fleet land a strong force farther south to take the defenders in the rear? The map will show how this danger could be removed. If the narrow channel left between the long island of Euboea and the mainland could be closed to the enemy's fleet, there could be no possible cooperation between the navy and the land-forces, and on this cooperation the Persians were absolutely dependent.

To guard this channel, the Greek fleet sailed north to Artemisium, while a land-force marched to Thermopylae. This force was composed of some 7,000 men, of whom 4,000 were Peloponnesians, including 3,000 Arcadians. The other 3,000 were from the districts of Phocis, Locris, and Boeotia, north of the Isthmus. Sparta was represented by its king Leonidas, who was in command of the whole force, and by the king's bodyguard of 300. More were promised from Sparta, but none were sent. The absence of Athenians was due to their presence in large numbers with the fleet, of which they furnished more than half.

Towards the end of August the host of Xerxes, which had set out in the spring, reached Thermopylae. For four days no attack was made; Xerxes expected that the mere sight of his vast army would make the Greeks withdraw. Then on the fifth day, in anger, he sent some troops to bring the Greeks captive into his presence. These having failed, others were sent, but equally in vain. Finally his famous 'Immortals' advanced but fared no better, for they were fighting in a confined space and so got no advantage from their numbers, and their spears had not the reach of the long Greek spears. For two days the incessant attacks went on. The Greeks, who were numerous enough to be able to relieve one another, had lost very few, and the Persians, after prodigious losses, were no nearer their goal. Then a native of the district, named Ephialtes, went to Xerxes and offered to guide a Persian force over a circuitous mountain trail that would bring them down in the rear of the Greeks. These latter were aware of the existence of the path and had posted the Phocians at the summit to guard it. But the Phocians were stupidly led, and let the Persians get past them.

When word was brought to Leonidas that the Persians were coming down the mountain path, a hasty council of war was held. As a result, Leonidas with a portion of the Greeks remained to hold the pass, while the main body withdrew and marched away to the south. The usual account is that

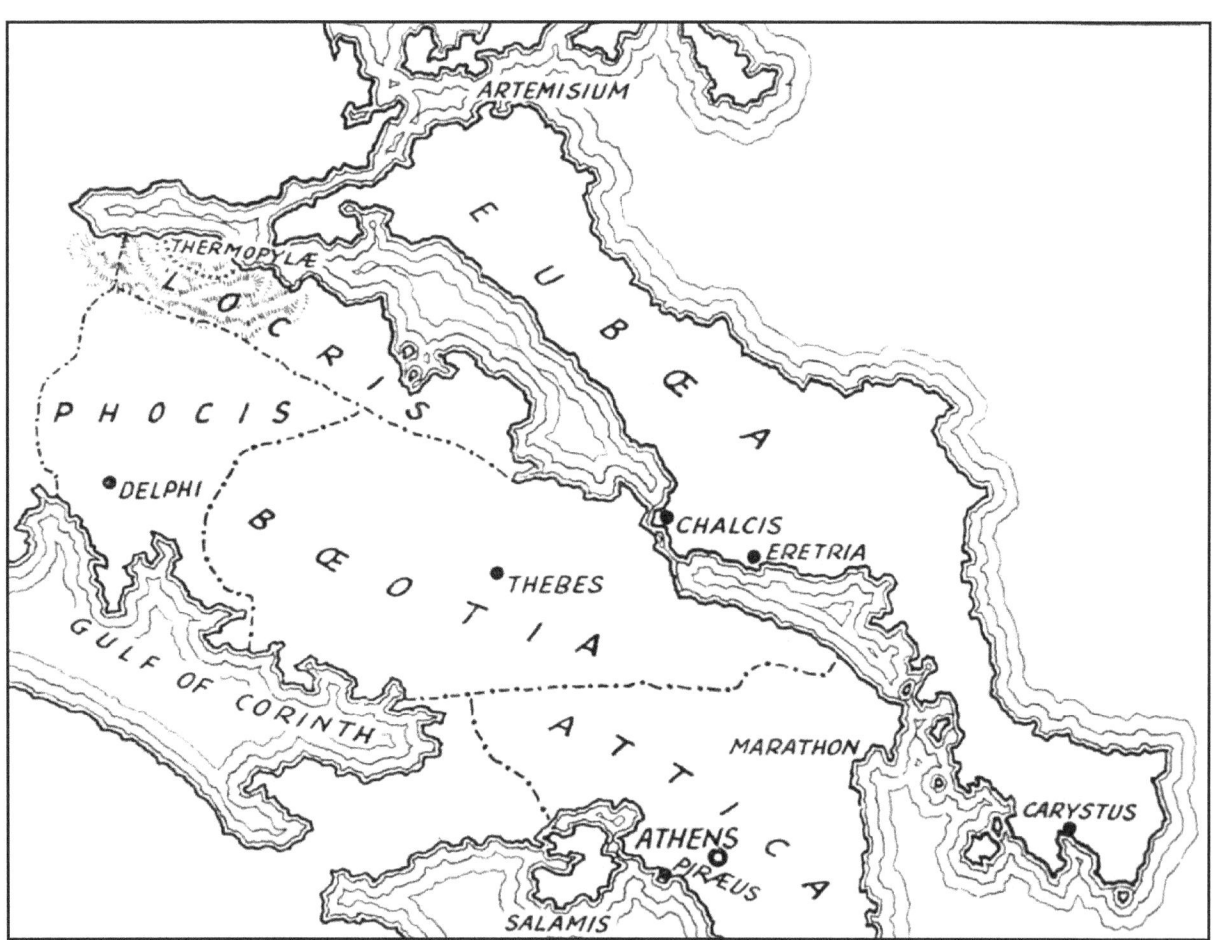

Thermopylae.

Leonidas and his bodyguard remained because, according to their traditions, Spartans could not in honor retreat in the face of an enemy, while he sent the others away that they at least might be saved to fight again. Many modern historians are inclined to believe that the larger force was sent back with orders to occupy some advantageous point where they could oppose the Persians threatening their rear, and that this for some reason they failed to do.

In any event, for Leonidas and the troops who remained with him there was now no retreat, and they resolved to sell their lives dear. His men, who besides the 300 Spartans included 700 from Thespiae in Boeotia, now advanced from the shelter of the narrow pass, that all might have room to fight, and the enemy fell in large numbers. Behind the Persians stood their commanders, whip in hand, smiting their men to drive them to the attack. After a time the Greek spears were all broken, but they went on slaying Persians with their swords. Leonidas fell; and a fierce fight raged over his body, which his men had four times to rescue from the onrush of the foe. At last the troops guided by the traitor Ephialtes were close at hand. Then the Greeks retired into the narrowest part of the pass; there, forming a circle, they defended themselves to the very last until everyone was slain. So fell the men of Sparta and Thespiae under Leonidas, leaving behind them an undying memory of devoted heroism. Perhaps the most famous epitaph ever written and the one most universally admired is that composed by the poet Simonides for the fallen Spartans. No translation of the brief two lines of verse has ever succeeded in reproducing the simple beauty of the original Greek; but its modest and dignified reserve may be seen even in the bald, literal rendering: 'Stranger, tell the Lacedaemonians that we lie here obedient to their commands.'

Meantime at Artemisium the rival fleets were engaged in a series of fights without any decisive result. Although the Persians had twice suffered heavy losses by storms on this dangerous coast, they had perhaps the better of the fighting. But they had not yet succeeded in forcing their way through the strait when word was brought to the Greek admiral that the defense of Thermopylae had failed. Obviously there was no longer any reason for the Greek fleet to remain at Artemisium, and it sailed down through the inner channel and cast anchor in the bay of Salamis near Athens.

Leonidas of Sparta, monument at Thermopylae [Photo credit: Praxinoa].

Questions

1. Describe the army of Xerxes.
2. Describe the make-up of the Greek army. Why were there no Athenians?
3. Describe the pass at Thermopylae. Why was it so well suited for the Greek's defense?
4. What took place in the first few days of the battle?
5. How were the Greeks finally defeated?
6. Write a description of the final battle at Thermopylae including a description of who was there and how they fought.
7. What role did the Greek navy play in the battle of Thermopylae?
8. Who won the battle of Thermopylae? Defend your answer.
9. Why was this battle important for the Greeks?

Vocabulary

disparity
circuitous

Chapter XXIII

Themistocles and Salamis

The heroism shown at Thermopylae should not blind us to the fact that it was a victory for the Persians, whose way to Athens was now clear of all likely opposition. They marched through Phocis and through Boeotia, where they burned Thespiae and Plataea and received the ready submission of Thebes, and then they entered Attica. Here, while the Persians were advancing southwards with their vast army and their fleet, a busy scene was being enacted on the seashore near Athens. As soon as their fleet returned from Artemisium, the Athenians had taken the heroic resolve to abandon their city, to leave the land that had been the immemorial home of their fathers, and to transport to a place of greater safety all their women and children, with such of their belongings as could easily be carried. Some were conveyed to Troezen, the fabled birthplace of Theseus, on the opposite coast of the Peloponnesus, others to Aegina and Salamis, the islands nearest to Athens. Everywhere, there were sad hearts, for not only were people parting from the lifelong associations of their homes, but there were many farewells to be said to husbands and sons and fathers who had to leave their exiled families and serve in the fleet—those 'wooden walls' to which the Delphic oracle had bidden them entrust their defense. It is interesting to read that the people of Troezen voted a daily allowance for the maintenance of each refugee family and arranged for the schooling of the children, who were also given leave to take freely of the fruit of any tree.

Before the middle of September the Persian army was encamped in the outskirts of Athens and the Persian fleet was riding off the shore close by. A few Athenians who had remained on the Acropolis sturdily defended it for some days, but at last the Persians scaled the heights, slaughtered all the defenders, and set on fire the temples and other buildings on the Acropolis. From their new temporary homes in Aegina, Salamis, and Troezen, as well as from the Greek fleet off Salamis, the Athenians could see the flames rising from their burning temples. Thus was Sardis avenged at last; and a messenger was sent off by Xerxes to his mother, Atossa, in Susa, to tell her how the irresistible might of Persia had accomplished the purpose of her husband Darius.

Meanwhile among the commanders of the fleet at Salamis there was much discussion of the next step to be taken. While the army of Leonidas and the fleet had been fighting in the north, the

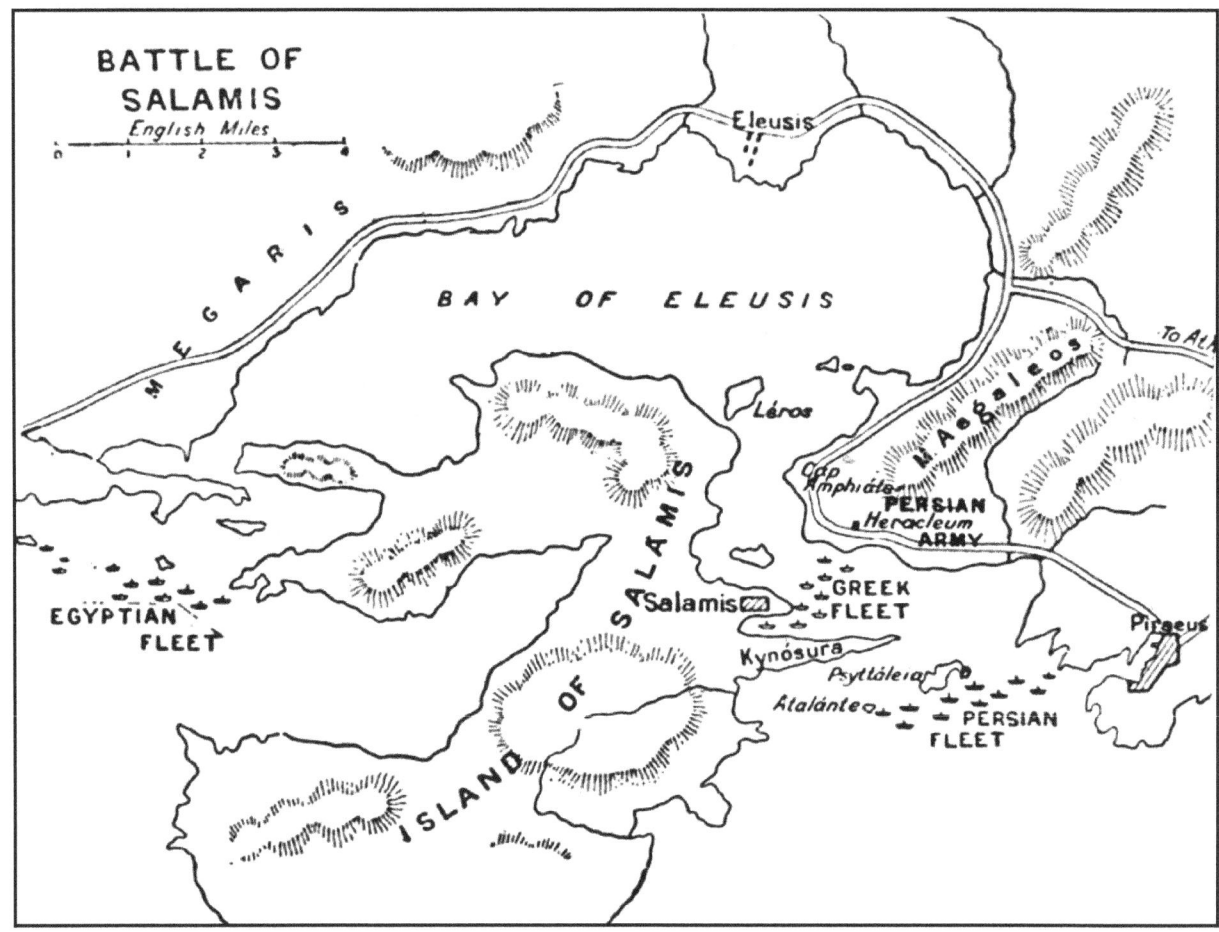

Plan of Salamis.

Spartans and the other Peloponnesians had been busy building a strong wall across the Isthmus. Apparently, in their self-centered short-sightedness they quite overlooked the fact that it would be easy for the Persians to land a force elsewhere on the coast of the Peloponnesus and thus make the wall of no avail. The Peloponnesian commanders were for retiring to the Isthmus to cooperate with the land-forces gathered there. This, of course, meant that Salamis, Aegina, and Megara, as well as Athens, must be abandoned, and the representatives of these cities, whose ships constituted more than two-thirds of the entire fleet, naturally protested. Moreover, Themistocles was anxious, for another reason, to bring about a battle in the straits near Salamis. The Persian fleet was larger than the Greek. Its ships, though bigger, were less heavily built and more easily handled; and the Phoenicians, Egyptians, and Ionians who composed the crews were more skillful seamen than the Greeks of the mainland, many of whom had as yet had little experience. It would, therefore, be greatly to the advantage of the enemy to have plenty of sea-room for fighting; but in the confined waters off Salamis this advantage would be lost, and with ships crowded close together the superior fighting qualities of the individual Greek would count for more than the enemy's greater skill in maneuvering. The argument that finally prevailed with the council of commanders was the threat of Themistocles that, if the selfish policy of the Peloponnesians were persisted in, the Athenians would withdraw their two hundred vessels, and, putting all their families on board ship, would sail away, as the Phocaeans had done some years before, and settle in the distant west.

But it takes two to make a battle, and Themistocles had as yet effected only one half of his purpose. It still remained to induce the Persians, contrary to their real interest, to engage in a fight at Salamis, instead of waiting for their army to reach the Isthmus. Themistocles' resourcefulness was equal to the task of convincing them that now, and not later, was their opportunity of victory. He sent a secret messenger to Xerxes, assuring him of his good-will to the Persian cause, and informing him that the Greek commanders were hopelessly divided, and that the fleet was on the point of breaking up and sailing away. If the Persians would only close the entrances to the strait, they would have the whole fleet at their mercy.

Soldiers of Xerxes' army. Left to right: two Chaldean infantryman and two Persians: Babylonian archer, Assyrian infantryman.

Xerxes swallowed the baited hook; and that night the Persian ships moved forward in two divisions: the Egyptians to occupy the farther exit near Megara, the major part of the fleet to prevent any escape by the eastern exit. The Greek council of war was again hotly debating the question of retirement, when Aristides, Themistocles' political rival (who, like the other Athenians at this time, had sunk all personal and party feeling in the presence of the common danger) came over from Aegina and brought the first news of the Persian blockade. There was but one thing now for the Greeks to do; they set about preparing zealously for battle when dawn should break.

Xerxes had a throne set up for him on a rocky platform under Mount Aegaleus overlooking the bay of Salamis, and here he and his courtiers came early to witness the spectacle of the Greeks' discomfiture. And a wonderful sight it must have been, to look down upon this narrow stretch of water in which some nine hundred war-vessels were fiercely engaged for hours in the clear Greek sunlight, undimmed by any smoke of battle. This sea-fight is vividly described for us in a Greek drama, *The Persians,* written by Aeschylus only a few years later. It is a unique thing to have a great battle described by a great poet, who himself took part in it. In this drama Queen Atossa is discussing with the nobles of the Persian court in Susa the chances of the king's victorious return, when a courier arrives with the news of the disastrous fight at Salamis. His account of that battle reads thus in part:

Soldiers of Xerxes' army, from left to right: Persian flag-bearer, Armenian soldier, Cappadocian soldier.

For with no thought of flight
The Greeks sang loud their solemn battle-hymn,
But eager for the fray and stout of heart;
And the trumpet's blare set all their ranks on fire.

. . .

And now from every ship was heard one cry:
'O sons of Greece, advance and freedom win;
Your country free, your children and your wives,
The tombs of your forefathers, and the shrines
Where dwell your gods. Now for all these ye fight.'

. . .

At first the onward-streaming Persian host
Held firm; but when in the strait our countless ships
Were crowded close, and none might help his friend,
Then by the impact of our own bronze beaks
Our serried banks of oars were broken short;
The while the Greeks, alert to seize the chance,
Circled about and smote; and everywhere
Floated our hulls o'erturned, until the sea
Itself no more was visible, thick strewn
With wrecks of ships and bodies of dead men.

A romantic version painting of the battle by artist Wilhelm von Kaulbach, 1868.

It was not on the sea only that Xerxes, horror-stricken, had to witness the slaughter of his men. At the entrance to the straight is a small island, Psytalleia, on which a considerable Persian force had been landed, in order to deal with any Greeks who might take refuge there during the battle. The rout of the Persian fleet left these men at the mercy of the Greeks, who, as soon as the fight began to go in their favor, sent over a body of troops from Salamis and slew them every one.

Immediately after the battle of Salamis, which was fought late in September, Xerxes with a large escort set out by land to return to Persia. Mardonius, with the more efficient portion of the army, numbering perhaps 200,000 men, went north to spend the winter in the broad plains of Thessaly, where he could more easily get sustenance for his cavalry. The remnant of the fleet sailed to the Hellespont to secure the king's passage to Asia, in case Ionia should revolt. Meanwhile the Athenians brought back their families to the ruins of their city. An amusing story, which is probably the invention of a later time, tells how the Greeks after the battle decided to award a prize to the man who had most distinguished himself at Salamis, and how each commander, on casting his ballot, wrote his own name first, but all agreed in placing Themistocles second.

Questions

1. After the battle at Thermopylae, what did the Athenians decide to do?
2. What did the Spartans do?
3. Why was Themistocles so eager to engage the Persians in a naval battle in the straits of Salamis?
4. What advantage did the Athenian navy have? What advantages did the Persian navy have?
5. How did Themistocles convince both the Spartans and the Persians to fight at Salamis?
6. What was the Persian strategy in the battle?
7. How was the much smaller Greek navy able to defeat the Persian navy?
8. What did Xerxes and the Persians do as a result of this battle?

Vocabulary

discomfiture
induce
sustenance

Chapter XXIV

The Final Repulse of Persia

Salamis was the turning-point of the war, but Greece was by no means yet safe. Danger threatened from two quarters: from the strong force left under Mardonius to complete the subjugation of Greece; and from the strange persistence of the Spartans in their selfish blindness to the necessity for the most complete cooperation. Even yet they do not seem to have realized that, even although the Peloponnesus should escape invasion for the present, to have the permanent frontier of the Persian empire pushed to the very Isthmus would be a perpetual menace to their freedom.

In the spring Mardonius came down to Boeotia, and by the most liberal promises sought to induce the Athenians to abandon the cause of the other Greeks. The Athenian answer was that, as long as the sun moved in its course, they would never make terms with the Persian king. Thereupon Mardonius invaded Attica, and the Athenians a second time removed their families by sea, this time to Salamis. The Spartans still showed no sign of sending their forces outside of the Peloponnesus; and it was obviously useless for the Athenians a second time to threaten the withdrawal of their ships, for Sparta had no longer any cause to fear the Persian fleet. Accordingly the Athenians sent word to Sparta that if adequate support was not immediately forthcoming, they would be compelled to do as Thebes had done and join the Persians. Sparta, realizing what this would mean, now for the first time in the war sent a strong army beyond the Isthmus. Mardonius retired into Boeotia, and here the allied Greek army followed him.

This was the largest army the Greek states ever put in the field in their whole history. It consisted of perhaps 100,000 men, of whom less than 40,000 were heavy-armed men, the rest being light-armed troops. The Spartans sent 5,000 Spartiates, and as many of the Perioeci, together with a surprisingly large number (35,000) of Helots—possibly as hostages. Athens contributed 8,000 heavy-armed men, Corinth 5,000, and Mycenae and Tiryns, now very unimportant places, sent, we are told, a combined force of 400 men. The whole army was under the command of Pausanias, the nephew of Leonidas and the guardian of his son, who was still a child.

The two armies confronted each other for days on the northern slopes of the range of Cithaeron, not far from Plataea. Pausanias was an able leader, but no Greek had had any experience in handling

North wall of Acropolis. (The sections of pillars are from temples destroyed by the Persians.)

so large a body of men, and all sorts of blunders were made by the Greeks, who were out-maneuvered by Mardonius and harassed continually by the Persian cavalry. But no mistake made by the Greeks equaled the culminating blunder of Mardonius, who, thinking to take advantage of certain confused movements of the Greeks, launched an attack on their isolated right wing. This, as it happened, was composed of the Lacedaemonian contingent, with 1,500 from Tegea in Arcadia. It was a fatal mistake, which Marathon should have taught him to avoid, to bring on a pitched battle between the Persians with their slight defensive armament and the best-disciplined and best-armed fighting men in the world. The Persians fought bravely enough, but they were no match for the Greeks. In the fighting, Mardonius was slain, and the whole Persian force fled in confusion to their stockaded camp on the plain. This was soon taken by storm, and the Persian army was practically annihilated. Simultaneously, the left wing, where the Athenians were, was engaged with a large body of Greeks who had joined the Persians; of these the Thebans were the most conspicuous. These 'medizing' Greeks (those who collaborated with the Persians) were also defeated; and in retaliation for their treachery to Greece, Pausanias laid siege to Thebes until the leaders of the medizing party were given up for summary execution.

The Athenian fleet had meanwhile gone to assist the Asiatic Greeks to regain their independence, and at the same time as the battle of Plataea—tradition says on the very same day—a battle

Head of Gelon I, diademed. Reverse: Biga driven by winged Nike (Boston Museum of Fine Art)

was fought at Mycale, a cape near Samos, in which the Greeks won a complete victory over a combined land and sea force. No Persian army ever again entered Greece, and within a few years all the islands and the Greek cities in Asia Minor and on the Hellespont were freed from the Persian yoke.

While the army of Xerxes was invading Europe, in the far western island of Sicily, the Carthaginians had landed a great army at their city of Panormus (now Palermo) and were marching along the coast to attack the Greek city of Himera. The motive of Carthage was not merely her ambition to extend her influence over this rich island, of which she held only the extreme western corner. There is no doubt that the attack was instigated by Xerxes, working through his subjects in Phoenicia. His aim, of course, was to make the powerful cities of the west so concerned for their own safety that they should send no help to their mother-cities in Greece. To that extent the plan succeeded. But the tyrant of Himera appealed for help to his son-in-law, Gelon, the brilliant and energetic tyrant of Syracuse, and Gelon's vigor in coming to the relief of Himera caused the utter failure of the expedition. Carthage was glad to purchase peace by paying a huge indemnity. As a result of this battle of Himera, which was fought in the same year as Salamis, Sicily remained Greek, and played no inconsiderable part in the spread of Greek civilization in the Mediterranean world.

The events of the Persian Wars have been set forth with exceptional fullness because of their exceptional importance. We have here one of the decisive moments in the history of mankind. Marathon and Salamis are much more than notable battles that chiefly concerned ancient Greece. What was there determined was that Europe should have a chance to develop a civilization of its own; and the destiny of the whole western world then hung in the balance. If the history were written of the way in which we of today have come by the rights and liberties that we prize most highly, the latest chapter might very probably describe the battles of the Marne, of Verdun, and of Amiens. But one of the earliest chapters would certainly describe how Greece defeated the attempt of Persia to substitute Asiatic customs and conceptions for European; the despotism of an Oriental autocrat over his obsequious subjects for free institutions and constitutional government; servile obedience to the will of a despot for freedom of discussion and the influence of public opinion; the rule of caprice and passion for the rule of law and reason. True, the Greek world had not yet achieved complete freedom or perfect self-government, but it had begun to tread the road that would lead to these in the end. Whereas whatever love of freedom the Medes and Persians may have brought with them from their northern European home had long been lost amid the luxury and servility and debasing customs of the Orient.

The Persian education consisted in learning to ride, to shoot with the bow, and to tell the truth; admirable enough, as far as it goes; but the inquiring mind of the Greek was opening the door to a whole world of interests of which the Asiatic had no conception. The Greek was fighting for the right to grow and develop as nature and reason should direct; he was fighting for freedom to investigate and discuss, for freedom of thought and freedom of speech, as well as for the freedom of self-government. And the reason he won was not merely his better equipment and his superior discipline; it was also because he stood for the rights of man (his own and his fellow-citizens) and saw clearly what he had at stake. His patriotism was narrow enough, being confined to his own city as a rule; but it was real, while the Asiatic fought because he was the slave of the Great King.

One of the numberless stories of Herodotus, the historian of this war, tells of a discussion between Xerxes and Demaratus, an exiled Spartan king living at his court. Xerxes could not see how the Greeks could possibly face his millions: 'If they were the subjects of one man, as with us, they might through fear of him go forward, few against many, under the compulsion of the lash; but left to their own freedom of action they would do nothing of the sort.' Demaratus answered: 'They are free, but not in all respects; they have a master over them, their country's law, which they fear more than thy subjects do thee. And whatever this master commands, that they do; and what it commands is ever the same, not to flee before any multitude of men, but to stand firm in their ranks, and either conquer or die.' Herodotus, in a word, puts obedience to a principle enthroned within the heart and understanding above obedience imposed by external authority and force, and therein finds the superiority of the Greek to the Persian.

Questions

1. What two dangers still threatened Greece after the battle of Salamis?
2. When the Persians invaded Attica, how did the Athenians convince Sparta to help them this time?
3. Who was the leader of the combined Greek force? How many soldiers did they have and what difficulties did they face?
4. How did the Greeks finally win at the battle of Plataea?
5. Where was the Athenian fleet at this time? What were they attempting to do?
6. What role did Carthage play in this war? Why did they get involved?
7. Describe the differences between the "Asiatic customs and conceptions" and the European.
8. What effect did freedom have on the Greek's fighting ability?

Vocabulary

culminating
obsequious
caprice

Athenians rebuilding their city under the direction of Themistocles. [Hutchinson's History of the nations, Volume I, 1914.

Chapter **XXV**

The Delian League and the Athenian Empire

A comparison has often been made between the repulse of the Persian invasion and the defeat of the Spanish Armada. In both cases a great national danger was averted by the resolute and undaunted resistance of the weaker side; in both cases the nation so signally delivered ascribed the victory to that divine power that scattereth the proud in the imagination of their hearts, and putteth down the mighty from their seats; and in both cases there followed an outburst of vigorous and many-sided activity and a new national pride. It was Athens, beyond question, that more than any other Greek state had been the soul of the steadfast resistance to Persia. And to Athens, as to England, the amazing victory brought a new energy, a quickening of the nation's spirit, and an enthusiastic confidence in her ability to achieve great things, undreamed of hitherto. From this time on, the history of Greece is virtually the history of Athens, especially in those enduring things which Greece left as a legacy to later ages.

As soon as the Persians retired, two matters called for attention: the rebuilding and fortification of Athens, and the liberation of the still-enslaved Greeks of the islands and Asia Minor. Athens was a complete ruin, and Themistocles seems to have suggested that, instead of rebuilding it, the people should shift their home to the Piraeus, close to the sea on which their power was increasingly to rest. Sentimental attachment to their old home was too strong, however, and soon hastily-built structures of sun-dried brick were rising over the devastated area. But the building of defensive walls was deemed by the Athenians an even more pressing need than shelter for their families. In these new city-walls, which by Themistocles' advice were made to enclose a larger circuit than before, all kinds of materials were used as they came to hand, whatever could be built into the new defenses. There was need for haste; for at the first rumor of rebuilding, the Spartans and other Peloponnesians made strong objection. They represented that it was folly to build what might prove to be merely a new stronghold for the Persians, should they come again. It would be better, they suggested, if all cities north of the Isthmus pulled down their fortifications and looked upon the Peloponnesus as their natural place of refuge and base of operations in case of invasion. Themistocles saw clearly that back of this advice lay jealousy of the rising power of Athens, but he did not think it wise for

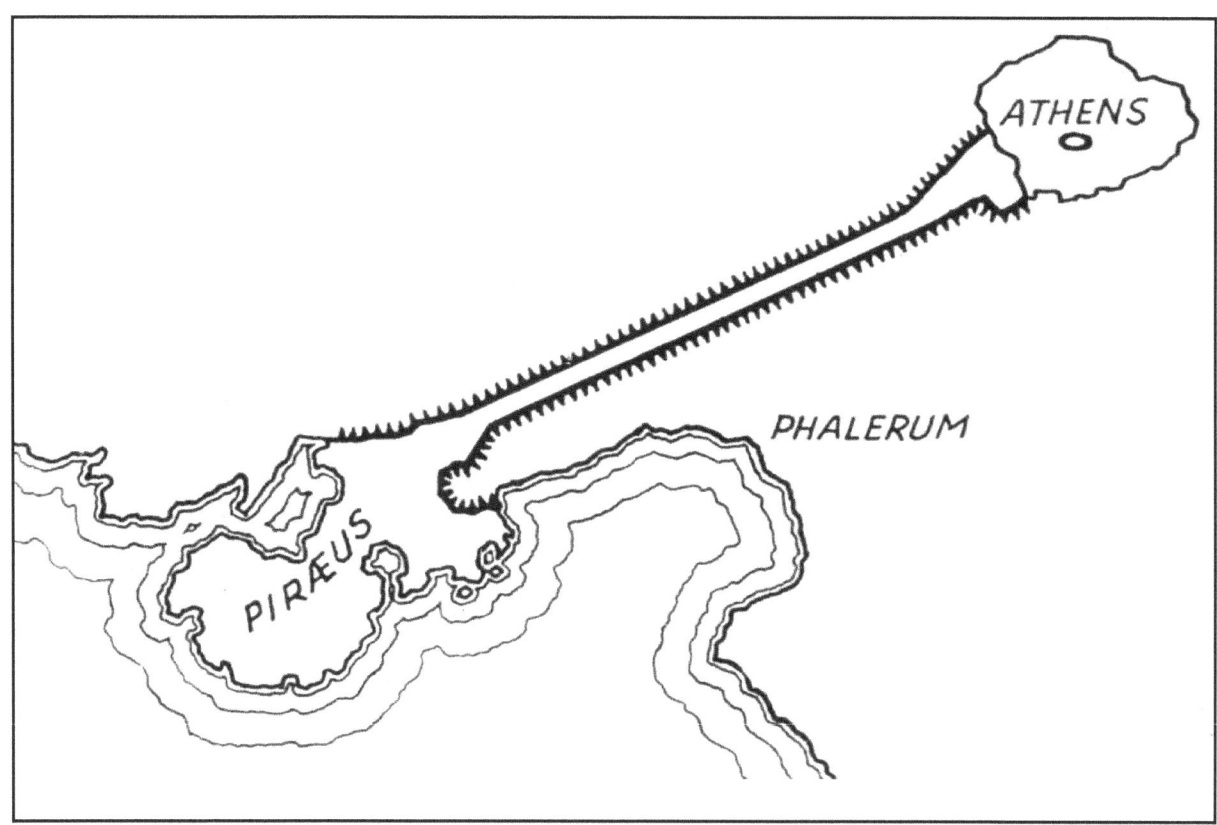

The Long Walls from Athens to Piraeus.

the moment openly to defy the Peloponnesian powers. He went in person to Sparta, and while at Athens men, women, and children devoted themselves to the rebuilding of the walls, he managed to temporize until word came that they were high enough to be defensible. Then he bluntly told the Spartans that the walls were up, and that Athens was quite competent to decide such matters for herself. This was virtually a declaration that the Athenians no longer acknowledged the hitherto unquestioned leadership of Sparta in Greek affairs.

The next step was to fortify the Piraeus. This had been proposed by Themistocles before the war and was now carried out under his direction. The wall ran about the whole circuit of the peninsula, seven miles in all, embracing not only the main harbor but also two smaller bays on the east side. Attracted by the growing importance of Athens, a great many Greeks engaged in commerce now came from other cities to live in the Piraeus. These 'resident aliens' could not become citizens, for in ancient times citizenship implied blood relationship and descent from the city's ancestors; but they brought increasing wealth and prestige to Athens. The Piraeus soon grew to be an important city, with wide streets and well-appointed residences, as well as the buildings needed for the growing commerce of Attica and the dockyards and shipbuilding yards for the strongest navy in Greece. About twenty years later, after the time of Themistocles, the two cities were united by the so-called 'Long Walls.' These defended the five or six miles of intervening space, and were strong enough to withstand any assault likely to be directed against them in the warfare of those days. This remedied the weakness Themistocles had seen in the position of Athens, for it was no longer possible for an enemy to invest the city and shut it off from its base of supplies at its seaport.

There remained the liberation of the Greeks from Persia. The defeat of the Persians at Mycale did not mean their retirement from the Aegean. They still held all their possessions both in Asia Minor and in Thrace. But to drive them out and liberate the Greek cities meant the maintenance of an efficient fleet in the eastern Aegean for a considerable time, and such a policy was, as might be expected, distasteful to Sparta. She, therefore, proposed that the Asiatic Greeks should leave their cities and migrate to new homes to be provided for them in Greece. Naturally this proposal was not acceptable to them, and before long, the lukewarmness of Sparta in their cause, together with the arrogance shown by Pausanias when he came out to command the Greek forces in the East, led the Ionian cities to turn to the Athenians and ask them to assume the leadership. Sparta was not averse to the change being made; it relieved her of an unwelcome responsibility; and so the Peloponnesian contingent withdrew from the fleet and returned home. In place of the earlier federation led by Sparta, it was now decided to form a new league under Athenian leadership, whose object should be the liberation of the Greek cities from Persian rule, and afterwards the weakening of Persian power in the West so that the Aegean should no longer be in danger of molestation.

Stele of a Doryphores (lance holder), parian marble, ca. 550-540 BC. Found in Athens, built into the Themistokleian wall. [Photo credit: Jebulon]

Besides Athens, the league included the cities of Euboea—except Carystus, which for some reason held aloof—the island states in the Aegean, and most of the cities on the coast of Thrace and Asia Minor; more than two hundred altogether, though many were very tiny and insignificant. The council of the league was to consist of one member from each state, large or small. The meeting-place of the council was to be the island of Delos, sacred to the god Apollo; and the league's treasury was to be under the guardianship of the god. Every state was to contribute an equitable share towards the maintenance of the necessary forces. Athens was to preside over the meetings of the council, and was charged with enforcing its decisions; it was, in brief, to be both president and executive of the league. A careful estimate was made of the probable annual cost of maintaining an efficient fleet of 200 triremes, and the duty of determining what should be the contribution of each state was entrusted to Aristides, in whose justice all had confidence. His assessment was so carefully and so conscientiously made that it was at once accepted. As some of the states might not desire or be able to equip and man their share of the triremes, it was agreed that any state might contribute a sum of money in lieu of ships. This money would, of course, be paid over to the state—in practice always Athens—which furnished these extra triremes. The money contributions of the allies were collected annually by ten Athenian stewards, and the command of the league's forces was controlled by Athens.

Base of a funerary kouros found in Athens, ca 510-500 BC, built into the Themistokleian wall. National Archaeological Museum, Athens.

The details of the operations of the Greek fleet in the Aegean have not been recorded. It is known, however, that Sestos, at the mouth of the Hellespont, was captured soon after the victory of Mycale, and that Cyprus and Byzantium were taken from the Persians while Pausanias was still in command. After the formation of the Delian League, its fleet was under the capable command of Cimon, the son of Miltiades, who spent several busy years gradually freeing the Greek cities from Persia. Finally, at the river Eurymedon, on the south coast of Asia Minor, he won a brilliant double victory over a great fleet supported by land-forces which Xerxes had collected to reassert his authority. This victory freed the Aegean and its coasts from any further danger from Persia for many years to come.

Although its primary object had been attained, the Delian League was not dissolved. Already things had happened which proved to be the first steps in transforming a voluntary league of free and independent allies into a compulsory empire of virtually subject states dominated by Athens—not that the change was planned or forecast. Neither Aristides nor Cimon would have sympathized with the establishment of an empire over free Greeks; yet both of them were whole-hearted supporters of the League and had done more than any other individuals to ensure its success. The part which Athens played in organizing the League was wholly commendable and unselfish; no one could possibly have foreseen what was to be the outcome of so praiseworthy a movement.

What were the steps which led in the end to a result so unforeseen, yet seemingly so inevitable? First of all, Carystus, which alone of the Euboean states had not joined the League, was forced to become a member; why should Carystus enjoy the benefits of the league and have none of its burdens? Next, the island of Naxos, one of the first to be freed, undertook to withdraw from the league; but why should Naxos be allowed to withhold from others the aid which it had itself received? Naxos was blockaded by the league's fleet, and as a punishment and also as a warning to others was deprived of its independence and made subject to Athens. Again when the victory at the Eurymedon was gained, it seemed to many that the league was no longer necessary; its objects had been attained. But the Athenians held, and events were to prove them right, that the Aegean would remain safe from Persian interference only so long as it was guarded by a strong Greek fleet. They therefore maintained the policy of keeping the League in being, and suffered no relaxation of effort, no withdrawal. Most of the islanders and Asiatic Greeks loved ease and were averse to exertion, while the Athenians, filled with a new sense of power and spurred on by new ambitions, were untiring in their ceaseless energy. The desire to escape personal service had led the majority of the states to contribute money rather than ships, and this had increased their weakness as it had made Athens stronger. To any dispute, therefore, there could be but one end, and in every case of default or of revolt the offending state was made subject to Athens. By the middle of the century the only states which had not been reduced to this position were Chios, Lesbos, and Samos, all large islands with strong fleets.

Athens treated her subject states with varying degrees of severity. All of them, of course, lost their vote in the council of the League; all of them had to pay tribute to Athens. In some of them an Athenian garrison was maintained; to others supervising magistrates were sent; and in practically all Athens saw to it that the local government was in the hands of the popular or democratic party, which as a rule was well disposed to the Athenian connection. Furthermore, in certain legal cases, both civil and criminal, the parties involved had to go to Athens for trial; and while it was well to have a more uniform system of law established over a wide area, yet this measure was opposed to the deep-seated passion of the Greek race for autonomy and self-government; so that any benefit accruing was forgotten in irritation and resentment. So, too, the tribute imposed was doubtless on the whole a very cheap insurance against Persia, but it was quite as galling to the former allies as positive oppression would have been.

The result was that the league became an empire (or tyranny, as the Greeks called it), and the allies of Athens became her subjects. At the beginning the action taken at each stage was, in the circumstances, reasonable and defensible; but in the end the Athenians came to be guided rather by the strong motive of self-interest, and some of the dominant imperialist party frankly defended the maintenance of the empire on the principle of 'might makes right.' About 454 BC the treasury of the League was formally transferred from Delos to Athens. In itself it was immaterial whether the League's funds were guarded by Apollo or by Athena; the real significance of the event was that it was an open avowal of the changed relation.

This chapter ends on a less heroic note than the last. It was not the only time in human experience when men who were willing to die in defense of their own rights were quite indifferent to the rights of their fellows, and denied to others the freedom which they passionately claimed for themselves.

Questions

1. In following the comparison between England and Athens, what two incidents do the authors compare?
2. What two matters required attention after the departure of the Persians?
3. What suggestions did Themistocles offer with regard to the rebuilding of Athens?
4. What was the reaction of the Spartans to the rebuilding of Athens? Why?
5. List the steps by which Athens came to rule over an empire.
    a. How did the Spartan's behavior contribute to Athenian domination?
    b. What was the Delian league and how was it formed?
    c. What was the primary object of the Delian league?
    d. Why, when this object was attained, did they not dissolve the league?
    e. What happened at the battle of Eurymedon?
6. How did Athens deal with cities that defied her authority?
7. What type of governments did Athens set up in cities under her control?
8. Describe the last step in Athenian domination.

Vocabulary

invest
contingent
equitable

Chapter XXVI

Athens Under Pericles

In most states, ancient and modern, there have usually been two parties, one more conservative than the other. Over much of Greece the conservative party was aristocratic, consisting largely of the well-born families which still retained many of their ancient privileges and powers. The other party, often much more numerous, was made up of those who were excluded from an equal share in the government. The existence of these two parties in most of the subject states of the empire goes far to explain, and in some measure to justify, its growth. For, more often than not, subjection to Athens meant that the democratic majority for the first time got anything like equal rights in the management of their own affairs. They evidently welcomed the domination of Athens as a protection against the domination of their own local aristocrats. So when a revolt against Athens occurred, it was practically always engineered by the oligarchic party, and, in suppressing it, Athens had usually the sympathy and often the active support of the larger part of the population. Even in the states which adhered to Sparta there was often a strong democratic party which was sympathetic to Athens, and which, if it could, would have transferred the state from Peloponnesian to Athenian leadership.

But in Athens itself, whatever certain individuals may have thought, there was no party that advocated a return to the days of a privileged class; both parties accepted the principle of democratic rule. The conservative or moderate party was made up largely of the landholders of Attica and the agricultural classes generally. The other party, which considered itself the more progressive element, but which its opponents deemed a radical mob, embraced the commercial and industrial interests which centered in Athens and the Piraeus, as well as the great mass of the city populace. The moderate party was led by Cimon until his death in 450 BC. The popular or democratic party was led by Ephialtes, who was assassinated in 461 BC and was succeeded by Pericles, a grand-nephew of Cleisthenes, and at the time about thirty years of age. Oddly enough, Cimon was a very genial and affable man, while Pericles was always dignified and reserved. Cimon's policy was to recognize Sparta's supremacy by land and be content with Athen's remaining a sea-power. He believed that the welfare of Greece depended on the cooperation of these two powers pulling together as

Bust of Pericles wearing a Corinthian helmet. Marble, Roman copy after a Greek original [Vatican Museums].

yoke-fellows. But it was not easy to avoid friction, and when certain disagreements and affronts discredited Cimon's policy in the eyes of the Athenian majority, the policy of Pericles was adopted instead. Pericles was a convinced imperialist who advocated making Athens the strongest power in Greece, by land as well as by sea. There is evidence that he saw clearly the dangers of a divided Greece, and that for a time he had before his eyes a vision of the Athenian empire expanding into a union of all Greece, so that an end might be put to internecine strife and an impregnable front presented to Persian aggression.

Athens had already complete control of the regions to the east, including the important trade route to the Euxine; Pericles now sought to extend her power westwards and similarly to control the trade with Sicily and Italy. The chief rivals of Athens in her commerce were Corinth and Aegina. In a quarrel between Corinth and its neighbor, Megara, the latter appealed to Athens for aid, and this led to war with Corinth and her Peloponnesian allies. The chief outcome was the conquest of Aegina, which now, instead of being a formidable rival, became one of the largest tributaries of Athens. By 450 BC her power extended from the Hellespont to Naupactus, commanding the western entrance to the Corinthian gulf, and northward as far as Thermopylae. A strong Athenian fleet was also sent to Egypt to assist a local rebellion against the Persian king, but this expedition completely failed. The Athenians were fighting in too many quarters, and their resources had been strained to the point of exhaustion. As it seemed more important to retain their gains in Greece than to continue attacking Persia, an arrangement was made with the latter which put an end to the forty years' hostilities. The Great King was too proud to surrender Ionia and the islands, but he was willing to leave them alone.

Athens had now reached the summit of her land-power. One by one her recent acquisitions began to fall away from her in uprisings assisted by the Peloponnesians, and in a very few years a peace was concluded by which the Athenians relinquished all the states on the mainland which they had recently added to their empire (Megara, Boeotia, Phocis, and Locris). The one solid gain which remained was Aegina. The most serious loss was that of Megara, for that mountainous little state had presented an almost impassable barrier to attacks by Peloponnesian armies.

These very meager results were not quite all that Pericles had to show for the first fifteen years of his leadership. Under his guidance the Athenian constitution became perhaps the purest form of democracy the world has seen; provided, that is, that one accepts the ancient limitation of citizenship to freemen of local descent. For in Greece aliens as well as women and slaves were excluded from the franchise, and there was no provision for naturalization. A man's political career lay in the city of his ancestors; elsewhere he must remain an alien. There had been no material change in the form of government since the days of Cleisthenes.[10] Nor did Pericles disturb the existing arrangements by which

---

[10] For the shifting of power from the archons to the generals see page 112113. Another change, of which the details are obscure and uncertain, had taken from the Areopagus, an ancient aristocratic court, any power of revision it may have retained, and left to it simply its ancient jurisdiction over cases involving religion or blood-guiltiness.

the sovereign people, acting through its assembly, council, and law-courts, as well as through its generals, archons, and other officials, determined and carried out the state's policy. But with the growth of the empire, both the assembly and the law-courts had more numerous and more momentous issues to decide. Pericles sought to have the whole body of the citizens take part in these decisions, and by habitual participation in public business learn to decide wisely.

The Athenians did not elect representatives to their parliament; every citizen was a member of the sovereign assembly. This body met on the Pnyx, a hill not far from the Acropolis and the market-place, to discuss the most varied aspects of national and civic policy: the question of war or peace, expeditions, foreign alliances, expenditures of public funds, and problems of all sorts—military, financial, or political—that concerned either the city or the empire. The regular meetings were held once a week through the year, and special meetings were often called. As the total number of citizens was about 25,000, every one of whom had the right to attend, to speak, and to vote, it would seem quite impossible for such a body to function as a deliberative assembly. But probably only a few thousand were present at even well-attended meetings. Many lived throughout Attica at a great distance from the city; many others were away, serving in the army or navy or engaged in commerce overseas; many were negligent or indifferent; and many of the poorer citizens could not afford the time to exercise their rights.

Theoretically, also, the whole body of citizens dispensed justice in both civil and criminal cases. But in practice, for the sake of convenience, 6,000 citizens were chosen by lot each year to represent the whole people. From these again, for each case as it arose, there was chosen a smaller committee,

View of the Acropolis from the Pnyx by Rudolf Müller (1883) in the Benaki Museum — Google Art Project.

it might be of 201 or 501 members or even some larger number, but apparently never a small number (to guard against intimidation) or an even number (to prevent a tie vote). It was before these sub-committees, or *dicasteries,* as they were termed, that the case was tried. In an Athenian court there were neither judges nor lawyers. The whole dicastery was both judge and jury, and each plaintiff and defendant had to plead his own case. True, he might engage someone to write a speech for him to learn and deliver as his own; and these 'speech-writers' were the nearest approach to the professional lawyer that Athens had.

One of the earliest measures of Pericles was to introduce the practice of paying citizens for service on a dicastery. The sum paid was quite small, but it was near enough to the living wage of workers for a poor man to feel that he could afford the time to discharge this civic duty. The measure undoubtedly strengthened Pericles politically and increased the support his policies would receive from the city populace.[11]

That this very amateurish way of deciding legal disputes secured less of substantial justice than our modern methods would be hard to prove. The speeches addressed to Athenian juries which have come down to us show two things clearly: that a great deal of irrelevant matter was introduced in order to win the favor of the audience, or prejudice it against the other side; and that, in intelligence and quickness of apprehension, the average Athenian audience was decidedly superior to any similarly chosen body of men today. Likewise, the speeches that we possess addressed to the Athenian assembly are quite equal, both in eloquence and in the demand made upon the understanding of the hearer, to any speeches in a modern parliament or congress of specially chosen representatives. The Athenian citizen, in fact, had a much better training in public business than most citizens of today. For Periclean democratic policy not only encouraged every citizen to share in the government of his country, but also presupposed the equal competence of every citizen. With us, democracy means that one citizen's vote is as good as any other's; with the Athenians it meant also that one citizen was as competent as any other citizen to hold office.

And so selection by lot was the established rule. Previously, the members of the council had been chosen by lot from a larger selected list; under Pericles, the selected list was dropped and the choice was purely by lot. Moreover, practically all the various magistrates, officials, and commissioners of the state were chosen by lot, and neither merit, nor favor, nor bribery, nor 'pull' could be a factor in the selection. As they held office also for but one year, and might not hold the same office a second time, the result was that an immense number of citizens had some first-hand personal experience of the working of the state's machinery. In particular there must have been at any one time many thousands who for one year had discharged the very important duties of member of the council. Nor must we overlook the effect of the 'scrutiny' which awaited each functionary at the end of his year of office, and the incentive this would be to do his very best, for his own, if not for his country's sake.

The one great exception to the practice of selection by lot was the all-important office of general, which Athenian common sense continued to fill by election. A member of the board of generals might also be re-elected, and it was by his re-appointment year after year to this high office that Pericles was able to guide Athenian policy, so that, as Thucydides, the Greek historian, said: 'Athens, while in name a democracy, was in fact under the absolute rule of her first citizen.'

---

[11] The members of the council were also paid, and probably most of the officials of the state. The principle of payment for civic services was extended early in the next century to include payment for attendance at the assembly.

The democratic equality of the Athenians was shown in other ways also. All citizens were alike under the obligation to render personal service in time of war, and, as was usual in Greece, each provided his own equipment. Every citizen able to equip himself as a heavy-armed soldier served in the phalanx of hoplites; a limited number of young men of wealthy families which could afford to keep horses composed the cavalry; and all the other citizens served either as light-armed foot-soldiers or in the fleet, where those too poor to provide weapons could at least be of use in rowing the triremes.

Hoplite soldiers featured on amphora from Attica, 560 BC. [Photo Credit: Bibi Saint-Pol]

Throughout the year in Athens there were a great many festivals and spectacles, including elaborate processions, musical and dramatic contests, races of various kinds, and athletic games; and these the whole free male population of Athens might attend as participants or spectators. Moreover, except when musicians or dancers were hired on the occasion of a banquet at some rich man's house, there were no entertainments in Athens, musical, athletic, or dramatic, that were not open, virtually without payment, to the whole body of citizens. The well-to-do in Athens had more leisure than others, and therefore a greater chance of being able to profit by the opportunities that were open to all for both relaxation and education, but otherwise they had no special advantages in the exercise of political rights or in the pursuit of culture. The great works of art that were produced in that age were equally to be enjoyed by all the people. The skill of architects was expended on public not on private buildings, and the productions of the great painters and sculptors of the day were all to be found in public places. And so the orator Demosthenes could say of the Athenians of this century: 'The public buildings they erected for us are of such beauty and grandeur that posterity is left incapable of surpassing them; but in private life so modest were they, so loyal to the spirit of our democracy, that the house of Aristides, or of Miltiades, or any other of the illustrious men of that period, is no more imposing than those of their neighbors.'

The great outstanding difference in civic life between the rich and the poor was that the former were expected to provide certain expensive public services. A large part of the public expense of the Athenian state, the mounting of its plays, the equipment of its warships, the arrangements for its games and festivals, its chariot and horse and torch races, its musical contests and regattas, were defrayed by private citizens who came forward voluntarily, and took pride in vying with their predecessors or with a crowd of rivals in the performance of the task. These services were for the benefit of all the citizens, but were not supplied at the public expense; they were financed by individuals,

Temple of Athena Nike, Acropolis of Athens Greece.
[Photo credit: Steve Swayne]

but not as private enterprises to make money. This was the Athenian equivalent for our modern graduated income-tax; the ancient method probably gave more satisfaction both to the rich and to the general public. All these things will show what is meant by the statement that 'there never was a people which made the principle that all its citizens were equal more of a reality than the Athenians made it.' Such, at least, was the aim of Pericles.

There was still another contribution of Pericles to Athenian life—one that in some measure still remains for the modern world to enjoy—the adornment of his city; so that, if Athens must give up the dream of leading a unified Greece, she might yet show how worthy she was of leadership, and might inspire where she could not rule. When peace was assured by the agreements with Persia and the Peloponnesian league, Pericles set about fulfilling a duty long deferred, the restoration of the temples destroyed in the Persian invasion. In the interval Athens had mightily prospered, and Pericles felt that more than mere restoration befitted her greatness. Gratitude to their patron goddess, Athena, also demanded of the Athenians the noblest structures that human skill could plan and build. There were funds available, for now that much less was required in peace time for the navy. There was a large surplus each year from the contributions pouring into the league's treasury from the subject states. We may not wholly approve of the way in which these funds were raised; but we owe a debt of gratitude to Pericles and the Athenians for the way in which they were spent.

Pericles had the assistance of Phidias, the greatest sculptor of the ancient world if not of all time, and of a brilliant group of architects, under whose supervision a series of noble edifices was planned and completed in a marvelously short period of years. The architects had two advantages: Mount Pentelicus close at hand was an inexhaustible quarry of gleaming white marble; and the Acropolis itself was admirably adapted for the group of buildings which they were planning. This hill rose in the center of the city to the height of about 300 feet. It had steep sides except at the west, where the approach was more gradual; and the irregularly shaped top was fairly flat, about 1,000 feet long and 400 broad. A hill of vaster size would have dwarfed the temples; a peaked summit would have made a group of buildings impossible; and both the area on top and the height above the plain were of almost ideal proportions.

The first building to be erected was that perfect Doric temple known as the Parthenon, which remained virtually intact for over 2,000 years. But in AD 1687, during a war between the Turks, who held Greece and the Venetians, a cannon-shot fired by the latter exploded a powder-magazine stored in the Parthenon and shattered it. Even yet in its ruins it is one of the most impressively beautiful of all the works of man. The temple was adorned after the Greek fashion with groups of statuary which were executed under the direction of Phidias, and doubtless in some cases by his own hand. The east and west pediments, 90 feet in length, held each a group of figures illustrating events in the story of Athena, and, though much mutilated, these are still counted among the finest statuary in the world and remain alike the inspiration and the despair of every sculptor. There was also a wonderful frieze, 534 feet long, running all round the building proper (see image on the next page). This represented in low relief the procession which, at the great Panathenaic festival every fourth year, approached the shrine of the goddess with votive offerings. The remains of the pediment sculptures and the greater part of the frieze were brought to England at the beginning of the nineteenth century by Lord Elgin, to save them from further destruction by the unappreciative Turks, and today, under the name of the 'Elgin Marbles,' these are the most notable treasures contained in the British Museum.

Within the temple was a costly statue of Athena made by Phidias himself. It had a wooden core, which was covered with plates of gold and ivory, the latter to represent the flesh. He also had a colossal bronze statue of the city's protecting goddess, in full panoply, erected near the western brow of the hill, so that miles away at sea the Athenian sailor returning home caught the flash of the sunlight on her helmet or spear-point. On a projecting bastion nearby, which commands a magnificent view of the Attic plain, the sea near Salamis, and the distant Peloponnesian mountains, was erected a charming little Ionic temple in honor of Athena, as 'giver of victory.' So perfect are the proportions of this temple that it does not suffer at all from its proximity to the grandeur of the Parthenon. About the bastion ran a parapet with lovely figures of Victories carved in relief.

Then, as the strength of the city walls rendered unnecessary special defensive works at the western approach to the Acropolis, Pericles planned an elaborate structure (called the *Propylaea*, or Entrance Gates) that would be a fittingly impressive introduction to the magnificence that lay within the Acropolis enclosure. Nowhere else in the world has there ever been a group of buildings to rival these, of such perfect proportions, of such serene and majestic beauty, and adorned with such a wealth of unsurpassed sculpture. Nor was the work of restoration confined to the Acropolis. A fine Doric temple was built in the lower city in honor of Hephaestus. This, which has long been mistakenly called the temple of Theseus, still survives, and is notable as the best preserved of all the remaining Greek temples. Also a temple to Poseidon was built on the rocky brow of Sunium, the outermost promontory of Attica towards the Aegean, and new buildings for the worship of Demeter were erected at Eleusis.

Acropolis of Athens panorama (panoramic view from Areopagus hill), Athens, Greece. [Photo credit: Ggia]

Parthenon, Athens Greece [Photo credit: Steve Swayne]

Portion of Frieze of the Parthenon.

Porch of the Maidens in the Erechtheum on the Acropolis. [Tilemahos Efthimiadis, Athens, Greece]

The last structure to adorn the Acropolis, while possibly planned by Pericles, was not completed until about twenty years after his death. This was the Erechtheum, called after an ancient Attic hero, whose shrine with two others was contained in one building. This fact explains the unusual shape of the building, which has two porches added to the normal rectangular temple. The building is Ionic, and has a wealth of delicate and beautiful detail unsurpassed in Athens. The south porch has the striking innovation of the figures of Athenian maidens replacing the supporting pillars, a feature which Greek taste did not approve sufficiently to copy or adopt elsewhere.

In this above all was the greatness of Pericles displayed: that he recognized that the city by ennobling the houses of her gods would ennoble herself; and that she could express her own might and her own ideals in no worthier way than by the erection of beautiful temples. It was not by the arts of a demagogue that Pericles swayed so long the people of Athens; it was by his lofty eloquence, his Olympian bearing, and by the appeal to reason and to what is best and highest in human aspirations. The Athenian democracy of his dreams, the ideal which he hoped by his policy to realize, was a state that should use the material resources of the empire in order to achieve for itself such intellectual and artistic greatness as to be a center of enlightenment to all Greece, while each citizen should so play his part and so use his opportunities as to develop a many-sided efficiency that would both enrich his own life and enable him to render more worthy service to his country.

Questions

1. Describe the two parties that existed in most of the Greek city-states. What kinds of citizens were in each?
2. How did the existence of these two parties contribute to the growth of the Athenian empire?
3. What party did Cimon represent in Athens? What did he think about the relationship of Sparta and Athens?
4. What party did Pericles represent in Athens? Describe Pericles' policy toward Sparta and Greece.
5. Describe the changes that took place in the Athenian empire.
6. What changes did Pericles make in the structure of the government?
7. Why did Pericles want all Athenians to participate in the government?
8. What measure did Pericles introduce to make sure that all citizens participated in government.
9. How did the average Athenian citizen's participation compare to an American citizen's? How did his abilities compare?
10. Describe the privileges and duties of the rich and poor citizens in Athens.
11. Describe how and why Pericles adorned the city of Athens.

Vocabulary

internecine
franchise
panoply

Chapter XXVII

Fifth-Century Culture

I. Art

There were other beautiful temples in Greece besides those in Athens. But Greek architecture was confined to temples. Even in Athens there were no great secular buildings comparable to the amphitheaters and basilicas and baths of the Romans. Greek life was lived as much as possible out of doors, and no elaborate structures were required for the conduct of public business or for amusements. Moreover, in his style of temple-architecture the Greek did not strive for variety and novelty. His one aim was to perfect the type which his sense of harmony and fitness had led him to adopt, composed of column and lintel and low-pitched gable roof. The path of advance was sought rather in the careful working out of symmetrical proportions for the various parts of the structure, and in striving for the utmost perfection in the sculptural work which adorned the building. This ornamentation was always kept subordinate to the architecture; the Greek never overloaded the structure with ornament or made his buildings a background or an excuse for the sculptured additions. Compared with Gothic cathedrals, the Greek temple may seem monotonous and bare; but in its own kind, though often copied, it has never been surpassed.

Athens again was not the only city where noble sculpture was to be found. All over Greece, but more particularly at the great seats of worship, such as Delphi and Olympia, each succeeding generation took pride in adorning their sacred places with appropriate statuary. The

Archaic Statue.

The Story of Greece

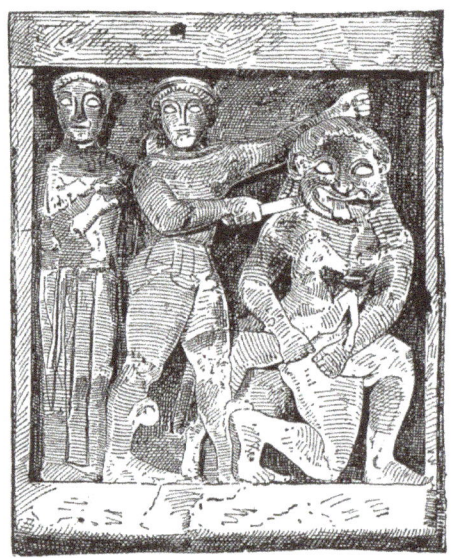

Early relief of Perseus slaying the Gorgon.

Head from Heraion, Museum at Olympia, Greece [Troy Mckaskle]

Venus of Milo, 3rd century. [Louvre, Paris]

most famous piece of sculpture in antiquity was the statue of Zeus made by Phidias for the temple at Olympia, and representing him as a kingly figure, equally majestic and benign. A Greek writer, Dio, of the first century AD, who had visited Olympia, writes thus of this representation of 'the giver of all good things and the common father of mankind:' *Methinks if one who is heavy-laden in mind, who has drained the cup of misfortune and sorrow in life, and whom sweet sleep visits no more, were to stand before this statue, he would forget all his griefs and troubles.* Like nearly all the work of the greatest Greek sculptors, this statue has long since perished. Of the best ancient statues that still exist, all but one are the work of unknown sculptors or are copies of famous originals made by less skillful hands in later centuries when wealthy patrons of art, especially among the Romans, wished to adorn their villas with copies of the masterpieces which their own age could appreciate but could not equal. And yet such was the amazing development of this art among the Greeks that, even after all the losses, what has been preserved to our time, fragmentary or secondhand as most of it is, challenges comparison with the very best sculpture that all the succeeding centuries put together have produced.

This is not the place to attempt any survey or history of Greek sculpture, or to describe the qualities which distinguished the work of its greatest masters, such as Phidias, Myron, and Polyclitus in the fifth century, and Praxiteles, Scopas and Lycippus in the fourth. There are, however, certain characteristics of Greek sculpture on which it is worthwhile to dwell.

1. It would be a great mistake to suppose that the Greek was born with some infallible sense of beauty which taught him instinctively how to achieve masterpieces of symmetry and grace. Greek sculpture began with very crude productions, and only gradually attained truly satisfying results.

What the Greek did have was a natural love of symmetry and a keenly critical mind, and by constantly striving through many generations he learned how to avoid this fault and how to correct that defect, and finally was able to turn failure into success. Doubtless the real advances were made by a small number of the most gifted men; but when once some difficulty had been overcome, there were many of lesser ability who could profit by the new discovery. The finest period of Greek sculpture was between 450 and 335 BC. After this time the loss of freedom seemed to dull the brilliance of the Greek mind and check the further development of its powers, and the later sculptors fell away from the high standards of the best period. Some of the illustrations of this chapter are intended to show the great improvement made on the first crude beginnings, as the Greeks learned gradually how to solve the problems of the proper representation of bodily attitudes, of graceful drapery, and of beautiful and expressive countenances.

2. Greek art aimed at, and in the end achieved, a perfect combination of lifelike realism and ideal beauty. On the one hand, until a later and degenerate age, ancient art never sought, on the ground of realism, to represent the mean or ignoble or morbid or ugly things in life. Such things exist, to be sure, but the Greek was not tempted to display his skill in portraying them; the portrayal of the noble and beautiful absorbed all his interest. On the other hand, in representing ideal beauty in the person of gods and goddesses, he never, like the Egyptians or Asiatics, made them other than human; but it must be humanity at its very best and highest. It is perhaps because of this that the Greek did not excel in portrait sculpture, more through lack of desire than lack of ability to represent the peculiarities and defects of actual living men. This branch of sculpture was developed chiefly in the Roman period.

Athena of Lemnos, Roman copy of Phidias, 5th century, Museo Civico Archeologico, Bologna.

3. Greek art never aimed at the sensational; the sculptor's works were marked by serenity and grace. This does not mean that they were graceful in a languid, sentimental way. There is plenty of life and vigor in the figures represented, but violent action or intense emotion is seldom portrayed. The Greek sculptor also produced his effects by a simplicity, which avoided affectation and extravagance. His figures and groups are never overloaded with superfluous detail or with ornamentation designed to display the sculptor's skill and amaze the spectator. These qualities of Greek art are illustrated in a representation of the parting of Orpheus from Eurydice. Orpheus, the great musician, had gone to the lower world in search of his dead wife, Eurydice. There he had so charmed the

Orpheus and Eurydice. [National Museum, Naples.]

nether powers with his music that they allowed him to take her back to earth, on condition that on their upward journey he did not once look back upon her as she followed him. But startled at something, Eurydice called out in alarm; Orpheus turned—and lost her forever. Hermes, the god who conducts dead souls to Hades, claimed her again for the realms of darkness. In the Greek sculpture, the simplicity and quiet serenity of the general effect are unmistakable. Yet there is complete success in portraying the love and tender yearning of the two who gaze on each other for the last time, as Hermes gently but inexorably interposes by the arresting touch on Eurydice's wrist. The same scene has been treated very differently by a modern sculptor. Hermes, the central and dominating figure, with godlike might holds husband and wife apart. With his right hand he thrusts Orpheus reeling back, as with arms outstretched in passionate despair he strives to reach Eurydice, who has sunk in the swoon of death and whose inert form Hermes with his left arm now holds in his firm grasp. It is not necessary to debate which is the more beautiful work of art; tastes will differ. The essential thing is to note that the violent action of the modern sculpture and a certain straining after dramatic effect are quite alien to the spirit of Greek art in its best period.[12]

The delicate reserve with which the Greek handled the fact of death is shown also in the funeral stele or gravestone (see page 156). This is one of the earliest of a great number of similar reliefs, which have been found in many parts of Attica. Many of these must have been cut by very ordinary workmen, but all have the same characteristics, with many variations of detail. The dead person who is commemorated is shown in some familiar quiet scene of home life. Occasionally he seems to be saying farewell as if going for a short journey; but there is never any exhibition of poignant grief or any exploiting of the morbid and sensational aspects of death such as are to be found in many a mediaeval or modern representation of the victims of the King of Terrors.

Nothing has survived to us, and little is known, of Greek painting or Greek music. In these two arts the modern world owes little to the Greeks. Their music was very simple, scarcely going beyond songs and chants, sung without harmonized parts, and accompanied by a single instrument such as the flute or the lyre. In painting there seems no reason to believe that the Greeks made any such progress as in the sister art of sculpture; their sense of form was keener than their sense of color. In one department only, that of vase-painting, was the workmanship wholly admirable; but this was due not to the coloring of the figures but to the spirited and graceful drawing, which is marked by the same simplicity and economy of detail as Greek sculpture.

2. Literature

In no way, perhaps, have the Greeks more profoundly and continuously influenced the modern world than through their literature, which remains one of the noblest achievements of the mind of man. It was the re-discovery of Greek literature, after it had been forgotten through the centuries of the Dark Ages, that brought about the revival of learning in the sixteenth century. Ever since that renaissance, or rebirth, of literary and scientific activity, the writings of the Greeks have been a constant source of quickening and inspiration to the human spirit. One indication of the indelible impression made by the Greeks on our intellectual life is the fact that we owe to them nearly all the

---

[12] The well-known Laocoon, which in this respect resembles the modern sculpture, is the work of a much later age (about 50 BC).

The Theatre of Dionysus on the south slope of the Acropolis of Athens [Photo credit: Rrburke].

various literary forms that are recognized in the world today, such as epic, lyric, dramatic, pastoral, and didactic poetry, the elegy, the ode, the epigram, and (in prose) history, oratory, the scientific or philosophical or critical treatise, the dialogue, the fable, the novel, and the essay. All these, as distinct forms of the literary art, originated among the Greeks, and most of them bear still their Greek names. To this list only one or two additions have since been made, such as satire, contributed by the Romans. It is one of the greatest evidences both of the vigor of the Greek mind and of the keenness of the Greek sense of appropriate form. Starting without any previous body of literature to guide them, in a few centuries they invented all these various kinds of literature, developed the form and style most appropriate to each, and also in most of them produced what have ever since been adjudged as masterpieces.

The special contributions of this century were history and the drama, including both tragedy and comedy. Few centuries, even in modern times with all the nations to draw from, can show such a galaxy of names of the first magnitude as the fifth century BC. The list includes Aeschylus, Sophocles, and Euripides, all writers of tragedy, Aristophanes, the writer of comedy, Herodotus and Thucydides, the historians, to whom should be added Pindar, the greatest of the Greek writers of lyric odes. All of these, except Pindar and Herodotus, were Athenians, and these two also lived in Athens for some years.

Three goddesses from the Parthenon pediment at the British Museum [Photo by Yair Haklai]..

The development of the drama in ancient times belongs entirely to Athens. It arose there in connection with the spring and autumn festivals held in honor of Dionysus, the god of fertility. At these, choruses in praise of the god were sung, with appropriate rhythmic movements, gestures, and dances. Out of this lyric pageant grew the drama, by the addition, first of a single reciter who supplemented with his narrative the songs of the chorus, and then of a second who made dialogue possible. It was Aeschylus who conceived the idea of the two actors, and before long Sophocles added a third. Beyond these Greek tragedy did not go. There might be more than three characters in the play, but by careful distribution all the parts could be played by three actors.

The dramas at Athens were always exhibited as part of the Dionysiac festivals, and consequently on only a few days in the year. They were played in the open air, on the southern slope of the Acropolis, and necessarily in the daytime. The Greek theatre was built by cutting out some convenient hillside for the rising tiers of seats, and the Athenians and afterwards the Greeks of other cities learned how to construct theatres capable of holding vast audiences—Plato mentions 30,000 in Athens—and yet with perfect acoustic properties. The chorus remained an integral part of the play, and the large circular space before the long narrow stage was occupied by them in the evolutions of their performance. There was no curtain; once the play had begun, the action was continuous. But the effect of division into acts was produced by the chorus filling in the interval between the various stages of the action. There was also no elaborate scenery or stage machinery. The dramatist depended for success on the construction of the plot, the eloquence and interest of the dialogue, the beauty of the choral interludes, and the effective rendering of his lines by the actor. There are other points of difference between Greek and modern stage performances, but the dramatic appeal of a

Theatre at Epidaurus. [Photo by Ronny Siegel].

good play seldom depends on these extraneous features. The Greek plays exhibit the usual Greek simplicity and economy, but do not suffer thereby. When presented today before a modern audience, a great play of Sophocles or Euripides is found to make as profound an impression as the very greatest of our English dramas.

One important difference between the ancient and the modern drama is that among the Greeks tragedy and comedy were always separate, and were presented at distinct festivals. A dramatist in Greece wrote only tragedies or only comedies; he never attempted both kinds. Still less did any Greek play mingle comic scenes with tragedy, as Shakespeare often does, by way of relief, or seek to evoke alternate tears and laughter, as a modern play may legitimately do.

The subjects of the ancient tragedies were drawn almost exclusively from the legends of the heroic age. But these were so treated as to give full opportunity for portraying the abiding human interests, for discussing the deep problems of life, and for presenting the great spectacle of our humanity in its sufferings, its conflicts, and its triumphs. The plays of Aristophanes, the comedian, on the other hand, exhibit plots of the most fantastical and topsy-turvy construction, combining political satire and the caricature of prominent citizens with scenes of uproarious and often ribald fun and choral lyrics of exquisite beauty.

Of the two great historians it will suffice here to say that Herodotus tells the story of the Persian invasions, prefaced by a long and picturesque account of the customs and traditions of the world of his day, both Greek and barbarian; and that Thucydides not only describes the Peloponnesian war, but mingles with the narrative of events so profound an exposition of the principles and motives which influence the actions of nations and individuals that his history is one of the richest storehouses of political wisdom that we possess. It is this that has made it a favorite study of so many great statesmen, and that has also prompted the saying that the chief importance of the Peloponnesian war is that Thucydides wrote its history.

Both works are more than a full and authoritative record of events, they are works of literature of the highest merit. Herodotus, the 'Father of History,' writes with transparent ease and charm, and is always a delightful companion. Thucydides is widely regarded as the greatest of all historians, not because of his style, which is often difficult and involved, but because of his penetrating insight.

3. Science

Ever since the time of Thales (page 112gs 92-93) in the early part of the sixth century, there was in many parts of the Greek world increasing evidence of the desire to discover order in the world about us and to learn the laws according to which nature works. At first men attempted to find some general principle that would explain the constitution of the universe as a whole. This was naturally too ambitious an endeavor to have much success. However, it led, for one thing, to certain thinkers in the fifth century (such as Democritus) formulating a doctrine of the atomic constitution of matter, and to another (Empedocles) reasoning that all things may be regarded as derived from four original elements—earth, air, fire, and water. This last theory had a life of over 3,000 years, and down to the birth of modern chemistry in the seventeenth century was regarded as an important scientific truth.

More valuable results were attained when the Greek thinkers narrowed their inquiries to individual branches of knowledge, and thus, as we now recognize, laid the foundations of many of the natural and physical sciences. In these attempts to penetrate the secrets of Nature's laws the Greeks were under a great handicap, as compared with modern scientists. They were entirely without such aids as microscopes, telescopes, and all the manifold appliances of our scientific laboratories. When we realize how absolutely dependent they were on what the unaided eye can reveal, it seems little short of marvelous what progress they made and how much they were able to establish merely by close observation and the exercise of their keen reasoning powers.

In one direction indeed this handicap did not exist. In the field of mathematics, pure reasoning can arrive at truth without assistance from either apparatus or experiment. The first great success of Greek science was in geometry. The demonstration of several important geometrical laws is attributed to Thales. Once the Greeks had entered upon this study, they went on from triumph to triumph. By the end of the fifth century Greek geometricians had formulated and proved the principal theorems of modern elementary mathematics, which concern parallels, triangles, quadrilaterals, regular polygons and, in part, circles. Further, they had laid the foundations of that rigorous conception of proof which was to set the standard throughout all Greek mathematics. There can be little in Books I, II, III, IV, and VI of Euclid's Elements which was not perfectly known before 400 BC. One result is that practically all the technical terms that we use in geometry are of Greek origin. From plane geometry they proceeded to annex other mathematical domains, such as spherical geometry, trigonometry, optics, and conic sections. And all this was done with such completeness that nothing they formulated has since had to be discarded or reconstructed.[13]

The Greek mathematicians were also greatly interested in the theory of numbers, especially in problems of proportion, progression, and irrational quantities. But they were hampered in their progress along this line by their system of notation, which indicated numbers by the letters of the alphabet.[14] The Arabic notation with its invention of zero has enabled schoolboys today to solve questions which only the most eminent of the Greek mathematicians would attempt.

The fact that the intervals in the musical scale are subject to mathematical laws was discovered quite early by Greek mathematicians. Some also busied themselves with the problem of the movements

---

[13] Euclid flourished about a century later, when he was able to draw up a systematic treatise on geometry in thirteen books, which has been the standard authority on this subject ever since.

[14] The difficulty under which the Greeks labored may be realized by comparing the very similar problem of making calculations with the Roman numerals; e.g. multiplying LXIX by CLVI.

of the heavenly bodies and elaborated the first theories of scientific astronomy. Some of their views were quite erroneous, others quite accurate. It is interesting to find that certain fifth-century Greeks came very near anticipating what is now known as the Copernican theory of the solar system.

Next to mathematics the most notable achievements of fifth-century science were in medicine. The whole secret of the success of Greek medicine was its systematic observation of the phenomena of health and disease, and the scientific reasoning with which it sought to understand the workings of Nature and build up a system of natural laws. The very word *physician* means one who seeks to know and follow Nature. One of the greatest physicians the world has known, Hippocrates of Cos, flourished towards the end of this century. The wonderful advances of modern medicine, most of them made within the memory of living men, and based on such recent discoveries as anesthetics, antiseptic treatment of wounds, and the germ theory of disease, have carried this science beyond anything possible for Hippocrates. But his methods of observation and diagnosis, his recommendations for the treatment of disease, and his lofty ideals for the profession are still the enduring foundation on which modern medical science is proud to build.[15] The subsidiary sciences of anatomy and physiology were beginning to be developed, but it was not until the next century that, under Aristotle, they became really important branches of scientific investigation.

Sophocles. [Lateran Museum, Rome.]

In still another development of this fifth century we can see the Greek's hunger for knowledge and his instinct for order and system, namely, in an endeavor to extend and systematize the education of

---

[15] The 'oath of Hippocrates' embodying these ideals is well known to medical graduates.

Stele of Hegeso.

youth. Until the middle of this century the education of the Athenian boy had consisted of instruction in reading and writing, with a little elementary arithmetic and a great deal of Homer and other poetry to be learned by heart. He also learned to play the lyre and sing to its accompaniment, and to practice those athletic exercises, which make the body strong and the carriage graceful. After this elementary education there was apparently no systematic training by which the youth could be prepared for the activities of his manhood, except that, before being enrolled as a citizen, he served for two years as a military cadet on garrison duty about the frontiers of Attica, and thus learned to take his place in the phalanx in time of war.

At this period, however, the growth of the Athenian empire and the development of democracy had made it highly desirable that the young man of good birth and ability, who was naturally looking forward to a political career, should receive some better instruction than was afforded by casual observation of the way things were managed in Athens and stray hints picked up from the conversation of his elders. Especially did it seem desirable that he should learn to speak effectively, for the assembly and the law-courts would be the chief arena in which distinction was to be won. For in those days success in life did not mean the accumulation of wealth, but playing a prominent part in the public activities of the community.

There was room then for some better education to fit one for the life of an influential citizen, and to supply this need there arose in the latter half of the fifth century a class of men who undertook to teach the art of public speaking. These were not always Athenians, but came from many parts of the Greek world, including Sicily. They went from city to city giving their instruction, for which there was such a demand that they were in receipt of handsome fees. Athens was, of course, their chief resort. These men were called *sophists,* a name which at that time meant merely 'men of special learning,' and had none of the unfavorable meaning that it afterwards acquired. The art of public speaking would include the study of the most effective arrangement of arguments; the proper ordering of one's thought in sentences; the use of adornment and figures of speech, and discrimination in the use of words. From this beginning have come the study of grammar and rhetoric and literary criticism, all of which were highly developed in later centuries among the Greeks.

But the art of the effective presentation of arguments was far from being the only subject on which these sophists gave systematic instruction. On all kinds of topics they were seeking to substitute system and reasoned theory for mere tradition or guesswork. We read of different sophists who gave lectures on such varied subjects as town planning, the treatment of horses, diet and cooking, scientific agriculture, stagecraft, tactics and warfare, musical theory and harmony, political science, and archaeology. Much of this learning may have had little permanent value, but the whole movement explains how, a century or two later, Athens came to be a great seat of learning, which in reality, if not in name, was the first university in the world.

Questions

1. Describe Greek architecture.
   a. What kinds of buildings did they build?
   b. What were the characteristics of these buildings?
2. How did Greek sculpture develop over time?
3. What combination of characteristics did the Greeks strive for in sculpture?
4. How did Greek sculpture differ from Egyptian and Roman sculpture? Explain the statement, "Greek art never aimed at the sensational."
   a. in love?
   b. in death?
5. What forms of literature did the Greeks come up with? Which form did they not?
6. What forms of literature were especially developed in the fifth century?
7. How has Greek literature affected subsequent generations?
8. Why does the author think that this influence of Greek literature is so impressive?
9. Name four Greek playwrights, and two Greek historians.
10. What form of literature belonged especially to Athens?

Vocabulary

sophist
rhetoric
antiseptic

Chapter XXVIII

The Peloponnesian War

An English scholar writes: 'The history of the world consists mostly in the memory of those ages, quite few in number, in which some part of the world has risen above itself and burst into flower or fruit.' Such a period was the fifth century BC in Greece; so striking were the conquests of the mind of man in this age, so remarkable the forward march of civilization, that one would seem justified in looking to the future with the assured confidence that this was 'to be the fair beginning of a time.' But instead we meet one of the tragedies of history. A civil war broke out in Greece with consequences so fatal to progress that this war is as epoch-making as the Persian wars, but in a different way. Instead of ushering in a new day for Greece and for humanity, it beclouded all the fair hopes of better things, and it so permanently weakened the capacity of the Greek race that, except for a few brilliant names, the following centuries are unmistakably a period of exhaustion.

This Peloponnesian war, as it is called, involved practically all the Greek world from Ionia to Sicily, and, before it was over, Persia also was drawn into the struggle. It started from certain comparatively trivial quarrels, but its true origin was in the inveterate jealousies of the Greek states. There was, to begin with, the antagonism between the Dorian and the Ionian sections of the race. There was the jealousy of Sparta and other states because of the rapid advance of Athens. There was the keen rivalry between the two chief commercial cities, Athens and Corinth. There was, on the part of the subject states of the empire, a constant feeling of resentment and irritation at the loss of their autonomy, and, on the part of the free states of Greece, a constant fear that Athens was aiming at the inclusion of all Greece in her empire. The Athenians, on their part, were resolute in their determination to retain, by force if necessary, the sovereignty they had gained, however much it might violate the Greek instinct for freedom and self-determination.

The immediate causes were two: a quarrel between Corinth and its colony Corcyra, in which the latter asked and received assistance from Athens; and the forcible quelling by Athens of a revolt on the part of Potidaea, also a colony of Corinth, but a member of the Delian league. In the former case Corinth resented the interference of Athens, and in the latter Athens resented the interference of Corinth. At the insistance of Corinth a congress was called of the Peloponnesian allies, at which

Sparta was induced to agree to a declaration of war. It was in fact the Corinthians who made the war; neither Sparta nor Athens was eager for it. The historian Thucydides ascribes to a Corinthian speaker at the congress the following contrast between the Athenians and the Spartans: 'They are revolutionary, equally quick in the conception and in the execution of every new plan; while you are conservative—careful only to keep what you have, originating nothing, and not acting even when action is most necessary. They are bold beyond their strength; they run risks which prudence would condemn; and in the midst of misfortune they are full of hope. Whereas it is your nature, though strong, to act feebly; when your plans are most prudent, to distrust them; and when calamities come upon you, to think that you will never be delivered from them. They are impetuous and you are dilatory; they are always abroad, and you are always at home.... If any one should say of them, in a word, that they were born neither to have peace themselves nor to allow peace to other men, he would simply state the truth.'

The combatants on the one side were Sparta with the other Peloponnesian states, Argos and Achaea alone remaining neutral, and on the mainland north of the Isthmus, Megara, Boeotia, Phocis, and Locris, together with Ambracia in the far west. Athens had with her, of course, her whole empire, consisting of nearly all the Aegean islands and the coast cities of Thrace and Asia Minor. On the mainland of Greece her only allies were Acarnania in the west and the city of Plataea in Boeotia. Of the western islands, Corcyra and Zacynthus sided with Athens, Leucas with the Peloponnesians. (See map on page 162.) The strength of the one side obviously lay in its fleet, of the other, in its land-forces; and this fact determined the strategy of the combatants, especially in the first part of the long struggle.

1. The Ten Years' War

In the early summer of 431 BC a large army invaded Attica, expecting that the Athenians, to prevent the devastation of their country, would risk a pitched battle, in which the Peloponnesians might naturally look for victory. But the Long Walls had been built by Pericles for just such an emergency. As years before on the approach of the Persian, so now again the inhabitants of Attica, at Pericles' bidding, removed their families and valuables, and left their country-homes and farms for the enemy to lay waste. The public places of the city, the temple-enclosures, and above all the open spaces between the Long Walls were given over to the refugees to erect temporary shelters for themselves, while the fleet could be trusted to keep the whole population supplied with food through the Piraeus. The invaders accomplished little beyond exasperating the country-folk, who could see the devastation going on in the plain outside the walls. Pericles with some difficulty restrained them from sallying out to offer battle, and contented himself with sending the fleet to retaliate by making descents here and there on the Peloponnesian coast.

Pericles' strategy, which aimed at tiring out the enemy by proving the invulnerability of Athens, was sound, and, but for an unforeseen calamity, would probably before long have proved successful. From some foreign port the plague was brought to Athens, and in the unsanitary conditions of the crowded city it found the best possible soil for its rapid spread. So virulent was the disease that, before it ceased, one-third of the population perished, and the remainder were greatly shaken in morale. Greatest of all the losses was the death of Pericles, who fell a victim to the pestilence in the third year of the war and the second summer of the plague. As so often and so naturally happens with men of such superlative ability, he left no successor to take his place. The smaller men, like Cleon, who now led the democracy of Athens, were not of noble birth, like Pericles, and much of their disrepute is traceable to the aristocratic scorn felt by certain Greek writers for any one of the commercial or industrial class who aspired to eminence in the state. They were fairly capable and well-meaning men, but they had not the long experience, the sound judgment, the self-restraint, and the clear vision of Pericles. As a result, their lack of foresight more than once led Athens into unwise projects, and the keenness of their partisanship prompted acts of unworthy violence.

The war went on for ten years without any decision being arrived at; which is just as one might expect in a case of the proverbial struggle between a whale and a lion. Several incidents of this period deserve notice for various reasons. Plataea, commanding the highway between Boeotia and the Peloponnesus, was besieged, and after a long resistance was taken. The women and children had been sent to Athens, and when its capture became inevitable about half the garrison made their escape. The rest were put to death on surrendering, and the city was destroyed. Again Mitylene, the capital of Lesbos, revolted from Athens. This was one of the few allied states that had not been made subject, and the Athenians so resented what they thought an inexcusable act of treachery that, when the city was recaptured, the assembly sentenced all the adult males to death and the other inhabitants to enslavement. Second thoughts soon brought a mitigation of this pitiless sentence. Although Cleon and others still urged that extreme measures were necessary to maintain the supremacy of Athens, only the ringleaders were punished. The spirit of ruthless ferocity shown in these two episodes indicates how great a blow was being struck at the cause of civilization and humanity by this civil war. And even more frightful excesses are recorded in Corcyra, where a bitter feud raged between the oligarchical and the democratic partisans.

The best commander Athens now had, Demosthenes, entrapped a considerable force of Spartans on the island of Sphacteria, on the west coast of Messenia. In the final assault these soldiers, to the amazement of all Greece, were taken alive. It was the accepted tradition that a Spartan would die rather than surrender. In order to recover these prisoners, Sparta was willing to make peace; but the Athenians were too elated by this success to meet her half-way. The next year, Sparta for the first time hit upon an effective way of attacking Athens. Brasidas, an unusually enterprising and attractive Spartan, conceived the idea of weakening the Athenians by getting control of some of her important subject states. Making his way with a small force to Thrace, he achieved considerable success. This was partly by the persuasiveness with which he presented Sparta as the deliverer of enslaved Greek cities, and partly by the vigor with which he used force when tact and argument failed. In that same year an Athenian army, while engaged in an inroad into Boeotia, met with a severe defeat at Delium and lost heavily.

Both sides were sufficiently discouraged by the course of events, and sufficiently weary of the indecisive fighting, to listen to overtures of peace. Finally, after a battle in Thrace which proved fatal to both Cleon and Brasidas—each of them an enthusiastic advocate of vigorous warfare—peace was made on the basis of a return to the conditions existing at the beginning of the war. On the Athenian side this peace was negotiated by Nicias, a prominent leader of the moderate party once led by Cimon, whose view he shared that friendship with Sparta was preferable to rivalry. By this peace of Nicias the Spartans recovered the prisoners taken at Sphacteria, and the Athenians were to regain the Thracian towns taken by Brasidas.

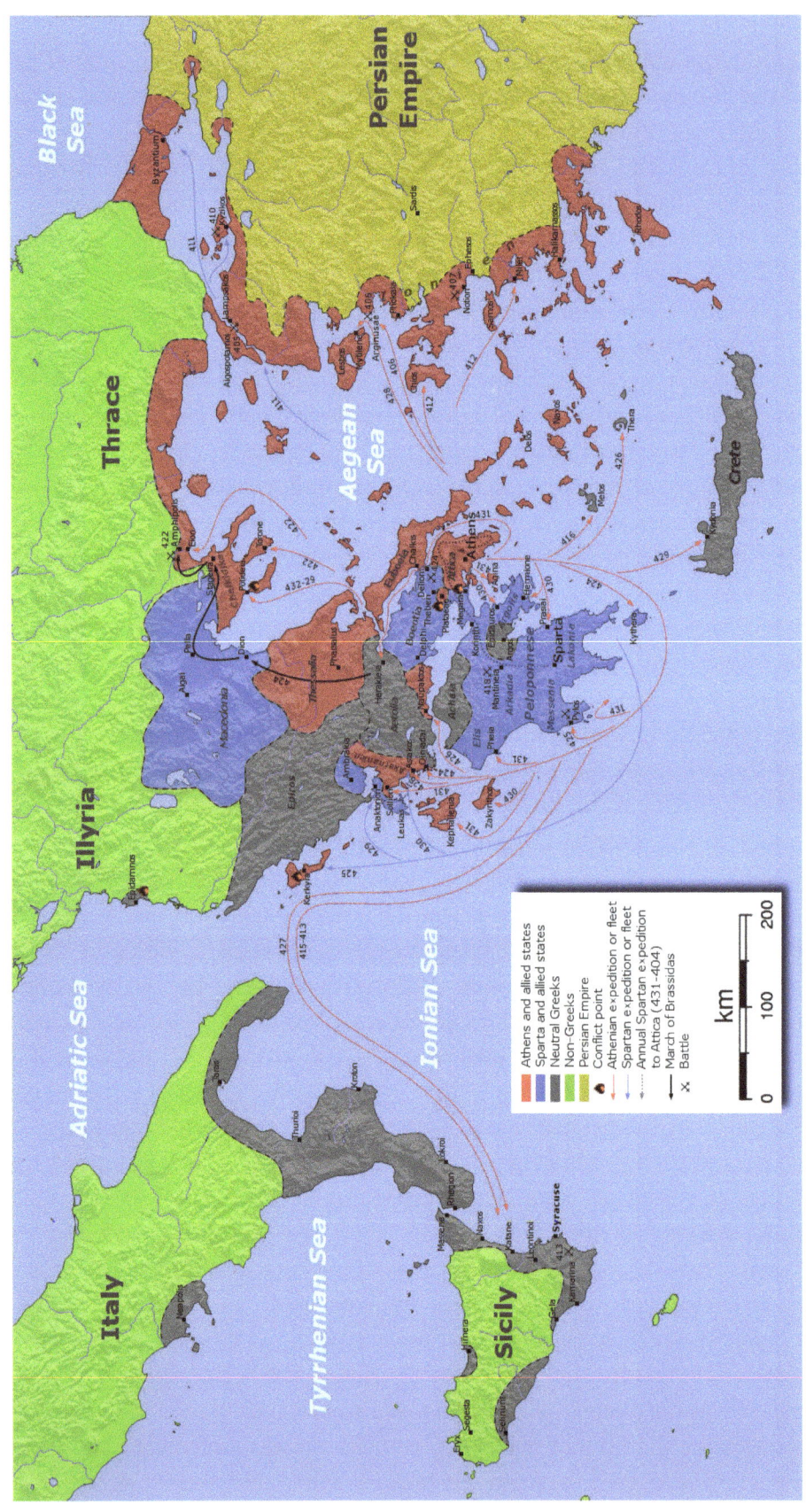

Though the peace was to be for fifty years, it brought but a brief interlude of quiet, and the preceding ten years are always counted merely the first stage in the whole Peloponnesian war. Dissension developed immediately, partly arising out of difficulties in carrying out the terms of peace, and partly due to the resentment of Corinth and Thebes at any such peace having been made. Attica was free for several years from invasion. The country-folk returned to their farms, and life in the city went on as usual. But many intrigues and various indirect acts of aggression showed that the fires of enmity were burning beneath the ashes.

2. The Sicilian Expedition

Meanwhile a young man was growing up in Athens who was destined to play a leading part in the remaining years of the century. Alcibiades was of noble birth, handsome, and wealthy. He had been brought up in the home of his kinsman Pericles and had every advantage an Athenian youth could possibly be given. No one in Athens had more brilliant abilities. He was to distinguish himself as a skillful political leader, a persuasive speaker, and a successful general. But he was self-willed and dissolute, as unstable as he was talented, and as unscrupulous as he was ambitious. Many stories were told of his youthful pranks and of his wild escapades in early manhood. He must have been a sore trial to Pericles, but there was something attractive in his high spirits, and he was popular without being respected, and followed without being trusted. At the beginning of his public career, shortly after the peace of Nicias, when he was about thirty years old, Alcibiades attached himself to the radical or war party, and opposed Nicias as Cleon had done. But later on we shall find him espousing the most diverse causes, as petulance or ambition dictated.

For many years the rivalries of the mother-cities had been reproduced in Sicily. There was the rivalry of Dorian with Ionian colonies, of oligarchical with democratic states, and of ambitious or quarrelsome cities with their neighbors. In particular Syracuse, a colony of Corinth and incomparably the strongest city in Sicily, and indeed second only to Athens in the whole Greek world, was pursuing a policy of aggression against the weaker Sicilian communities. It was natural for a threatened Ionian colony to invoke the aid of Athens, but no serious intervention was possible while the war with Sparta was in progress. But when a later appeal came from Segesta, it seemed to the ardent war-party in Athens a golden opportunity for including in the empire this rich island of the west. Nicias, cautious and peace-loving, opposed the scheme. He was overborne, and then was himself appointed to take command of the expedition, with Alcibiades

A Hermes Pillar.

Bust of Alcibiades.

and Lamachus as his colleagues. Excitement ran high at Athens, for the people entertained the wildest hopes of gaining empire and riches and glory. The expedition was the finest ever organized in Greece. There were 134 triremes with many smaller vessels, and 30,000 men of whom 5,000 were heavy-armed infantry. When the fleet was ready, all Athens thronged the Piraeus to see it set sail—never to return.

On the very eve of departure it was found one morning that the stone pillars which stood at each house-door and which bore the head of the god Hermes carved at the top had all been mutilated. This sacrilegious act horrified the devout and alarmed the superstitious. The reason for the mutilation of the *Hermae* was not apparent nor was it ever discovered. But the reputation of Alcibiades for recklessness and irreverence prompted his political enemies to attribute it to him. They refrained, however, from laying any formal charge until he had sailed, taking with him a large section of his warmest supporters. With these out of the way, his enemies easily secured a decree recalling him to Athens to be tried on a charge of impiety.

The order of recall reached Sicily before anything had been accomplished. Syracuse was so unprepared that a prompt attack such as Lamachus advised would probably have been successful, but Nicias and Alcibiades had favored a more gradual approach. Alcibiades was in no mood to submit his conduct to the Athenian courts, and instead of returning to Athens he made his way to Sparta. There, being given a hearing before the assembly, he declared that he had never really sympathized with the Athenian democracy, and that the policy of Athens was first to conquer Sicily, and then with this increase of power to make herself mistress of the Peloponnesus and all Greece. He strongly recommended two measures: to send a capable general to Syracuse to organize and direct its defense; and to seize Decelea as a permanent strategic post in Attica from which the Athenians could be more effectively harassed than by the brief annual invasions. Was Alcibiades a traitor who sought only revenge? Or was he rather aiming at humbling his country and thus preparing the way for his return as its deliverer, after which it might perhaps be possible to make himself, like Pisistratus, tyrant of Athens?

The Spartans were deeply impressed by this speech and acted as he advised. They sent Gylippus to Syracuse, accompanied by a strong force from Corinth, and his arrival gave fresh courage to the hard-pressed Syracusans. Indeed, in a short time, it was the Athenians who were on the defensive, thanks to the energy of Gylippus and the cautious stupidity of Nicias, who, now that Lamachus had fallen in battle, was sole commander. Nicias was at last obliged to appeal to Athens for help. A second expedition of seventy-three triremes, with an army nearly as strong as the first, was sent under Demosthenes and the struggle became truly gigantic, when one considers the intensity of the fighting, and the large issues involved—for Athens, wider dominion or ruinous failure; for Syracuse, freedom or subjection.

But even the arrival of reinforcements failed to bring victory, and after several reverses by land and sea Demosthenes advised withdrawal. Nicias hesitated to take so serious a step, but finally consented. However, on the night before the forces were to re-embark, an eclipse of the moon took place, and the pious Nicias and the simple-minded sailors alike took this to be a warning not to depart before the next full moon. The delay was fatal. The Syracusans had been building up a strong fleet and were becoming steadily more expert and more confident. They now blocked up the great harbor in which both fleets lay, so that the Athenians could not sail out without a battle. The desperate fight that followed was in full view of the land-forces lining the shore about the harbor. No tragedy ever enacted on a stage was witnessed with such agonized suspense, as the spectators followed every movement, realizing that their own safety and the survival of their empire were at stake that day, and perhaps the very existence of Athens. The utter defeat which followed left the Athenians no recourse but to attempt to escape by a long and arduous land-march to some friendly city. The sick and wounded had to be left behind to the doubtful mercies of their enemies, and the army had to march practically without supplies. They found every road blocked, and in a few days were forced to surrender to the triumphant and vengeful Syracusans. Nicias and Demosthenes were put to death, and the survivors from the army and the fleet, after a long imprisonment under harrowing conditions, were sold into slavery by those whom they had come to enslave.

3. The Ionian War

The completeness of the Syracusan victory, followed by so cruel a vengeance, proved the turning-point of the war. To be sure, most of the troops lost were not from Athens but from the subject states. New ships could soon be built, but the skilled sailors who had kept the seas clear of enemies, both Persian and Peloponnesian, were not to be replaced. The war now enters on its third and final stage, and the scene shifts to the eastern Aegean, where for nine more years Athens made a brave but ineffectual struggle. The weakening of Athenian sea-power led directly to three results: The Peloponnesians for the first time in the war ventured to send a strong fleet into the Aegean; the subject states of the empire saw in Athens' extremity their own opportunity to revolt; and Persia also proceeded to reassert her authority over the Greek cities and islands that had once paid her tribute. Sparta was ready to assist the island states to remain free, but at the same time made a discreditable bargain with Tissaphernes, the satrap of Ionia, by which, in return for Persia's financial support of the fleet, the Greek cities in Asia Minor were to be given back to the king. This was the price Sparta was willing to pay for victory.

Syracusan Coin. (Commemorating the victory of 413 BC) [British Museum, London]

We now find Alcibiades leaving Sparta, which had taken his advice but had done nothing for him in return, and enjoying the favor of Tissaphernes. By representing to this satrap that it was to Persia's interest to let Athens and Sparta wear each other out, he induced him to refrain from giving Sparta any really effective aid. With great skill he so cultivated both parties in Athens that before long he secured his recall to his native city. The past was forgiven and he was made one of the Athenian generals. The Athenians were putting forth tremendous efforts, and for a time made head against their enemies, largely because of the vigor and military skill of Alcibiades and the lukewarmness of Tissaphernes to Sparta. At this juncture the Persian king, dissatisfied with Tissaphernes' conduct of affairs, sent down his younger son, Cyrus, to replace him. Simultaneously the Spartans sent out a new admiral, Lysander, who won the confidence of Cyrus and also proved to be the most efficient leader the Peloponnesian fleet had yet had. And unfortunately at this time the Athenians, displeased by a slight naval defeat, deposed Alcibiades from his generalship, although he had not been present at the battle and was indisputably their ablest leader. He withdrew to a fortified place of his own on the Hellespont from which he could watch events.

Conon, who succeeded Alcibiades, was either inefficient or unlucky, and was quite unequal to coping with the strong combination of Lysander and Cyrus. Two years after his appointment, the battle of Aegospotami, fought in the Hellespont, brought the war to a close. It was less a battle than a surprise, due to the carelessness of Conon, to whom Alcibiades had sent an unheeded warning. Virtually the whole fleet was captured without resistance. When the news of the disaster came, a wailing cry ran from the Piraeus through the Long Walls to the city, and that night in Athens no one slept. Expecting momentarily the approach of the victorious enemy and having neither time nor resources to build a new fleet, the people prepared as best they could for a siege. The city was soon invested by land and by sea. No assault was needed; in a few months famine compelled an unconditional surrender.

Corinth and Thebes were eager to destroy the city and sell its citizens into slavery, as Athens herself had done more than once. But Sparta refused to destroy a city which had done so much for Greek freedom. She was less implacable in her enmity than the commercial rivals or the close neighbors of Athens; and probably also the Spartans had sufficient foresight to see that, with Athens out of the way, Corinth and Thebes might be difficult to deal with. The terms imposed were, however, hard enough for the imperial city which had ruled over so wide an empire and had dreamed of uniting all Greece under her leadership. The Long Walls and the fortifications of the Piraeus were to be razed. All her territory outside Attica, except only Salamis, was to be taken from her, and all but twelve of her warships surrendered, and Sparta's leadership was to be acknowledged. The victors proceeded to level the walls to the sound of music, believing that that day was the beginning of freedom for Greece.

In reality, the subject states were but exchanging one master for another. Greece had missed its one chance of becoming a united nation under enlightened leadership, and was returning to the old chaos of conflicting interests and chronic warfare. Sparta not only surrendered to Persia the Asiatic cities which the Delian league had set free, but also began to exercise over the other states of the league a much more oppressive rule than that of Athens. In each city the local government was set aside, and a Spartan governor installed, supported by a Spartan garrison and ruling through a small selected group of subservient partisans. In pursuing this imperialistic policy the Spartans were not only setting at naught their promise of freedom to the subjects of Athens, but they were also abandoning their age-long avoidance of foreign entanglements. They had had no experience in managing subject states, and the Spartan, when given authority abroad, was apt to prove arrogant, tyrannical, and rapacious. If this change of policy was not devised by Lysander, it was he at any rate who brought it into effect, and with his armed force imposed a harsh autocratic rule upon the former members of the Athenian league.

In Athens itself something similar took place. There had always been a small oligarchical element that scorned democratic institutions. In the confused years that followed the disaster at Syracuse, an effort was made by this party to have the government of Athens limited to a comparatively small body of citizens. It was argued with some force that an assembly containing thousands of unenlightened voters, easily persuaded by demagogues and apt to be swayed by prejudice and to vote in ignorance, was not a fit body to determine the city's policy in critical times. But the Athenians were still a free people, and as soon as they realized what was being aimed at, the attempt to set up the oligarchy of 'the Four Hundred' quickly collapsed. Now, however, conditions were more favorable, and with the support of Lysander and his armed forces a small oligarchical group of thirty came into power. Nominally they were merely a commission authorized to draft a new constitution for submission to the assembly. They really proceeded to exercise despotic power in Athens and inaugurated a reign of terror such as that city had never known. Wealthy or obnoxious citizens to the number of 1,500 were put to death and their property confiscated; thousands more fled to save their lives. The rule of 'the Thirty' was too intolerable to last long, even though supported by a strong Spartan garrison. The exiles, led by Thrasybulus, gathered a small but resolute force and finally established themselves in the Piraeus, where they defeated the more numerous forces of the Thirty, slew their leader Critias, and restored the democracy. There was sufficient moderate opinion in Sparta to prevent Lysander from intervening again in Athenian affairs, but the general policy of establishing a military despotism throughout Greece was persisted in by Sparta for a generation.

A story from Plutarch's *Parallel Lives*: Lysander

The Peloponnesian war had now been carried on for a long time, and after their disaster in Sicily it was expected that the Athenians would straightway lose their control of the sea, and presently give up the struggle altogether. But Alcibiades, returning from exile and taking the command, wrought a great change, and made his countrymen again a match for their enemies by sea. The Lacedaemonians, accordingly, were frightened again, and summoning up fresh zeal for the war, which required, as they thought, an able leader and a more powerful armament, sent out Lysander to take command upon the sea. When he came to Ephesus, he found the city well disposed to him and very zealous in the Spartan cause, although it was then in a low state of prosperity and in danger of becoming utterly barbarized by the admixture of Persian customs, since it was enveloped by Lydia, and the King's generals made it their headquarters. He therefore pitched his camp there, and ordered the merchant vessels from every quarter to land their cargoes there, and made preparations for the building of triremes. Thus he revived the traffic of their harbours, and the business of their market, and filled their houses and workshops with profits, so that from that time on, and through his efforts, the city had hopes of achieving the stateliness and grandeur which it now enjoys.

When he learned that Cyrus, the King's son, was come to Sardis, he went up to confer with him and to accuse Tissaphernes, who, though he was commissioned to aid the Lacedaemonians and drive the Athenians from the sea, was thought to be remiss in his duty, through the efforts of Alcibiades, showing lack of zeal, and destroying the efficiency of the fleet by the meagre subsidies which he gave. Now Cyrus was well pleased that Tissaphernes, who was a base man and privately at feud with him, should be accused and maligned. By this means, then, as well as by his behaviour in general, Lysander made himself agreeable, and by the submissive deference of his conversation, above all else, he won the heart of the young prince, and roused him to prosecute the war with vigour. At a banquet which Cyrus gave him as he was about to depart, the prince begged him not to reject the tokens of his friendliness, but to ask plainly for whatever he desired, since nothing whatsoever would be refused him. "Since, then," said Lysander in reply, "thou art so very kind, I beg and entreat thee, Cyrus, to add an obol to the pay of my sailors, that they may get four obols instead of three." Cyrus, accordingly, delighted with his public spirit, gave him ten thousand darics, out of which he added the obol to the pay of his seamen, and, by the renown thus won, soon emptied the ships of his enemies.

Lysander resumes command with the approval of the people.

Questions

1. Dissect the quote by the Corinthian speaker who contrasts the Athenians and the Spartans. Who is the imprudent and who is the feeble though strong (who is the "you" and who is the "they")? What are the qualities of each side according to this speaker?
2. Based on the information in this chapter, make a timeline of the Peloponnesian War, entering the events on the timeline.
3. How did the war end and how did it affect the lives of the Greeks?

Vocabulary

inveterate
dilatory
mitigation

Chapter **XXIX**

Socrates and His Circle

In the midst of the promise of brighter days for Athens, now that the democracy had been restored, came an event that has always been made a reproach to the Athenian people. This was the sentencing to death, on a false charge, of Socrates, who of all the Greeks that ever lived deserved most to be revered for his exemplary life and character.

Socrates was one of the poorest of men, but he was indifferent to wealth. No one ever knew better than he that 'a man's life consisteth not in the abundance of the things that he possesseth.' Entering the agora one day and seeing the booths unusually crowded with merchandise, he said: 'Bless me, what a multitude of things there are that one can do without.' Among a people remarkable for beauty and graceful bearing, Socrates was conspicuous for his ugliness and his grotesque figure. Rather he prayed to the gods that he might have 'beauty in the inward parts' and that also he might ever count wisdom to be true wealth.

But although devoted above all others in Athens to the search for knowledge, Socrates dissociated himself both from the scientists and from the sophists of his day. Knowledge of the external world about us he thought infinitely less important than knowledge of ourselves. Human beings were to him far more interesting than trees and animals, and the study of human nature and human life he considered the most fruitful and necessary of all studies.[16] As for the sophists, he thought that what men most needed was not instruction in how to win success in life, as success is usually interpreted, but in the earnest and lifelong search for the greatest of all treasures, namely, perfection of character and uprightness of life.

To attain these, he reasoned, we must know what they are. For if we know accurately what justice, for example, and courage are, we shall be more likely to attain them than if we have imperfect and inconsistent notions about them, or have never tried to think out what it means to be just and courageous. Thus an important part of Socrates' search for truth consisted in the attempt to get exact definitions of the virtues and of other matters that concern our life and conduct. His interest

---

[16] This was in harmony with the famous motto inscribed on the temple at Delphi, 'Know thyself,' which Socrates often quoted.

in these questions led to the development of the new studies of ethics, that is, of the science of moral conduct, and politics, or the science of citizenship and government. Moreover—though he did not himself dream of this further application—the natural and physical sciences, in which he himself took so little interest, have made great use both of his discovery of the value of exact definitions, and of his method of working out definitions by proceeding from particular cases to general principles.

The Athenians spent a large part of their time in the agora, the gymnasia, and other public places. And there, for the last forty years of the fifth century, Socrates was a familiar figure, as he discussed with all sorts of people the questions that interested him so deeply, and sought to induce others to share his search for truth. There never lived a more acute reasoner than Socrates. Quick to detect and expose any loose reasoning in others, he was, at the same time, humble about his own wisdom, which, to his mind, consisted chiefly in knowing how ignorant he really was. He held, therefore, that the first step in helping others to attain true knowledge was to help them to realize their ignorance, and this he would proceed to do by a merciless, yet perfectly courteous and urbane, cross-questioning. One Athenian is represented as saying: 'When we are drawn into a discussion with Socrates, no matter what the subject may be, we are always led on by him until we find ourselves giving an account of ourselves and of our way of living, and Socrates never lets us go until he has thoroughly sifted us.'

He made enemies at times by his exposure of dangerous error, of hypocritical pretense, or of confused thinking. And he also made enemies by his criticism of Athenian democracy as a principle of government, and especially of its assumption that all citizens were so equally competent that the magistrates could be chosen by lot. No one, he argued, would ever dream of choosing a man by lot to act as pilot or as doctor, and surely governing a state is a task that calls for expert knowledge and careful training just as much as directing a ship or curing a disease.

He insisted, moreover, that we need some surer ground for our morality than mere custom or tradition, and that we should be able to give a reason for our beliefs, and know precisely why we hold them. This was mistaken by some timid Athenians for an attack on the time-honored standards of their fathers. Socrates was, of course, simply trying to find a stronger defense for the time-honored morality, to which he himself loyally adhered. He was trying to save morality from the insidious

Alcibiades Being Taught by Socrates, by François-André Vincent - Musée Fabre.

attacks of those who argued that morality is nothing more than custom and fashion, and that the moral law does not bind any man who is strong enough to disregard it. Might does not make right, he protested; nor again is a thing right just because it is the custom, or the law. It is right because of what it is in itself, by reason of its own essential nature. To understand what this is he counted man's highest privilege and his supreme duty.

Finally, when he was now seventy years of age, some of his enemies who had great influence in the city publicly accused him of corrupting the youth of Athens by his teachings. The newly revived democracy was anxious to purge the city of the evil influences that had brought disaster during the last generation, and, by shrewd appeals to their fears and prejudices, the jury of 501 citizens before whom Socrates appeared was induced by a small majority to declare him guilty and sentence him to death.

Socrates might have saved himself by promising to remain silent henceforth, or by offering to withdraw from Athens altogether. He scorned any compromise, however. In a noble speech he defended the principles that had guided him throughout his long life, and declared that so long as he had breath, he would never abandon the search for truth or cease to exhort his fellow-citizens to think more of their character than of their bodies or their possessions. To this mission he felt that he was called by God, and he must obey God rather than man. The court might kill his body, but he was convinced that neither in life nor in death could any real harm come to one who sought to obey God and serve his fellow-men.

In due time he was given the usual cup of poisonous hemlock to drink and met his death with perfect calm and confidence. Few things in literature are more moving and more quietly impressive than the account in Plato of the last hours of Socrates on earth. It closes with this eulogy, expressed with all the customary Greek simplicity and restraint: 'Such was the death of our friend, who, we believe, was, of all the men that we have known, the best, the wisest, the most upright.'

So unusual a man as Socrates was sure to attract the attention of the brightest and most promising of the youth of Athens, who were drawn partly by the brilliancy of his conversation, and partly by the nobility of his character. On some of these he failed to make a lasting impression; on Alcibiades, for example, and Critias, the foremost of the Thirty. Alcibiades in his youth was an especial favorite of Socrates, who failed, however, to cure his self-willed waywardness. One of the criticisms leveled at Socrates was that such men as Alcibiades and Critias had been much in his company, and that few men had done so much harm to Athens. The truth is that Socrates, instead of corrupting Alcibiades, had tried to save him from corrupting influences, but had failed.

Of the other members of his circle special mention should be made of Plato and Xenophon, to whom our knowledge of Socrates is chiefly due. For Socrates left no writings of his own, and yet no one in the ancient world has had a greater influence and a more continuous influence upon modern thought than Socrates, speaking through his disciples, Plato in particular. Plato had all that fortune had denied to Socrates of good birth, wealth, and comeliness. When he came under the influence of Socrates, he was a young man of about twenty, and already a budding poet of great promise. He threw aside both poetry and the prospect of political eminence, and attached himself to Socrates until the latter's death some eight years later. Socrates' teachings had sunk deeply into his mind, which was one of extraordinary power. He proceeded to develop the truths that he found in them, and to build up one of the most famous of those great systems of thought which we call philosophies.

To set forth his views, he wrote a series of dialogues or conversations in which his master Socrates had the chief place—a tribute of admiration and gratitude to his master. These dialogues have many a lifelike picture of Socrates and his acquaintance as they moved amid the familiar scenes of Athens, and are written in the most perfect style achieved by any Greek prose writer. Indeed the combination in Plato's writings of profound thinking, of vivid imagination, of humor, of moral elevation, and of beauty of style has never since been matched.

In addition to doctrines which require a mature intellect to comprehend and estimate, the philosophy of Plato includes as one of its central teachings the belief in the immortality of the soul. This doctrine Plato sets forth with a clearness unequalled anywhere until the coming of Christianity. Being immortal, the soul, he teaches, is of infinitely more importance than the body and its powers, or than all our material possessions and interests. The development of our mental and spiritual powers is, therefore, man's supreme concern. Much of his writing sets forth what would be the consequences, in our present life on earth, of this estimate; how this view, if followed up consistently, would affect the whole organization of society, our laws, education, economic system, literature, art, amusements, our whole lives in short. Plato was thus the forerunner of all writers of utopias, picturing a perfect life of mankind upon earth.

There were those in his day who were inclined to point to the frequent prosperity of the wicked, and argue that one is justified in seeking his own advantage regardless of others, after 'the simple plan that they should take who have the power, and they should keep who can.' In reply Plato presents a powerful argument to prove that uprightness and virtue are to the soul what health is to the body, its true welfare and only real satisfaction; that even if we did find 'Truth for ever on the scaffold. Wrong for ever on the throne,' yet the man who once sees the true issues at stake, who sees virtue and vice for what they really are, will unhesitatingly choose the former, no matter what the consequences may be. There is something in man, Plato teaches, that is akin to the beast. There is also something akin to the divine, and this latter is the true man. To strengthen the nobler of these and to curb the baser must be man's highest good, even if there were no hereafter. But when we take into account the fact that the soul does not perish with the body, Plato holds that to gain the whole world at the cost of ruining the soul is the most foolish and indefensible of choices.[17]

Xenophon was by no means so great a thinker or so consummate a writer as Plato. He was simply a high-minded Greek gentleman, who could write with clearness and ease on a variety of topics that interested him. Among his works is an account of the character and conversations of Socrates, under the name of *Memorabilia* (or Memoirs) of Socrates. In another work, under the guise of a description of the early life and upbringing of Cyrus the Great, he really sets forth his view of what an ideal education should be. He also wrote a history of Greek affairs from the point where Thucydides' unfinished history was broken off by his death. But his best known work is the *Anabasis,* in which he gives a graphic and detailed account of a famous military expedition in which he himself took part and which ended in a great adventure.

On the death of Darius, his elder son Artaxerxes became king of Persia. Cyrus, the younger son, formed the design of supplanting his brother by securing the assistance of some of the Greeks whose courage and capacity he had learned to appreciate while he was satrap of Asia Minor. Now

---

[17] For fifty years until his death, Plato taught his philosophy in some public gardens near his house on the outskirts of Athens. This resort was called the *Academia,* from an ancient Attic hero, and hence it came that his successors, who founded a school of philosophy to perpetuate his teaching, were known as the *Academy.*

that the Peloponnesian war was over, Cyrus, with the secret support of the Spartan government, was able to enlist many thousands of men trained to war, and with these and a much larger body of Asiatics set out for Babylon. Xenophon accompanied the Greeks, not as an officer, but as a personal friend of one of the commanders. At first the Greeks were told that the expedition was to attack some district in Asia Minor; when they learned the truth, they were already far on their way and promises of increased pay induced them to continue.

Xenophon's record of this march is the first detailed account in literature of travel in strange lands. We can follow with ease and interest every stage of the long march through Asia Minor and Syria to the Euphrates, and then down that river and over the Arabian desert until they were within a few days' march of Babylon. Here the king's army, vastly superior in numbers, met them and offered battle. Cyrus' confidence in his Greek troops was fully justified; they had no difficulty whatever in vanquishing the troops opposed to them. But on returning from the pursuit they found that when Cyrus caught sight of his brother he had been unable to restrain himself, and in a rash attack on the king's bodyguard had been killed. With his death, the object of the whole expedition was gone, and the Asiatic troops would not continue the struggle.

Undaunted by the fact that they were overwhelmingly outnumbered and were far in the heart of a hostile and unknown continent, the ten thousand Greeks undertook to march back home again. The Persians prudently refrained from attacking them; but before long, by an act of treachery, the generals of the various Greek groups were seized and put to death. In this emergency Xenophon came forward and assumed direction of the leaderless army. The route chosen by the 'Ten Thousand' was not that by which they had come. This would have taken them again through a desert where no supplies were available, and where they would be constantly harassed by the hordes of Persian cavalry. Instead they had decided to head straight north for the Euxine Sea. The return march took them eight months. They were dogged for weeks by Persian troops, and when they reached the mountainous region north of the Tigris valley they had to fight their way through the fierce and savage hill-tribes and march in winter weather over snow-covered heights. Finally one day the vanguard, climbing a hill, caught sight of the Euxine. Their shout of *The sea! The sea!* brought the whole army hurrying to rejoice at the sight, which to them meant deliverance and home.

This expedition had important consequences. It revealed to the Greeks in an unmistakable way that Persia was far from invulnerable. The demonstration that a few thousand men could penetrate to the very center of the empire and fight their way back without serious losses was to bear fruit before the century was over in the complete collapse of Persia in the invasion of Alexander the Great. No exploit in their whole history gives a more vivid impression of the invincible courage and ready resourcefulness of the Greeks, especially when we remember that the 'Ten Thousand' were by no means the flower of the nation, but mere mercenaries and adventurers. It gives evidence also of the degree to which the habit of self-government had become part of the Greek character. It is a remarkable spectacle, this large society of soldiers belonging to no state, responsible to no authority, but managing their own affairs, deciding what they would do, determining where they would go, seldom failing to listen to the voice of reason in their assemblies, whether it was the voice of Xenophon or of another.

Questions

1. Describe Socrates and his approach to life.
2. What kinds of things did he ask his students (and his fellow citizens) to consider?
3. Why did the elite consider him a threat?
4. Describe Plato and his contribution to Greek society and Western Civilization.
5. Retell the story of Xenophon's adventures invading Persia and returning to Greece.

Vocabulary

ethics
insidious
consummate

Chapter XXX

Epaminondas and Philip

The first sixty years of the fourth century present a bewildering maze of incessant warfare and shifting alliances in every part of the Greek world. Each state sought its own immediate advantage; no sign can be detected of any step towards a stable union or some form of fair and reasonable cooperation based on mutual concessions in the general interest of all Greece. The best minds of Greece could create noble political and social ideals which have ever since been an inspiration to the civilized nations of the world. But the Greeks were apparently incapable of evolving a political system in which these ideals might be realized. Of the course of events in this period only an outline can here be attempted.

The understanding between Sparta and Persia, which had proved so disastrous to Athens, did not survive the expedition of Cyrus. The Persian king was naturally displeased at the encouragement given to Cyrus by Sparta, and Sparta was influenced by the evidence of Persia's weakness. Before long we find a Spartan army under its able king, Agesilaus, carrying on successful warfare against Persia in Asia Minor. Persia retaliated by stirring up trouble for Sparta in Greece, an easy thing to do, as Sparta's aggressive and domineering attitude towards her late allies was causing deep resentment everywhere, especially in Thebes and Corinth. We now find these cities, as well as Persia, welcoming the support of Athens, which, since the expulsion of the Thirty, had been quietly regaining her former commercial pre-eminence. A Persian fleet was put under the command of the Athenian Conon, who soon avenged his defeat at Aegospotami by winning an overwhelming victory over the Spartan fleet off Cnidus. Conon then sailed to the Piraeus, and, with the approval of Thebes and others of her late enemies, had the Long Walls and the other fortifications of Athens rebuilt.

The growing opposition in Europe had already led to the recall of Agesilaus and his army from Asia, in order to maintain Spartan supremacy. At last, the inconclusive warfare in Greece brought about an agreement with Persia by which Sparta abandoned the Greek cities in Asia to the king in return for the latter's ceasing to support Sparta's enemies in Greece. This brought the war in Greece also nominally to an end; but Sparta continued her practice of interfering in the internal affairs of other states and of breaking up any alliance which might prove too strong for her to dominate.

A Spartan army which was on its way to Thrace on such an errand seized the citadel of Thebes, with which at the time Sparta was at peace, installed a Spartan garrison in it, and put in power a small oligarchical group of its own adherents. Many of the Thebans fled from the city, and a few years later a small band of these patriots who had received shelter in Athens set out under a vigorous leader named Pelopidas, made their way in disguise into the citadel, slew the Spartan officers, expelled the garrison, and set up a democratic government of their own again. In effecting this revolution they had the assistance of many of the Theban youth, who had remained in Thebes and had been secretly prepared for a day of reckoning by Epaminondas, a close friend of Pelopidas. The Spartans and their partisans had looked upon Epaminondas as a harmless philosopher and teacher, but all the while, with an eye to the future, he had been directing their physical training and instilling ideals of patriotism and liberty.

By her ruthless policy Sparta had seemed to have succeeded in destroying all effective opposition in Greece, but from now on her difficulties began to increase. Athens formed a new league of the Aegean states on fairer terms than the former Delian League. And Thebes, under the shrewd guidance of Epaminondas, began to develop a strength and an activity never shown in all her previous history. The Boeotian League was restored under Theban leadership, and much attention was paid to the training of the Theban youth for war. Her bold and independent attitude soon showed that Thebes in her turn was aiming at the supremacy in Greek affairs which Sparta had held so long.

Sparta at last sent a strong army to invade Boeotia and chastise Thebes for her presumption. But when the two armies met at Leuctra, Epaminondas, though with inferior numbers, won a complete victory. This was due principally to the new tactics he had devised. Hitherto in Greece the whole line of battle, ten or twelve spears deep, would advance simultaneously against the opposing line. Epaminondas massed his well-trained Thebans on one wing in a column fifty deep, which he launched in an irresistible charge on the opposing wing. Meanwhile, the rest of his line, made up of the weaker Boeotian allies, advanced much more slowly, so as to hold the attention of the enemy facing them, without coming to any actual engagement until the enemy's line was already shattered. The new principle thus introduced into battle-tactics was destined to have a long career—the principle of launching an overwhelming force at one selected point in an enemy's position. At Leuctra the battle was decided by this one charge, in which the Spartan king and hundreds of his best troops were slain.

This victory not only shattered the tradition of Spartan invincibility, but also made Thebes the most powerful state in Greece. With Greece at last freed from the crushing military despotism of Sparta, and with so high-minded a patriot as Epaminondas guiding the policy of Thebes, one might hope that Theban supremacy would bring a new spirit into Greek political life. Trained by the philosophers to a simple and almost ascetic life, skilled in bodily exercises and passionately devoted to intellectual culture, a great orator and a great captain, but even more remarkable for his moral qualities, his modesty, his frankness, and his humanity, Epaminondas deserved to be taken by the ancients as the finest type of the Greek genius. But with all his noble qualities, his culture, his uprightness, his eloquence, and his military genius, he lacked the one thing which Greece most needed, the gift of constructive statesmanship that should have some wider policy and ideal than the aggrandizement and supremacy of his own city.

With the active support of Thebes, Arcadia and other parts of the Peloponnesus asserted their independence from Sparta. An Arcadian confederacy was founded, for which a new capital city, Megalopolis, was built. Epaminondas led an army into the Peloponnesus, and, for the first time in its history, Spartan territory was invaded. The city itself, though threatened, was too strong to attack, but Epaminondas proceeded to set Messenia and its Helots free from the Spartan yoke. A new city, Messene, was built on the slopes of Mt. Ithome, where, three centuries before, the Messenians had made their last desperate stand for liberty. The weakening of Sparta brought anarchy, however, rather than freedom to the Peloponnesus, and twice more Epaminondas had to march south to intervene in the persistent quarrels of the various states.

Whenever one nation attains a dangerous preeminence, it is natural for its neighbors to combine in self-defense. Thebes and Sparta had opposed the Athenian empire; Thebes and Athens had united in opposition to Sparta; and it was not long before Sparta and Athens found themselves in alliance to resist the supremacy of Thebes. The northern Arcadians also had begun to resent Theban interference, and finally Epaminondas for the fourth time entered the Peloponnesus to crush the combined opposition that was developing. At Mantinea in Arcadia he met the forces of Sparta and her allies, and, by using again the tactics of Leuctra, to which Spartan conservatism had not learned to adapt itself, he was again victorious. But in the moment of victory he was himself fatally wounded. Pelopidas had fallen the year before in Thessaly, and there was no one left capable of continuing the work begun by these two men.

For some years comparative peace, the peace of exhaustion, reigned in Greece. There were still innumerable petty conflicts, but no one state aspired to impose its rule upon the rest. The political unity which was the great need of Greece, and which individual Greeks here and there were advocating, was to come more quickly than the condition of affairs would lead one to suppose, and from a quite unexpected quarter.

In the north-western corner of the Aegean, north of the Chalcidian peninsula, was the kingdom of Macedonia, lying between the fringe of Greek colonies on the coast and the mountainous interior occupied by wild Thracian tribes. This region, which was fertile and well-watered, was partly plain and partly hill-country. The Macedonians lived in scattered villages, not in towns organized as city-states; they were probably of kindred race with the Greeks, but so backward in their development and speaking so uncouth a dialect that they were regarded by the other Greeks as little better than semi-civilized barbarians. The kings of Macedonia were of somewhat purer descent than their subjects, whom they ruled after the fashion of the chieftains of Homeric times. Towards the close of the fifth century, Archelaus, the most energetic of these kings, had firmly established his authority and built up a strong army, and had sought to introduce something of contemporary Greek culture. In the fourth century, the Thebans, while engaged in extending their power over the north country, took Philip, a young member of the reigning family, as a hostage to Thebes. Here he remained for three years, during which time he became acquainted with the Theban military tactics, learned something of the culture and institutions of the Greeks, and saw at close range their jealousies and their consequent weakness. A few years later, at the age of twenty-four, he became king and at once set himself to consolidate and extend his power.

Philip was no ordinary man. He was a consummate diplomatist, who to an acute and powerful mind united adroitness in managing men, skill in taking advantage of every opening, patience in biding his time, and utter unscrupulousness in his methods. Very early he seized certain rich gold mines on his eastern frontier,[18] and these gave him unlimited resources to use in building up his army and in bribing men and states to serve his ends. He had also real military genius. Not only did he fashion his fierce tribesmen into a well-disciplined and formidable army, and make more extensive use of cavalry than was usual in Greece, but by a new device he made the Macedonian phalanx more than a match for the best of the Greeks. He had the spears of his warriors so lengthened that the first ranks could come into action before the enemy was able to retaliate.

For a long time Philip met with no vigorous opposition from any quarter to his steady and insidious advances, although Athenian interests especially were often affected. At last a young Athenian came forward in the assembly to denounce Philip. At the time of his *First Philippic,* Demosthenes was thirty-two years old. He had made a resolute effort in youth to overcome natural defects in his speech, and had for some time been engaged in writing speeches for delivery in the law-courts. Now for the rest of his life his activities alternated between the courts and the assembly; the eloquence there displayed has gained for him the reputation of being the greatest orator of antiquity. There were many other orators in Athens at this period whose speeches have been preserved to us. A century of democracy had fostered the practice of public speaking, both before the assembly and in the courts, and this, combined with the teaching of rhetoric by the sophists, had brought the art of oratory to such a pitch of excellence that it was now entitled to rank as a new department of literature. The oratory of Demosthenes, like that of all the best of the Greeks, was simple rather than ornate, terse and direct rather than diffuse. Above all, it was full of intense earnestness and showed consummate art in its persuasive reasoning and its impassioned appeal.

Demosthenes desired to see Athens the champion of Greek freedom and the leader of a Greek confederacy. But he had to contend with a decline in the old civic spirit of the Athenians, who, for a generation, had, like other Greeks, grown more and more averse to personal service in time of war, preferring to engage some soldier of fortune to fight for them with his army of professional hireling soldiers, gathered together from all parts of Greece. He had also to contend with opponents who in some cases honestly doubted the existence of danger or the need of exertion and sacrifice, and who in other cases were in Philip's pay and working in his interest. The result was what we might expect. By 348 BC Philip was master of the whole Chalcidian peninsula, and soon his power extended from the Hellespont to Thermopylae. On his first attempt to send a force through this pass, he was prevented by the prompt action which, for once, Demosthenes was able to induce the Athenians to take.

Before long, however, war between the Phocians and their neighbors gave Philip his opportunity. He managed to get himself invited by the enemies of the Phocians to intervene and put an end to the war. The devastation of Phocis which followed roused such feeling in the country and so opened the eyes of the Greeks to the danger which threatened them

Demosthenes. [Louvre Museum]

---

[18] To the mining town close by he gave the name of Philippi, a name of importance in the later history of Augustus and of St. Paul.

that Demosthenes was able to form a confederacy of nearly all the states south of Thessaly and north of the Peloponnesus to oppose Philip. Ten or fifteen years earlier this achievement might have changed the course of history; now it was too late. Philip had grown too strong to be successfully resisted, and at the battle of Chaeronea, fought near Thebes, he gained the undisputed mastery of Greece.

All opposition was crushed, and further resistance was hopeless. Philip at once called representatives of the Greek states to a general congress at Corinth to form a league of all Greece. He then had himself chosen as commander-in-chief of the forces with which he proposed that united Greece should make war on her ancient enemy, Persia. In this new league every state was to be free and independent, and each was guaranteed by the whole league against attack by any other state. In reality, the only freedom left to the Greek city-state was the management of its local or municipal affairs; foreign policy was dictated by Philip. Unity had been attained, but at the expense of liberty; the excessive assertion of individual and separate interests had brought its own nemesis. Greece had failed to solve the difficult problem, how to combine freedom with order, how to reconcile the rights of the separate parts with the good of the whole.

There has been much controversy over the question whether or not the victory of Philip at Chaeronea and the eclipse of Greek liberty should be regarded as a deplorable tragedy. It is clear that the failure of the Greeks to grow into a united nation weakened their power for good in the ancient world, and that they were wasting their unique gifts in their constant quarrels. And the sequel makes it equally clear that the unity and peace enforced by a stronger power would prove a gain to the world at large. Macedonia was inferior to Greece in culture, but it had the strength which comes from unity of command and policy, and it had a more vigorous national spirit. Greece lost her political freedom, but gained another glory, that of civilizing the whole Mediterranean world, with consequences that persist to this day—not that Philip himself had any such lofty and far-sighted aims in his mind. His policy was dictated by ambition, not by any desire to render a great benefit to civilization. One can, therefore, sympathize with Demosthenes in his fight for his ideals, and yet, because of the larger issue, be well content that fate doomed his cause to defeat.

Philip himself did not live to carry out his project of attacking Persia. On the eve of setting out for Asia he was assassinated, and was succeeded by his young son, Alexander, whose brilliant achievements were rendered possible only by the less spectacular but equally masterly success of his father in transforming a petty semi-barbaric tribe into the Macedonian empire.

Monument Philip of Macedonia.

Questions

1. What concessions did both the Persians and Spartans make to get a kind of peace between them?
2. What were the accomplishments of Epaminondas? What gave him the advantage over the Spartans?
3. Why was Philip able to raise such an impressive army?
4. How did Philip choose to rule over Greece after his conquest?
5. Do you think this was good or bad for the Greeks? Explain why.

Vocabulary

retaliate
presumption
nemesis

Chapter XXXI

Alexander and Aristotle

As soon as news came of Philip's death, there was a general disposition in Greece to throw off the Macedonian yoke. Thrace on the east promptly rebelled and with Illyria on the west prepared to attack Macedonia. The youthful Alexander, but twenty years of age, found himself king of a territory no larger than his father had started with, twenty-three years before. This kingdom Philip had extended cautiously and by slow degrees. Alexander was of a different temperament. Ardent, impetuous, brave even to recklessness, he was very like the passionate Achilles whom he so admired and from whom he fancied himself to be descended. A swift march into Greece before the cities were ready for open rebellion at once awed them into submission, and as Alexander had a genuine respect for Greek culture and was anxious to conciliate the Greeks and be regarded by them as their leader, no harsh penalties were inflicted.

Two short victorious campaigns reduced Thrace and Illyria and also revealed Alexander as a bold and resourceful military genius, whose brilliant successes cowed his enemies and endeared him to his soldiers. To ward off the threatened invasion, Persia was still seeking to incite the Greeks against Macedonia, and when it was reported that Alexander had been killed in Thrace, there was great rejoicing in Greece. With the support and sympathy of Athens and other cities, the Thebans openly rebelled, slew some Macedonian officers and besieged the Macedonian garrison in the citadel. Suddenly Alexander appeared with an army before Thebes. The Thebans were speedily routed, and, as a warning to all Greece, the city was utterly destroyed and the inhabitants sold into slavery. Only the temples of the gods and the house of the poet Pindar were spared. Satisfied with this demonstration of his power, he accepted the submission which the Athenians hastened to offer.

Alexander now considered it safe to undertake the invasion of Persia, and next spring he crossed into Asia with some 30,000 men, of whom few were Greeks. Nor had he the support of the Greek navy, so that for some time he ran the risk of being cut off from return to Europe in case of need. He seems to have been supremely confident of success and so preferred not to insist, like a despot, on unwilling contingents of infantry or ships. Not far from the Hellespont, at the river Granicus, a Persian force of about equal strength was swept away in an impetuous charge, and Alexander

Alexander the Great.

then marched triumphant through western Asia Minor, stopping only to reduce two cities which made a brief but futile resistance.

After wintering in Asia Minor, Alexander marched the next year into Syria, where the Persian king was waiting for him in person with an army of greatly superior strength. The road into Syria led through a narrow strip of country between the mountains and the sea, and here Darius sought to cut off his retreat by crossing the mountains in the rear of Alexander's army. Against an Asiatic enemy this movement might have been successful; but in fact the Persian army was cramped for room in the narrow space, and its vast numbers, which might have been overwhelming further inland, were a hindrance rather than a help. Alexander swiftly turned and attacked with his well-seasoned troops, and the battle soon became a rout. Darius himself fled in such haste that he left behind his mother, wife, and children to fall into the hands of Alexander, who treated his prisoners with a courtesy unprecedented in the warfare of those days.

The enormous extent of the Persian empire made it certain that the king could raise another and even larger army to oppose Alexander, but it also made the collecting of an army a very slow process, so that after the victory at Issus, Alexander was sure of being undisturbed for at least a year. He realized that he would eventually have to invade the very heart of Darius' kingdom, but he also realized that it would be suicidal to do so while the Persian fleet commanded the Aegean. His plan was to get control of all the sea-coast, especially of Phoenicia and Egypt, from which the king's naval strength was drawn. Then, with his rear defended and communication with Macedonia secure, he might venture to go in search of Darius and his hosts. The city of Tyre, built on an island close to the coast, caused him several months of the hardest fighting he ever experienced before it was finally taken. The capture of this important naval station was followed by the forcing of the stronghold of Gaza, farther south. By the end of the year Alexander was in Egypt, which made no resistance whatever, having never been a willing part of the Persian empire. In each country that he subdued, Alexander set up a permanent organization, showing that he was not engaged in a mere military raid, but contemplated establishing an enduring sovereignty. In Egypt he also chose a site for a new seaport, Alexandria, at the mouth of the Nile, and himself superintended the planning of its streets. He meant this city to take the place of Tyre and be the center of the trade between Greece and the Orient. The subsequent history of Alexandria, which ever since its foundation has been one of the great commercial cities of the world, shows that Alexander's genius was not confined to the battlefield.

In the spring Alexander returned to Tyre to prepare for his march into the interior. About midsummer he set out with 40,000 infantry and 7,000 cavalry, knowing that he would encounter a force vastly outnumbering his own and would have to fight on ground of Darius' own choosing. Neither at the Euphrates nor at the Tigris was his crossing opposed. At last near Arbela, in the plain beyond the Tigris, he came upon the Persian army, twenty times larger than his own. Incredible as it may seem,[19] the Persians were completely defeated; 30,000 were killed and even more taken prisoners, while the Macedonian loss was but a hundred. Darius himself fled in panic from the field, and sought refuge in the highlands of Media towards the east.

Postponing for the present the pursuit of Darius, Alexander marched south and occupied the great cities of that land, Babylon, Susa, and Persepolis, where he found immense treasure, the accumulated hoardings of many reigns. In the following spring, the pursuit of Darius began. It led Alexander to the southern shores of the Caspian Sea before he came up with the dying king, slain by some of his own faithless subjects. The body of Darius was sent to Persepolis to be buried with royal honors. Alexander was already far beyond any region known to the Greeks, but, fired with ambition and lust of conquest, he pressed on still farther into the interior of Asia, defeating every force that offered resistance. First, turning south, he conquered the highland tribes of Afghanistan—something no European nation has ever since done; then he marched north over the high snows of the Hindu Kush range into Bokhara beyond Samarcand; then turning southwards again he entered India through the Khyber pass and conquered the whole vast region of the Punjab. Here on the Hydaspes river he fought with king Porus the last and fiercest of the four great pitched battles of his wonderful career. Imagining that he was now close to the eastern limits of the world, he was eager to advance. But his Macedonians refused to go farther, and reluctantly Alexander agreed to lead them back.

His route was down the Indus to the sea, then along the coast of the Indian Ocean through fierce desert heat, a terrible march that cost far more lives than he had lost in all his battles, and so at last to Susa. He had been gone six years and had accomplished a feat not to be matched in the world's record of exploration and conquest.[20]

More important than the mere conquest of the Orient was Alexander's policy, consistently pursued, of organizing the countries he now ruled into a homogeneous empire, in which Asiatics and Europeans should be assimilated into one people. To this end he founded numerous cities (more than seventy we are told) throughout Asia. In these he settled large numbers of Greeks and Macedonians who should serve both as a military garrison and as the pioneers of Greek civilization. He also had large numbers of the youths of his eastern provinces trained according to Greek military methods, and thus built up a strong reserve army. In many cities where he visited he had Greek games celebrated, with musical and dramatic performances. The results of this penetration of the eastern world with Greek culture will be found to have had more important and permanent results than his political arrangements.

Leaving Susa towards the end of the year, Alexander went north to Babylon. Here he was met by delegations of ambassadors from all the countries of the Mediterranean, even from Carthage, Spain, Etruria, and southern Italy. Only from Rome there is said to have been no embassy. These had come to do homage to the conqueror of the eastern half of the world and to bespeak his favor should he turn his conquering armies to the west, as he seemed likely to do. Vast as was Alexander's

---

[19] Yet not so incredible, if one remembers the tremendous odds successfully faced by the conquerors of India, Wellesley at Assaye and Clive at Plassey.

[20] In these far eastern countries to this day marvelous tales are told of the exploits of the great 'Iskandar.' Candahar in Afghanistan still bears his name.

Alexander in Battle, from the Sidon Sarchophagus. [Istanbul Archaeological Museum]

empire—extending from the Adriatic to the Punjab, and from Egypt to Turkestan—he busied himself with plans for further exploration and conquest, beginning with an expedition to Arabia and the Persian Gulf, by which trade-routes might be established between India and Egypt. The next summer, just as all was ready for this expedition, he died in Babylon at the age of thirty-three. His brief illness was brought on by his intense grief at the death of his dearest friend, Hephaestion, followed by a fever due to excessive indulgence in wine at a banquet.

The two greatest names in Greek history in the last half of the fourth century are Alexander and Aristotle. The achievements of the latter, though less imposing, have been equally important in the history of western civilization. As it happens, these two men were well acquainted; for when Alexander was twelve years old, his father Philip put him for several years under Aristotle's charge. It was doubtless while Aristotle was his tutor that the young prince learned to know his Homer by heart and conceived such an abiding admiration for Greek culture.

Aristotle, who was born in Macedonia, was the son of the court physician to king Amyntas, Philip's father. He had spent twenty years in Athens studying under Plato before he returned to his northern home and became Alexander's tutor. After Alexander's accession he returned to Athens and taught philosophy and science in the grounds of a gymnasium called the Lyceum. His followers were known as the Peripatetic school, from Aristotle's habit of pacing up and down the walks of the gymnasium gardens as he discoursed.

Aristotle was a man of immense learning, 'the master of those who know' in Dante's phrase. Except perhaps in the higher mathematics, he possessed all the knowledge of his own time, and even to the present day no one man's authority is so great in so many diverse fields. Of more consequence to us than his great learning were his contributions to human knowledge; these contributions lay equally in the extension of knowledge and in its organization. The voluminous writings which still survive—and a whole library has been lost—may be divided into four groups. First are the treatises on logic, which as a science we owe to Aristotle. Second are the treatises on psychology, and the analysis of the operations of the senses and other powers of living creatures. Third is a group of works dealing with various branches of human activities and the practical problems of life; of these the *Ethics,* the *Politics,* and the *Poetics* are of permanent value and are widely read to this day. Fourth comes a long series of works on natural history.

Aristotle added enormously to the knowledge of the life and nature of the animal world by his unwearied investigations. In these he was aided by Alexander, who ordered collections of strange varieties and rare specimens of both plants and animals to be sent back to Aristotle from the new lands he was traversing. Not only did Aristotle eagerly absorb all the minute knowledge of nature possessed by the hunter, the farmer, and the fisherman; he was himself an extraordinarily keen observer, and had in addition a special gift of detecting in each organism what is really significant and essential. His possession of 'the systematic grasp which brings order into everything, and the gift for finding analogies and similarities' enabled him to establish a truly scientific classification of species, and entitles him to be regarded as the founder of scientific zoology and comparative anatomy. Moreover, under his direction his pupil Theophrastus worked out the classification of plants and thus founded scientific botany.

Aristotle's way of thinking, in philosophy and logic and natural science, dominated the minds of men for centuries. In the Middle Ages his authority was even more absolute than in ancient times. Until the Renaissance his classifications and principles, his methods of investigation and proof were unchallenged, though not always rightly understood. And now when a clearer knowledge has been gained of what his principles really were, it is found that much of the advance in knowledge which recent generations have made, especially in political philosophy and the biological sciences, has been in the true spirit of Aristotle's thought, so that scientists and philosophers alike have conceived a new and profound respect for his magnificent intellect.[21]

Bust of Aristotle. Marble, Roman copy after a Greek bronze original by Lysippos from 330 BC; the alabaster mantle is a modern addition. [Photo credit: Jastrow]

---

[21] Thus Darwin wrote: 'Linnaeus and Cuvier have been my two gods, though in very different ways; but they were mere schoolboys to old Aristotle.'

Questions

1. How did Alexander maintain and/or reconquer the Greek city-states?
2. After making a conquest, how did Alexander set up the government? What did this show about his ideas of conquest?
3. How did he spread Greek culture?
4. What are the contributions of Aristotle to Western Civilization?
5. What are the four groups of his writings surviving from antiquity?

Vocabulary

conciliate
contingent
unprecedented
assimiliated

CHAPTER **XXXII**

THE HELLENIZED EAST

Greek history is regarded by some as ending with the death of Alexander; others hold that it really ended with the victory of Philip and the loss of Greek independence at Chaeronea. Undoubtedly the political history of the city-states is henceforth of little significance; from the point of view of world history what Athens or Sparta did may from now on practically be ignored. But with equal truth we may also say that Greek history was only now beginning; that all that happened before Chaeronea was but a preparation for the real mission of Greece, when the animosities and ambitions of its many separate units were curbed by a stronger power, and when, as a result of Alexander's conquests, the language and culture of Greece became known over half the ancient world. This was the unity to which Greece finally attained—not a political unity, but a unity of influence upon civilization. The Greeks, having been conquered by force of arms, were able, in their turn, to conquer the rest of the eastern world by teaching the nations to speak and think and live as Greeks. After the third century BC, Greek culture ceased to be a matter of race.

In the new Greek cities, of which scores were to be found in Asia, the citizens proper were the Greek settlers, mostly retired soldiers or traders. The native inhabitants would seldom have any voice in the city government, which followed Greek models, with council, assembly, and magistrates. In these well-planned new cities, where buildings, furnishings, and dress, as well as the language, were Greek, the interests and activities of the community were those of the universal Hellenic world: commerce, art, poetry, discussion, the athletic contests of the gymnasium, and religious festivals, these last including music and drama. It was the civilization of this larger Greek world of the last three centuries BC, rather than that of the smaller Greece of the fifth century, which the Romans learned to know, and which they admired, copied, assimilated, and then passed on to western Europe. The Romans might perhaps have given little heed to the culture of a small nation quite inferior in strength to themselves. But when they found that everywhere to the south and to the east of Rome, wherever their legions marched, the same language and civilization met them, they could not but be impressed. And it was through the eyes of Rome that the western nations saw Greece for the first fifteen centuries of our era.

Bust of Ptolemy I Soter, king of Egypt (305 BC–282 BC) and founder of the Ptolemaic dynasty, Louvre Museum. [Photo credit: Marie-Lan Nguyen]

There were few regions, however, in which the native culture was wholly displaced. The farther east Greek civilization went, the less conspicuous was its influence. Moreover, it was mainly an urban civilization, and flourished only in and near the countless cities in which, under Alexander and his successors, Greeks and Macedonians were settled. The peasants of Syria and Egypt, to say nothing of the remoter east, remained quite untouched by it, but the official classes, the commercial classes, and the city populations generally, whatever their racial origin may have been, spoke Greek, followed Greek customs, and if they were often unappreciative of the finer aspects of Greek life and thought, had at least a veneer of Greek culture.

One of the clearest indications of this generalized Greek culture was the adoption everywhere of a uniform Greek language. Instead of the many dialects which prevailed in the earlier Greek world, one common tongue, called the *Koine* (common or universal), came to be used in every center where Greeks were found. As befitted the eminence of Athens, both in literature and in commerce, it was the Attic dialect that, with slight modifications, came into general use. The traditional dialects still lived on in their own districts, and Doric and Ionic were still used in poetry; but the *Koine* was the language of prose literature, of official documents, of commercial correspondence, and of social intercourse.

The framework of political history in which this widespread civilization was set need be described only in a general way. When Alexander died, much confusion was caused for some years by the rivalry of his Macedonian generals, several of whom aspired to succeed to his power. By the end of the century three leading subdivisions had emerged: Egypt, Macedonia, and Syria, which last included the greater part of Alexander's Asiatic empire. The rulers of each division took the name of king, and, except in a few of the older Greek centers which retained a measure of independence, monarchy was for the next two centuries the normal form of government.

In Egypt the king was the Macedonian Ptolemy, one of Alexander's astutest generals, who founded a dynasty which lasted until the death of Cleopatra, its last representative on the throne. The three first Ptolemies were able and enlightened monarchs who made their chief city of Alexandria a great center alike of commerce and of learning. Besides its manufactures of linen and glass, Egypt was one of the great grain-exporting countries of the ancient world, and the papyrus used for manuscript scrolls, which were becoming very common in the Mediterranean world, was all grown and prepared for use in Egypt. Beyond Alexandria the Greco-Macedonian culture scarcely penetrated. Egypt as a whole remained as it had been and was to be for ages, a land of toiling peasants and unchanging customs. But from the time of the first Ptolemy, Alexandria was full of life and activity above all other cities of the East. Its residents were of many nations. Besides Greeks, Macedonians, and Egyptians, the most important element was a large colony of Jews, who were settled here in the first place by Alexander and who increased in number until Alexandria was the largest Jewish city in the world. They had their own quarter, observed their own customs, and had special privileges granted them. In course of time they adopted the Greek language, and this led to the famous Greek translation of the Jewish scriptures called the *Septuagint*, which was used by Jewish communities all about the Mediterranean.[22] As a meeting-place of Greek and Jewish thought, Alexandria had a very considerable influence on the development of religious belief both before and after the introduction of Christianity.

Portrait of Seleucus I Nicator, king of Syria, 1st or 2nd century, Louvre Museum. [Photo credit: Carole Raddato]

The immense library of Alexandria, founded by the first Ptolemy, was one of its chief glories. Nowhere in the ancient world was there to be found so great a number of scholars and scientists as composed the Alexandrian Museum (or 'Home of the Muses'), founded and liberally endowed by the Ptolemies. An immense amount of erudition was devoted to the collection, criticism, and explanation of Greek literature. Here also was the seat of the most important school of medicine of these centuries. The Egyptian custom of embalming the dead led to the Alexandrian physicians abandoning the Greek prejudice against dissection of the human body, which had retarded knowledge of the structure and organs of man. Mathematics and astronomy also nourished in Alexandria. It was here that Euclid lived, and here also Eratosthenes, the most eminent of ancient scientific

---

[22] It was in this Greek version that the early Christian centuries knew the Old Testament.

geographers, worked out a calculation of the circumference of the earth which came strikingly close to the estimate of modern scientists. By this time Greek astronomers had established the spherical shape of the earth, using precisely the same arguments that are advanced today. Archimedes of Syracuse, the greatest of Greek mathematicians and the inventor of many ingenious machines, such as the screw named after him, lived for some time in Alexandria, published his books there, and, on his return to Syracuse, kept up communication with his brother scientists in Alexandria.[23]

Seleucus, another of Alexander's generals, established his claim to the kingdom of Syria, but neither he nor his successors, the 'Seleucid' kings, found it possible to retain under their rule all the Asiatic conquests of Alexander. First the Punjab, and then the other regions east of the Tigris valley had to be resigned to native rulers. But Greek civilization did not at once die out in these far distant regions. Indian art and architecture show many traces of Greek influence. The Parthian power, which grew up south of the Caspian, gradually expanded westwards until, in the first century BC, it included Babylonia and Mesopotamia. But the native Parthian kings, although at war with the Seleucid kings, continued to style themselves 'Phil-Hellene.'

In northern Syria and all through the region watered by the Tigris and Euphrates the Seleucid kings established scores of new cities with Greek organization, activities, and interests. The chief of these, and serving as the western and eastern capitals of the kingdom, were Antioch in northern Syria near the sea, and Seleucia on the Tigris, almost on the site of the later Mohammedan city of Bagdad. The importance of these two cities, which were for centuries among the largest in the world, was due to their commanding position on the natural caravan routes over which passed the trade between the Mediterranean and the far East.[24]

The number and importance of these new cities, with their persistent Greek atmosphere and tradition, accounts for the fact that, when in the seventh century the Mohammedan power arose to conquer all the East, Arabian learning throughout the Moslem world contained so large a Greek element. Arabian science and philosophy were based almost entirely on the Greek scientific and philosophic doctrines, associated especially with the name of Aristotle, which were current all through the East. The vast reputation of the Moorish scholars of Spain, at whose feet European learning was content to sit, was due to their possession of the Greek science which Europe, having more pressing practical problems on its hands, had by that time forgotten. Long before western Europe at the Renaissance recovered direct contact with original Greek literature, European scholars had learned from the Moors their Greco-Arabian philosophy and science (medical, astronomical, and mathematical) and were translating into Latin the Arabic versions of the works of Aristotle and other Greeks. Indeed, the unbounded reverence for Aristotle in the Middle Ages was in large measure a reflection of the Arabian or Moorish acceptance of him as the ultimate authority in philosophy and science.

Asia Minor also early broke away from Seleucid rule and became divided into a number of small kingdoms. These were continually at war with one another or with the kings of Syria, who made various attempts to re-establish their control over the country. In the third century BC, the Gauls, a Celtic tribe from northern Europe, invaded Asia Minor and finally settled in the central highland

---

[23] Archimedes himself valued his famous inventions far below his discoveries in pure mathematics, a truly scientific and truly Greek estimate. He directed that on his tomb should be engraved a sphere inscribed in a cylinder, with the ratio 3: 3 added, indicating that he regarded the proof of their relative volumes as his greatest achievement.

[24] Antioch was named after Antiochus, the son and successor of Seleucus. The name Antiochus was borne by many others of the Seleucid kings.

district thenceforward called Galatia. Asia Minor became another center for the building of Greek cities and the extension of Greek civilization. It was no longer along the coast merely that Greek cities were to be found, as under the Persian empire. Not only did Ephesus and Smyrna awake to renewed prosperity, but many a city in the interior, such as Tarsus, Laodicea, Philadelphia, and the Pisidian Antioch, became to all intents and purposes Greek, while the courts of the native kings welcomed and encouraged the literary and artistic refinements of Greek culture. At a later period, when Roman rule put an end to strife and warfare in Asia Minor, the process of Hellenizing the whole of Asia Minor, including finally Galatia and Armenia, was gradually completed, at least in the cities and large towns.

The third great division, that of Macedonia, had a very checkered history. Not till sixty years after Alexander's death did an end come to the strife over the possession of the throne of Macedonia. Very early in the third century the ambitious Pyrrhus secured for himself an independent kingdom in Epirus on the Adriatic coast, and both he and his son made determined efforts to get control of Macedonia also. Finally, Antigonus, the grandson of one of Alexander's generals, succeeded in establishing himself, and several generations of his descendants ruled over the Balkan peninsula as kings of Macedonia. While this prolonged struggle was going on, the Macedonian king naturally could not assert his authority strongly over Greece proper. The Greek cities, therefore, while still nominally subject to Macedonia, were able to resume much of their former independence, and therewith also their former dissensions. More than once Macedonia intervened, and towards the close of the third century Philip V was engaged for some years in a struggle to maintain his supremacy in Greek affairs. In the course of this struggle he was unlucky enough to come into collision with the growing power of Rome, and the further political history of Greece now becomes part of Roman history.

Tanagra Figurine, 325-310BC. [Altes Museum]

While Athens was always famous because of its glorious past and still remained a center of philosophy and rhetoric, as Alexandria was of science and medicine, her preeminence as the chief commercial city of the Aegean was lost. Rhodes, which became prominent in the third century, was better situated to be the distributing center for the immense traffic which passed into Europe from the Euxine and the cities of Alexandria and Antioch. This island-republic was in many ways like mediaeval Venice. It possessed little territory, but had a strong fleet with which it suppressed piracy in the Aegean, and jealously maintained its independence for nearly three centuries after the death of Alexander. Its trade brought it immense wealth and made it a notable center of art and culture. At the school of oratory, for which Rhodes was famed, Cicero, Brutus, and Caesar studied in their day.

Inevitably, the character of Greek civilization was altered by its extension over the Oriental world. The very success of the Greeks who found themselves masters of so rich an empire tended to impair the high standards of their best period. The opening of the East to commercial enterprise, the dispersion and circulation of the hoarded treasures of its kings, the setting up of so many royal courts where any able and ambitious Greek might rise to high position, all created a situation in which hundreds of traders and officials grew wealthy and immense fortunes were made by not a few. The wealth of the Orient introduced also the enervating luxury and the effeminate manners of the Orient. Literature and art both showed that Greek taste was deteriorating. The Corinthian column, for example, with its highly ornamented capital came into vogue, instead of the quieter Doric and Ionic orders. The poetry of the period is less robust and spontaneous, more a matter of skillfully framed phrases and conscious literary artifices. Fastidiously polished little poems and epigrams, of refined elegance and perfect in technique, were written, but nothing worthy of being classed with the great literature of the past. With the exception of Theocritus, the Sicilian writer of pastoral poems and idyls, there is no poet of even the second rank. The great words of Pericles are quite inapplicable to the Greeks of the post-Macedonian period: 'We love the beautiful, but with simplicity of taste; we pursue culture, without becoming effeminate.'

Yet if, in the realms of art and literature and political action, this age accomplished little of distinction, in philosophy and science the Greek still showed his creative power. Some account has already been given of the scientific activity which was centerd at Alexandria but not confined to it. This period also saw the rise of two important philosophical systems which flourished for many centuries, the Stoic and the Epicurean. Both systems aimed at giving men a principle that would guide them to perfect living. Because of the conditions of the age and the downfall of the city-state system, both turned from the normal Greek belief that the ideal life for man is to be found in active citizenship in a well-organized city-state. Rather, both held that man should hold aloof from external interests and find his resources in himself; and both taught that one who has a clear grasp of truth and orders his whole life accordingly cannot fail to attain perfect satisfaction and felicity. But when it came to defining what is truth and what is perfect satisfaction, they parted company. Epicurus held that the highest good is pleasure and avoidance of pain; only the way to attain true and lasting pleasure is not by indulging appetite, but by living the simple life, by frugality, contentment, and serenity of spirit. He also taught that all our mental disquiet about destiny and the gods and death and the hereafter will vanish if we accept his theory that everything is the result of chance, by which material atoms happen to come together to produce living beings, who at death are merely dissolved again into unconscious atoms.

The Stoic school, on the contrary, held that the universe is controlled by a supreme reason, which directs all things and is both providence and fate. Each man has imparted to him some portion of this universal reason, which animates all nature, so that there is one law of nature for all mankind. The ideal life must therefore be to live in harmony with this universal nature and in obedience to the law of reason. If this be attained, nothing else matters. To the good and wise man, health, wealth, freedom, friends, are indifferent things that add nothing to wisdom and virtue, which are the sole good of man. The Stoics also held that our feelings and emotions, being different from reason, must be opposed to reason. So the wise and virtuous will indulge no feelings or emotions; pity, joy, and sympathy should be banished as well as hate or envy or anger. Each philosophy had some admirable features. But Epicureanism was apt to become selfish and sensual indulgence; and Stoicism was equally self-centered and tended to produce a harsh and repellent austerity. It was hard for the Epicurean to keep from sinking to a mere voluptuary; it was even harder for the Stoic to climb to the impossible heights of his ideal.

Stoicism was to grow in importance among the Romans, whose stern, unbending temper it suited. If the high-minded Roman during the first centuries of our era had a religion, it was Stoicism. It was something in that ancient world to proclaim that virtue is supreme, that one universal and natural law of reason binds all mankind together, and that virtue disregards the accidents of poverty and slavery. All this paved the way for a fuller recognition of the brotherhood of man. And political history was working in the same direction. His intense local patriotism was the mainspring of much that was admirable in the Greek; but it prevented him from identifying himself with anything outside his own narrow group. The Macedonian, and later the Roman, rule broke down the barriers of this particularism, and thus tended to abolish the distinctions, not merely between Greek and Greek, but also between Greek and barbarian.

Finally, by its contact with the Orient, the Greek world was thrown open to a multitude of eastern religions, too often combined with debasing superstitions and more or less exciting rites of worship. Probably many were attracted by some hunger of the soul which their own Greek religion did not satisfy; more often it was love of novelty and sensation that made the new faiths and rituals popular. Such influence as the Greeks, in their turn, had on the religions of Asia was apparently very slight, although in the course of centuries it becomes quite evident that, in Syria and Alexandria, a blending of Asiatic religious faith and of Greek thought had been quietly going on, which had most momentous consequences in the development of Christian theology. It is significant, too, that, during the first centuries, Christianity spread in the East only within the limits of the area ruled by the Greco-Macedonian monarchies and permeated by Greek civilization. The Greek himself, however, had none of that instinct for religion which so distinguishes the Oriental peoples, who have given the world all its great religions. The Greek spirit is rather that of humanism; that is, the full development of all man's powers and faculties; keen interest in everything that the human intellect can achieve or apprehend; and free, untrammelled inquiry into anything that concerns the life of man. It was by pursuing these ideals, and by leaving them to inspire the races after them, that the Greeks did their greatest service to mankind.

Several times in the last few pages reference has been made to the Greeks coming in contact at various points with the power of Rome. Greek and Roman history may be compared to two great rivers, arising at a distance from each other, and for a long time flowing separately, out of sight or sound of each other, but finally coming together to flow onward with commingled waters. The course of Greek history has now been followed to the point of confluence; it is time to trace similarly the course of Roman history, the other great contributing influence to the growth of the modern western world.

Questions

1. According to this author, what kind of unity did Greece finally achieve?
2. Describe, compare and contrast the ideology of the Epicureans and the Stoics.
3. How did Greek culture affect the regions of the east, and what was the effect of the eastern ideas on Greece?
4. Explain Greek humanism.

Vocabulary

veneer
erudition
enervating
voluptuary

The Story of Rome

Chapter XXXIII

Rome and the Roman People

The history of Rome is the story of a small city-state in Italy which gradually extended its power in ever-widening circles until it had conquered all the countries of the Mediterranean region and held practically all the civilized communities of antiquity under its control. Not merely did this empire persist for centuries, but even when in outward form it passed away, the spirit and influence of Rome lived on and left their impress deep upon both mediaeval and modern Europe.

How was this single city able to achieve such widespread power? Mere military skill and ambition cannot account for it; other explanations must be found. Briefly, they may be said to be two: an unusually favorable strategic position, and, what is far more important, a unique national character. For the conquest, first of Italy, and then of the rest of the ancient world, was due, not to some Roman of exceptional military genius, or to a succession of them, but to the Roman nation. That is why Rome's dominion was so firmly established and endured so long.

The map shows that the peninsula of Italy occupies a central position in the Mediterranean world. The Apennines, which form the backbone of the peninsula, are much closer to the east coast than to the west; and, as the eastern coast is also destitute of harbors, it possessed no important cities. Italy faced the west, as Greece—with the Aegean archipelago at its doors—naturally looked towards the east. From the harbors on the west coast, Spain and France are easily reached, while on the south the large and important island of

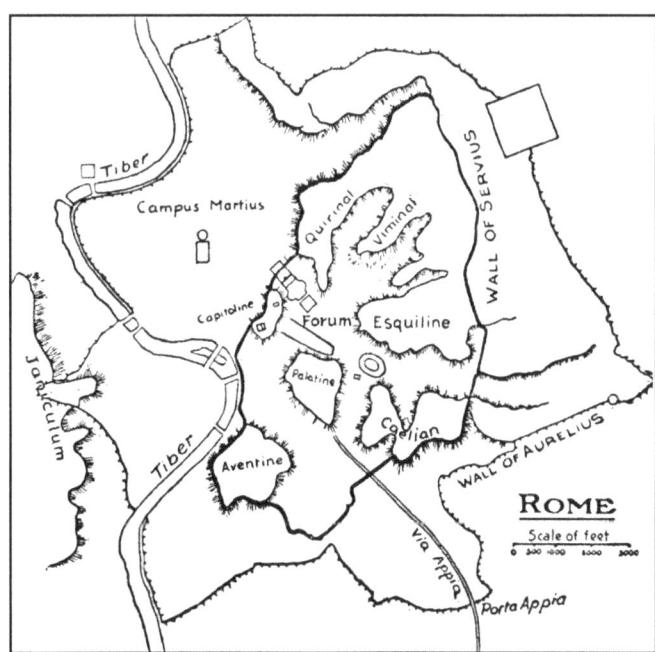
Ancient Rome.

199

Sicily is virtually a continuation of Italy; and from Sicily in turn the African coast is not far distant. At the south-east of the peninsula are harbors from which the ships of ancient times could easily cross to Greece, and thence to Egypt and Asia Minor. Finally, on the north, the barrier of the Alps, while protecting Italy from easy or frequent invasion, is pierced here and there by passes which made communication possible by land with central and western Europe.

Within the peninsula the situation of Rome was equally favorable. Near the center of the west coast the Tiber empties into the sea, and fourteen miles from its mouth, at the head of navigation in ancient times, is a group of hills commanding the crossing of the river at this point. This site, where the city of Rome grew up, possessed several advantages. It was connected with the sea by a navigable river, and was yet sufficiently far from it to be safe from raids by pirates, an important consideration in early times. Its hills formed natural defenses against land attacks, while the river was an additional protection against enemies from the north. And, as opportunity came for Rome to extend her territory, her central position enabled her gradually to advance north and east and south, until she was mistress of all Italy and was the center from which radiated a system of strategic roads that was afterwards extended throughout Europe and gave rise to the saying that 'all roads lead to Rome.'

But Rome's success was due still more to the character of her citizens, which pre-eminently fitted them for leadership. All classes of society were loyal to the state and public-spirited to an unusual degree. The citizen-body displayed a high sense of duty and discipline, while the leaders developed a remarkable genius for government, for conciliating and assimilating conquered peoples, and for so organizing the ancient world as to ensure the preservation of its civilization. The Romans had not the intellectual and imaginative powers of the Greeks, and originated very little. On the other hand, they had the capacity, which the Greeks so signally lacked, for united action and readiness to subordinate the individual to the group. If they were not of so adventurous a spirit as the Greeks, their advances were made with caution and maintained with dogged tenacity. Their mission was not so much to add to the treasures of ancient civilization as to safeguard them, and for this task their practical, orderly, persevering character was well-adapted.

The Palatine Hill from the Forum. [Photo Roger Wollstadt]

Tiber River in Rome. [Photo credit: Mr. Ajedrez]

Comune di Flumicino and the mouth of the Tiber emptying into the Tyrrhenian Sea. [Photo credit Doc Searls]

From a panel of an altar dedicated to Mars and Venus, 117 AD: the Tiber River represented as a god (Tiberinus) here bottom right revealing the twins. [Photo credit: Marie-Lan Nguyen]

Questions

1. Describe the two major factors that the authors give as reasons for Rome's achievement of widespread power.
2. Describe the geographic advantages of Rome both with respect to the rest of the Mediterranean and with respect to its situation on the Italian peninsula.
3. Describe the general character of the Roman people.
4. How did the Romans as a people compare to the Greeks?
5. What characteristics did the Romans have that the Greeks lacked?

Vocabulary

preeminently
conciliate
assimilate

Chapter XXXIV

Rome under the Kings

Of the founding of Rome and its early development many stories have come down to us. Unfortunately most of these are legends or traditions handed down by word of mouth. For many generations the people were satisfied with these stories and no attempt was made to write anything like an authentic history of their city. Yet these legends are of great value to the modern student of history, for even if they cannot be accepted in detail, they often contain some kernel of truth. And even when purely fictitious, they reveal the character of the people by showing us what qualities they admired and what kind of men they honored. Legend after legend tells of Romans who resolutely endured private loss for the sake of the public good; whose patriotism showed itself in sacrifice rather than in 'flag-waving'; whose integrity was proof against all appeal to ambition or personal gain; who met disaster without panic, and by steadfastness of purpose and refusal to admit defeat achieved victory in the end.

One of these legends tells how Aeneas, one of the princes of Troy, escaped from the city after its capture by the Greeks, and after many wanderings made his way to the coast of Italy and there founded a new city, Lavinium, near the mouth of the Tiber. Aeneas was the ancestor of a long line of kings who continued to rule in the neighboring city of Alba Longa. At length there was dissension in the royal house. A usurper seized the throne, drove out the reigning king, and gave orders that his only male heirs, his infant grandsons Romulus and Remus, should be taken to the bank of the Tiber and left there to perish. According to the story, they were found and protected first by a she-wolf, and later by a shepherd. When they grew to manhood, they restored their grandfather to his throne and then determined to build a new city on the spot where they had been rescued. Thus was the site for Rome chosen. During the building of the walls, a quarrel arose in which Romulus slew his brother, and thus became the sole founder of the city and its first king. Another tradition tells how Romulus, in order to increase the population of his new city, proclaimed it a place of refuge to which exiles and outlaws were welcomed. The real significance of this legend lies in its reflecting the policy followed by the Romans in later times of admitting outsiders to a share in citizenship much more readily than was done by the Greek city-states.

The Capitoline Wolf with Romulus and Remus in front of Rome City Hall. [Photo by Mr. BrittonJ]

In reality Rome had a quite different origin. Italy was settled in prehistoric times by tribes speaking an Indo-European language, who came down from central Europe, as the kindred Greek tribes were coming into the Balkan peninsula. They did not, like the Greeks, come in contact with a superior civilization, and their progress was therefore much slower. Italy was far more fertile than Greece, and had few harbors; so that while the Greeks became a seafaring and trading people, the Italian tribes remained home-keeping landsmen, tilling the rich plains and valleys and pasturing their herds and flocks in the upland country. When the historical period begins, we find these Italian settlers in four main divisions: a lowland tribe, the Latins, occupying the plain of Latium south of the Tiber; and three highland tribes, the Umbrians, the Sabines, and the Samnites, in the hilly central districts of Italy. All these tribes were of kindred stock and spoke closely related dialects.

We also find three other races occupying large districts in Italy, in which they had gained a footing long after the coming of the Italian tribes. Earliest of these were the Etruscans, who held Etruria, the district lying north of the Tiber, and who for a time were also able to extend their rule over Campania, south of Latium. This race had migrated to Italy from Lydia in Asia Minor, probably as a consequence of the disturbances in the Aegean area connected with the downfall of the Cretan power. Like feudal barons, they had their strongholds on the hills that abounded in the Etrurian plain; and like the Norse rovers, they sailed the western seas, establishing themselves where opportunity offered. Corsica came into their possession, and they dominated the sea to the west of Italy, which the Romans continued for centuries to call by their name.[25] The Etruscans brought with them from the East a culture far more advanced than existed in Italy at that time; and when, some centuries later, Greek civilization was developing, the Etruscans were quick to import its products. Both directly and indirectly they exercised a refining influence upon the somewhat rough simplicity of Rome.

The southern coasts of Italy were occupied by Greek cities founded in the colonizing period of Greek history. The absence of harbors on the Adriatic and the strength of the Etruscans on the west coast prevented them from settling farther north. These cities also were of service in introducing the Romans to the superior civilization which had developed in the eastern Mediterranean. Finally, in the extreme north is the great valley of the Po, separated from the rest of Italy by the Apennine range, which here crosses the peninsula from west to east; this part of Italy was occupied by Celtic or Gallic tribes which crossed the Alps about the beginning of the historical period, some centuries after the Italic tribes.

---

[25] The words *Etruscan*, *Tuscan*, *Etrurian*, and *Tyrrhenian* are apparently all variants of the same name.

A Remnant of the Ancient Wall of Rome. [Macmillan & Co Ltd.]

The Greek settlers lived on terms of peace with their Italian neighbors, but it was otherwise with the aggressive Etruscans. The plain of Latium was in those days much more fertile than now, but, for safety against marauders, the Latins who tilled the lowlands built their settlements on the adjacent hills. Thus the group of hills by the Tiber also came to be occupied as a place of refuge from attack; and as Rome was the stronghold closest to Etruria and guarded an important crossing of the Tiber, this outpost of the Latins was of special importance, and its inhabitants had abundant opportunity to become sturdy warriors as well as farmers.

The government of early Rome resembled that of the Greek communities of Homeric times, both being an inheritance from their Indo-European ancestors. We again hear of a king, a council of elders (in Rome known as the senate), and an assembly of citizens. As in Homer, the king appears in the threefold capacity of military leader, priest, and judge, but his powers, while extensive, were not absolute. Motives of prudence, if nothing else, would lead him to consult the senate, a body made up of the most experienced citizens; and even the assembly could not be entirely disregarded, though it appears to have had little opportunity of expressing its collective views, meeting as it did chiefly to hear announcements or to witness ceremonies and festivals. Another influence which tended to act as a check upon the power of the king was the Roman respect for the *mos maiorum* (the 'custom of their ancestors'), a sentiment so strong that only the most self-willed ruler would attempt to go counter to it. The Romans always looked upon their inherited customs as the product of generations of accumulated wisdom and experience; hence they thought that they should not be disregarded or altered unless the circumstances were most exceptional. We find this influence constantly operating in Roman political life as a check upon rulers and people alike. The Romans were temperamentally conservative, a quality which is but another aspect of the persistence and tenacity which they showed so often in their wars. They altered their customs and institutions only under pressure and after long consideration. They were satisfied with the smallest possible change that would effect their ends; and they were apt to cling to ancestral usages long after they had become almost meaningless forms.

The Roman kings of the legends were seven in number. Every Roman was well acquainted with their exploits and the events of their reigns, but historians are sceptical about the truth of these popular traditions, particularly in the case of the first four kings.[26] These legends describe in great detail the reigns of Romulus, who founded the city and consolidated its power; of Numa, a man of peace, who devoted himself to the development of laws and religious institutions for the young city; of Tullus Hostilius and Ancus Martius, warlike kings, who extended its power over the other towns of Latium, and built a seaport town, Ostia, at the mouth of the Tiber; and finally of Tarquinius Priscus, Servius Tullius, and Tarquinius Superbus (or Tarquin the Proud), an Etruscan line of kings who ruled over Rome for a considerable period.

According to Roman tradition, the first Tarquin was an Etruscan adventurer, who came to Rome, won the favor of Ancus Martius, and on his death was chosen king. This account conceals the undoubted fact that Rome had really been invaded and conquered by the Etruscans, whose power was then at its height. The legends represent Rome as greatly enlarging her dominion at this time and ruling over Latium and southern Etruria. In reality, the lords of southern Etruria during this sixth century BC extended their sway over Rome and Latium, and introduced their customs and manner of life into the Roman state. For the first time Rome had now fine temples, a well-drained city, a well-organized army, and other indications of the change from a small town to a capital city. The control of the whole district enabled the rulers of Rome to build up their city by causing all traffic between Etruria and the south to pass through Rome rather than farther inland. The great road up the Tiber valley by which the hill tribes transported salt from the sea also passed through Rome, which thus came to be the center of the trade-routes leading north and south and east and west. The community, though under the rule of foreign princes, remained predominantly Roman, and suffered no permanent change

At length the rule of Tarquin the Proud became so cruel and oppressive that an uprising took place and the Etruscan lords were expelled. While the details of the traditional story may be questioned, there is no doubt that these foreign rulers left a legacy of such intense hatred that the very name of king was forever odious to the Romans. The traditional expulsion of the kings was thus in fact the regaining of independence. This explains what the traditional story leaves unaccounted for—why it was that the Roman state now became again a single small community in the midst of a number of similar Latin towns, which were now its allies and no longer its subjects.

---

[26] From this year [753] the Romans dated the events of their history, as happening *e.g.* in the 364th year from the founding of the city.

Questions

1. If many of the legends of Rome's founding are not true in whole or in part, how do they still help us to understand Rome and the Roman people?
2. Briefly recount the tale of Romulus and Remus.
3. Name the four main divisions of Italian settlers within the vicinity of Rome.
4. Name and describe the other races of people occupying large districts in Italy.
5. What was the "Mos Maiorum?" What effect did this have on the government of Rome? How did this act as a check on the power of the king?
6. Name the seven kings of Rome. How did the last three differ from the first four?
7. What do historians think about this change in kings?
8. What happened to the seventh king of Rome? Why?

Vocabulary:

resolutely
dissension
tenacity

Brutus in the Forum denouncing Collatinus as a traitor who delighted in war and the profits of tyranny.

Chapter XXXV

Patricians and Plebeians

After the revolution which expelled the Tarquins, a republic was set up. In place of the kings there were now two elected magistrates known as consuls. In theory these inherited the powers which had previously belonged to the king; they exercised jurisdiction in the city and were in command of the army. Like the kings, they were attended by 'lictors,' officers bearing the 'fasces' (a bundle of rods encircling an axe), as the symbol of supreme power and the right to punish even with death.[27] In practice the power of the consuls was limited in two ways. In the first place, they held office for a year only, and in so brief a period were not likely to acquire excessive power. Further, they were colleagues, exercising authority jointly, and the disapproval of either would nullify any action of the other.[28] The senate and the assembly of the people continued to act as they had under the kings. The senate, however, whose members had taken the leading part in the revolution, gained increased influence. The ancient practice by which they were consulted in all important matters now became transformed into a right to give or withhold approval to all new legislation or to any election held by the assembly. Various factors will be found combining to make this authority of the senate of the utmost importance in the subsequent development of the Roman state.

The new republic was by no means a democracy. Like the Greek states after the fall of their monarchies, it was distinctly aristocratic. There was a sharp division of the citizens into two orders, and the first two centuries of the republic are marked by the efforts of the less privileged class to gain equal social and political rights. The two orders were known as patricians and plebeians. It is not known how the distinction originated. It appears to go back to the very beginnings of Roman history and to depend on the accepted predominance of certain leading families. The plebeians were citizens with a right to vote in the assembly; but the law, or the custom—which in Rome was equally potent—left them under serious disabilities. The patricians jealously guarded their privileges and had two things in their favor: the fact that both the magistrates and the senate were chosen from the patricians only, and, instead of being rivals for power, always cooperated in resisting the plebeian

---

[27] The Fascists of present-day Italy have taken their name from this emblem of law and order.

[28] This is an early example of the theory of checks and balances in government, an idea which plays an important part in many modern constitutions, conspicuously so in that of the United States.

Fasces.

demands for equal rights; and the fact that the Romans, with their characteristic conservatism, habitually made the fewest and slightest possible changes in their government.

Among the disabilities under which the plebeians labored, in addition to their exclusion from the senate and the magistracies, was the fact that the system of voting in the assembly made their vote practically valueless. In the assembly, or *Comitia,* which controlled elections and legislation, the Romans voted by groups called 'centuries,' a name which is far from exact, as some centuries contained fewer and others many more than one hundred. The system had been organized in the time of Servius on a military basis, and especially on the principle that a small number of heavy-armed soldiers would be equal to a much greater number of light-armed troops. The patricians, whose wealth enabled them to serve in war as cavalry or as heavy-armed troops, constituted a majority of the centuries (98 out of 193); the rest of the citizens, though far more numerous, were grouped in a smaller number of centuries and could therefore always be outvoted. Something, again, in the origin of the two classes involved the separation of the orders on religious grounds, as completely as in the case of Jews and Gentiles. The plebeians could not represent the state in religious ceremonies; to do so would be to offend and estrange the ancestral gods. Not only was this made one of the reasons for confining the magistracies to the patrician order; on the same religious grounds, plebeians could not intermarry with patricians.

The plebeians had other grievances which were perhaps more serious. Patrician magistrates often used their power in an unjust and oppressive manner, and this was all the easier since the laws of the land and the rules of legal procedure were known only to patricians, who were loath to share this valuable secret. Moreover, the use of the state pasture-lands was reserved to the patricians, and, when conquered land was seized, its distribution was so manipulated that the plebeians did not receive a fair share of it. The plebeians were mostly small farmers, with little capital, and were often kept from attending to their farms by service in the army in Rome's frequent wars. Their unfortunate position was aggravated by a harsh law of debt, which permitted a creditor to imprison an insolvent debtor and even to sell him and his family into slavery.

The plebeians did not submit tamely to these injustices, as men of a less virile race might have done. At the same time, their characteristic Roman loyalty, self-control, and moderation generally kept them from taking any action that would disrupt or weaken the state. They continued to press for their rights and gradually won them, for the most part by constitutional means and without resorting to violent or revolutionary measures.

This long struggle passed through two phases. During the first, the plebeians aimed at security against harsh laws and the unjust acts of magistrates; during the second, having realized that their civil rights were not secure without political equality, they aimed at obtaining an equal voice in the government and the right to hold office.

The first serious clash between the orders occurred when resentment at unjust treatment and the cruel laws of debt led to the plebeians withdrawing from the city, refusing to serve in the army, and threatening to found a new settlement if redress were not given. This secession, which was virtually a 'strike' of a large part of the state's fighting forces, resulted in the plebeians being given the right to elect special magistrates of their own, called *tribunes*. The tribunes had no administrative duties; their office was simply to aid and protect oppressed plebeians, and to this end they were empowered to forbid any act of any magistrate within the city, by pronouncing the one word *veto*. To interfere with a tribune in the exercise of this right was made a capital crime. This extraordinary power, designed at first as a compromise to prevent individual cases of injustice, became in time a powerful political weapon, as it enabled a tribune easily and effectively to block any objectionable proposal.

The body by which the tribunes were to be elected was not the assembly voting by centuries. There had grown up in Rome another assembly, composed of plebeians and voting by tribes. These tribes, which eventually numbered thirty-five, four urban and thirty-one rural, were arranged practically like modern parliamentary constituencies on a basis of residence and ownership of property within a certain area. The resolutions of this plebeian assembly had not the force of legal enactments, and theoretically were binding only on the plebeians who passed them; but they represented too important a section of public opinion to be ignored, and gradually they obtained binding force upon all citizens if approved by the senate.[29]

The tribunate was not the first new magistracy to be established by the republic since the first creation of consuls. At the very beginning of the republic it was recognized that in critical times the divided authority of the consuls might prove dangerous. In such cases a dictator might be appointed instead of the consuls, with all the powers of the former king, but in no case for a longer period than six months. It says much for the loyalty of the Romans to their republic that no dictator ever sought to take advantage of the trust thus reposed in him in order to make himself master of the state, like a Greek tyrant.

Next we hear of an agitation for the publication of the law, comparable to the movement at Athens which resulted in Draco's legislation. This demand led to the publication of the Twelve Tables. These for the most part simply recited the existing laws and usages without seeking to amend them; but merely to have the laws set up where all might learn them would check any arbitrary administration of justice. This marks the beginning of the development of the great legal codes of later centuries, whose principles are still of authority in modern courts of law. A few years later a measure was passed permitting intermarriage between the orders, and providing that children should take the rank of their father. This broke down a great social barrier separating the orders, for there were among the plebeians certain wealthy families of long descent, who were directly affected by the removal of such a stigma of inferiority.

One of the most important landmarks in the advance of the plebeians was the passing of a group of rather miscellaneous measures known as the Licinian laws, from the tribune Licinius, who after years of struggle succeeded in carrying his proposals. Of these, two in particular deserve mention. In order to improve the lot of the small farmer and prevent the monopolizing of public lands by wealthy land-owners, it was provided that no citizen should hold more than 500 acres of public land or keep more than 500 sheep and 100 cattle on the common pasture-lands. A second law, which prescribed that at least one of the two consuls must be a plebeian, indicated that the struggle had entered on its second phase and that the plebeians were now seeking political equality.

---

[29] In the course of time the restriction of this assembly to plebeians seems to have become a dead letter, and patricians were not debarred from attending and voting, if they wished. Because of the different system of voting, however, the vote of the patrician minority would have little or no effect.

When these laws were passed two new magistracies were instituted, both of which were to be filled by patricians only. A praetor was to be elected to superintend the administration of civil law, in place of the consuls, and two aediles to exercise control of markets, police, festivals, and other matters. One reason for the creation of these offices was the growing complexity and extent of the state's business, which could no longer be efficiently handled by the two consuls; but another reason was the determination of the patricians to keep what power they could in their own hands. It is noticeable that, when they did give way, it was always on the basis of some compromise. In this case, when a magistracy was thrown open to plebeians, some of its powers were transferred to a newly created office, which was reserved to patricians. This policy, however, merely postponed the inevitable. The plebeians were coming more and more to feel their strength, and before long all the important offices had one by one been opened to plebeians. Thus, a plebeian was dictator in 356, another was praetor in 337 BC, and in 300 BC, plebeians were made eligible for all the priesthoods of the state religion.

Finally, after more than two hundred years of controversy, the danger of a popular rising led to the passing of the Hortensian law, which provided that the decrees and legislative measures of the plebeian assembly should have equal validity with the laws passed by the other assembly without requiring the approval of the senate. With the passing of this law the struggle for social, political, and religious equality is ended. Patrician and plebeian are now equal before the law, and the distinction between the orders has ceased to have any real meaning.

Perhaps it would be more correct to say that the struggle for equality assumed a new form. Rome had by no means attained democracy. Indeed the unhealthy distinction between rich and poor had increased. Moreover a new nobility had grown up, which included both the old patrician families and the more wealthy and influential plebeians. These had on the whole served Rome well, providing her with able leaders, and the Romans, conservative as usual, preferred always to fill the slate-offices from families that had already given them efficient and successful magistrates. In theory, any citizen might be elected to office; in practice, it was well-nigh impossible for anyone to be elected whose ancestors had not held office. Such a man, if elected, was called a 'new man' *(novus homo)*; those who counted magistrates among their ancestors were 'nobles' *(nobiles,* the well known).

Equally important was the composition of the senate at this period. It had gradually become the custom to fill vacancies in this body by choosing ex-magistrates, and in the course of time this custom had received the sanction of law. The senate was thus composed of men who, after holding an important office, passed, practically for life and automatically, into its ranks. The Roman senate, thus constituted, has with good reason been called 'the most effective assembly of men of capacity and experience in practical life that the world has ever seen.' Its prestige was therefore enormous, and while legally its chief function was still to give advice to the magistrates, yet these had such respect for the authority of the senate that advice and direction were in practice indistinguishable.

Thus, while much had been gained by the people in dethroning privilege and resisting injustice, yet the position of the 'nobility' (the office-holding class) and of the all-powerful senate still gave the Roman constitution an aristocratic complexion. An aristocracy of office had succeeded to an aristocracy of birth.

Questions

1. Describe the government set up in Rome after the time of the kings.
2. Was the government a democracy?
3. How was the power of the consuls limited? What was the most powerful branch of the government? Why?
4. Name the two groups or orders of citizens in Rome. Along what lines, or by what criteria was this division made? Could all the citizens vote in the assembly?
5. What advantages did the upper group have?
6. What grievances did the Plebeians have?
7. Describe the two phases that the struggle between these classes went through. What were the Plebeians attempting to gain in each case?
8. What did the Plebeians do in the first clash? What did they want? What did they receive?
9. What were the main responsibilities of a tribune? How were they elected?
10. What other measures were taken to appease the Plebeians?
11. What did the Licinian laws do for the Plebeians?

Vocabulary

plebeian
patrician
estrange

The map includes the 12 cities of the Etruscan League and notable cities founded by the Etruscans.

Chapter XXXVI

The Conquest of Italy

While these social and political changes had been taking place, the Romans had found time to extend their borders at the expense of their hostile neighbors. A glance at the map (pg. 218) will make clear the position of Rome and of the different peoples of Italy: the Latins, Rome's near neighbors and kinsmen, occupying the northern part of Latium; beyond these, to the east and south, other small Italic tribes, the Aequi and Volsci; farther south, the Samnites, one of the main branches of the Italic race; in the extreme south, the fringe of Greek colonies known as Magna Graecia; face to face with the Romans across the Tiber were the Etruscans; to the east of these were the Umbrians and the Sabines, both of Italic stock; and finally in the northern part of Italy were the Gauls.

The successive stages of Rome's conquest of the Italian peninsula must now be traced. After the expulsion of the Tarquins, repeated attempts were made by the Etruscans to recover their lost power. It is to one such attempt that the legend of Horatius and his defense of the bridge refers. For a century the Etruscan stronghold of Veii was a constant source of danger and annoyance. On the other sides, the Aequi and the Volsci, after the manner of hill-tribes, made constant forays into the lowland districts of Latium. To defend themselves, the Romans and the Latins formed a league, of which the Romans were the leaders. The long series of border wars in which the Romans were engaged tested their courage and gave them an invaluable schooling in military affairs. By the end of the fifth century Latium had been made secure, and soon after Veii was taken and destroyed.

The defeat of the Etruscans was probably due in part to the inroads at this period of the Gallic tribes to the north. Always a restless and warlike people, the Gauls were easily led to make forays across their borders, and at times these expeditions assumed serious proportions. It was not long before even Rome made the acquaintance of these roving warriors. An unusually adventurous band, coming probably from across the Alps, made its way south through Etruria, defeated the Roman forces in a great battle, and then captured and sacked the city of Rome, only the citadel being successfully defended against them. Fortunately this band was bent on plunder rather than on conquest. They left the city almost as quickly as they had come, and before long Rome had recovered

Italian Warriors. [Macmillan & Co., Ltd.]

from the effects of the invasion. Yet one serious consequence of the sack of the city deserves notice. All the official records were destroyed by the Gauls, so that future historians were deprived of this important material, and even in ancient times had to rely upon legends rather than official documents in reconstructing the history of the period before 390 BC.

During all these wars, Rome's Latin allies had stood by her loyally, but at length they grew alarmed at her increasing power, and rose in revolt. After a short struggle they were defeated and reduced to a subordinate position. Campania also, which had allied itself with the Latins, was conquered. The civil rights of the conquered Italians were not curtailed, but they were forbidden to form any union with one another and each was compelled to look upon Rome as its leader. We have here the beginning of Rome's general policy of isolating her subjects from one another and binding them closely to herself, while allowing them autonomy in local affairs. This practice was later expressed in the Roman saying *Divide et impera* ('Divide and rule').

This first stage in the expansion of Rome brought her into closer contact with the Samnites. These, originally a hill-tribe, had recently overrun the Campanian plains south of Rome's territory. A series of stubbornly contested campaigns, lasting over half a century, was required before this enemy was overcome. The final crisis of these wars was the battle of Sentinum. The Samnites had put in the field a great army consisting of their own forces and those of the Etruscans, Umbrians, and Gauls, whom they had united in an alliance against Rome. The alarm at Rome was great, and energetic efforts were put forth to meet this powerful combination. At length the Romans, who had the advantage of operating on interior lines, succeeded in separating their foes, and the Samnites and Gauls were defeated after a long and stubbornly-contested battle. As a result of this victory, the greater part of Central Italy came under the rule of Rome. Roads were built and fortresses established to bind together the territories which had been won.

Rome was now approaching the territory of the Greek cities in the south. With many of these she had had friendly commercial and diplomatic relations, but the great city of Tarentum was jealous and hostile, and viewed Rome's advance with disfavor. Hence, when a pretext offered, the Tarentines provoked a war. Feeling themselves unequal to the task of defeating Rome, they invoked the aid of Pyrrhus of Epirus, a Greek prince of boundless ambition and great military skill. In the war which followed, Pyrrhus won two great battles, thanks to his well-trained army and his formidable elephants, with which the Romans had never before been confronted.

Pyrrhus of Epirus from the National Archaeological Museum of Naples. [Photo credit: Cataloan].

But so stubbornly contested were the battles and so great the cost of victory that he realized that Rome could not be conquered. 'Another such victory, and I am ruined,' he is said to have exclaimed, and on viewing the Roman dead, he declared, 'Had I been king of this people, I should have conquered the world.' Eventually Pyrrhus was forced to acknowledge defeat and retire from Italy, and Tarentum soon surrendered.

Rome had now nearly completed the successive stages of her conquest of Italy. From the Apennines southward the whole peninsula was now under her control, and within a few decades she had added the district of Cisalpine Gaul by defeating the Gallic tribes in the valley of the Po. Her method of dealing with her conquered territory showed that in her magistrates and senate she possessed a body of able organizers. The policy was followed of building great connecting roads and of founding colonies in different parts of the country. These settlements served as centers of Roman influence in time of peace and as fortresses in time of war. Two types are met with: Roman colonies, whose members retained full Roman citizenship, and the so-called Latin colonies, which possessed all the rights save that of voting. The rights of other communities also were graded, some retaining local self-government, while others were governed by prefects from Rome. Above all, leagues and unions of all kinds were forbidden and all were taught to look upon Rome as the leader in all foreign relations and as the preserver of order, from whom alone further privileges and a higher status might be obtained. Rome's far-seeing policy in granting even partial citizenship to colonies and distant towns was in marked contrast with the practice of the Greek states, and in many ways the conquered peoples were made to realize that Roman rule was not a despotism but that they had been taken into partnership.

Italy, showing principal Races.

Questions

1. Describe the stages in the Roman conquest of Italian peninsula.
2. What factors led to the Roman victory over the Etruscans?
3. Explain the practice of *divide et impera*.
4. Why did this method work to the advantage of the Romans as opposed to the way the Greek states, for example, dealt with their conquered peoples?

Vocabulary

foray
formidable
prefect

Chapter XXXVII

The Romans of the Early Republic

In reading of the development of Rome one may easily form the impression that its people were interested exclusively in politics and war. But the Romans were not naturally an aggressive race, bent upon conquest; the incessant warfare of the first two centuries of the republic was due rather to the aggressiveness of others and the constant danger from their restless neighbors. The Romans were a resolute, unyielding people, and when confronted with hostility and turbulence on their borders, both instinct and self-interest prompted them to advance rather than to give way. Again the Roman was not keenly interested, as was the Athenian Greek, in political discussion or controversy for its own sake. He would fight to secure justice and the recognition of his rights; but beyond that, the great majority of the Roman people had little interest in political struggles, and none at all in theories and ideals of government. The Roman's heart was in his family and his farm; all other occupations and interests—war, politics, trade, education, religion—were subordinate to these.

The family was the basis of the Roman state and included not only the father, mother, and children, but also the grown-up sons with their wives and families, and the daughters until they married and joined another similar family group. The household slaves also were regarded as members of the family, and this tended to make the institution of slavery less odious. If the family was noble and powerful, there were also a number of subordinate retainers, called 'clients,' who were under the protection of the head of the house and, though freemen, bound to render him service. The father of the family *(paterfamilias)* had absolute power throughout his lifetime over every member of it; but he was expected to exercise his authority reasonably and in accordance with ancestral custom. The Roman matron, though legally under tutelage, occupied a position of dignity and authority, managing the household and directing the work of the women, both slave and free. The status of women at Rome was much more satisfactory than in Athens or in most eastern lands. Although debarred from politics, they did not live in seclusion, and the history of Rome contains many records of women who played an important part in the life of the community and were held in high esteem.

The typical Roman of this period was an independent farmer, managing his own farm, whether large or small, and working with his men. As far as possible, all the needs of the household were provided by its members, clothing, buildings, implements, as well as food. Education also was a matter for the family circle, there being as yet no regular schools. It was the task of the parents to see that their children were trained not only to help in the work of the farm and the household, but to honor and practice the Roman virtues of obedience, courage, devotion to duty, honesty, and frugality, and thus to become worthy citizens of Rome. The children were taught the story of the deeds of their ancestors, with common proverbial sayings and some traditional songs; but there were no books, nor had the Romans any literature as yet.

Religion also was intimately connected with the family group. It was not a personal matter, but was concerned with the religious observances that were traditional in the household. According to the earliest Roman conception, the gods were not like the Greek gods, divine beings thought of as like mankind, only far superior, with individual characters and distinct appearance. They were powers rather than persons, powers that manifested themselves by helping or hindering the various operations of the household. Such were Vesta, the spirit of the hearth, the Penates, the spirits of the storehouse, Saturnus, whose care was the sowing of the seed, Faunus, who made the cattle to breed, Robigo, who kept away the mildew, Janus, the god of the door and so also, god of all beginnings, and many others. It was the duty of the head of the family to secure and keep the favor of these powers and spirits. Hence at certain appointed times he offered appropriate sacrifices on behalf of the family, according to the rites that had been handed down from generation to generation, while at other times the whole household joined in the observance of some religious festival.

The state also had its religious ceremonies, and one of the duties of magistrates was to represent the whole family of the citizens in its relations with the gods. The religion of the state shows many resemblances to that of the family. Thus Vesta was worshipped not only in private homes but also as the goddess of the civic hearth, in a temple where the sacred fire was kept burning by the Vestal Virgins, who were chosen by the state and held in high honor. Other deities worshipped by the state were Jupiter, the god of the sky, Juno, the goddess of marriage, Mars, the war-god, and Minerva, the goddess of arts and crafts. These were mostly introduced under Etruscan influence, and differed from the earlier and original Roman gods in having temples and statues like the gods of Greece and Asia. As the Romans came in touch with other peoples in their conquests, they often established the worship of new deities in Rome. Thus the worship of Diana and Venus was introduced from Latium, and later on, after contact with the Greek cities, temples were from time to time erected to many of the gods of Greece.

Our knowledge of the character and moral ideals of the Romans is derived very largely from their legends, which, by describing the exploits and virtues of the heroes of their race, reveal to us their own point of view and their moral standards. From these legends we learn of the frugal simplicity of life among even the more wealthy citizens, who remained for generations plain-living farmers with no desire for luxury or ostentation; we learn of their strong sense of justice and their fidelity to their pledged word; of that inflexibility that made them so strong and persevering in action, but also made them often hard and unsympathetic, and at times even cruel; and of that hard-headedness and lack of imagination which left them without a native literature or art and without interest in science or philosophy, but which made them the most efficient and practical of ancient peoples. Naturally the majority of the legends picture the stout-hearted resoluteness that

Relief representing a farmer driving his cow to market.

endured every evil and never acknowledged defeat, and the devotion to the welfare of the state which shrank from no sacrifice.

One of the most famous of the stories, too well known to need repetition here, tells of the heroic resistance of Horatius to the Etruscans who sought to capture Rome and reinstate the Tarquins. To this same war belong two other tales of heroism. A Roman youth, named Mucius, undertook to enter the Etruscan camp by stealth and slay the king, Lars Porsenna. He succeeded in penetrating to the center of the camp, but mistook one of the officers for the king. When he slew this officer, he was at once seized and brought before the king. Fearlessly he told how a band of Roman youths had sworn to repeat the attempt until, sooner or later, some one should succeed. The king, desiring to learn more of the plot, caused a fire to be kindled, and threatened torture. To show his contempt for this, Mucius deliberately thrust his right hand into the flames and held it there. The king, amazed at his courage, ordered him to be released and sent home, where he was ever after called Scaevola, the Left-handed.

Not long after this, the Romans, being hard pressed, had occasion to give a number of boys and girls to Porsenna as hostages. One of the girls, named Cloelia, persuaded her companions to make their escape by night and swim back to Rome across the Tiber. The Roman leaders thought it would be a breach of faith to connive at the escape of hostages, and sent them back to the Etruscans. Porsenna, struck with her courage and enterprise, set Cloelia free, and soon after made peace with Rome. One interesting feature in these legends is the broad-minded spirit that was not too prejudiced to attribute magnanimous acts to an enemy.

Another legend from the same period shows how strict and uncompromising the Romans could be in their devotion to duty. A conspiracy was formed by some of the young nobles in Rome to restore the Tarquins. The plot was detected and the conspirators were brought before the consul Brutus for judgment. There could be but one penalty, death. But among the traitors were the consul's own two sons. He had to decide between his duty as consul and his feelings as a father. Unhesitatingly he condemned them to death with the rest, putting the claims of the state before the ties of flesh and blood.

As Roman sternness sometimes had an unattractive side, so too, sometimes, had the indomitable pride of the race, when it degenerated into arrogance. Indeed the patricians as a class were often accused of arrogance and overbearing conduct as well as of selfishness and exclusiveness. An example of patrician pride at its worst appears in the story of Coriolanus. He had won great renown and popularity as a successful general, and was in many ways a man of high ideals, but he was lacking in sympathy and humanity. In particular he was bitterly opposed to the cause of the plebeians, for whom he had a great contempt. At a time of famine in Rome, the king of Syracuse had sent a gift of grain to feed the people, but Coriolanus proposed that it should not be distributed unless the plebeians would give up the right to elect tribunes. This so angered them that they demanded that he be tried before the assembly. Even the patricians did not sympathize with his arrogant attitude, and in his pride and resentment he scorned to defend himself, left the city, and joined himself to Rome's enemies, the Volscians. These gave him command of their army, and such was his success that the Romans in despair sent envoys to sue for peace. He haughtily refused to make any reasonable terms, and the Romans knew not where to turn. At last an embassy of the Roman women approached him, led by his own wife and his mother. The latter's reproaches and his wife's appeal broke his proud spirit, and with the words 'Ah, my mother, you have saved Rome, but have lost your son,' he led his army back. He could never return to Rome, and the Volscians resented his sparing the city when it was in his grasp. He lived but a short time after, unhappy and discredited. This story of the evil of excessive pride is also a tribute to the influence and loyalty of the Roman matron.

Another striking figure of the period of Rome's early wars is the dictator Cincinnatus, who represented to the Romans the ideal combination of dignity and simplicity. During a war with the Aequi, an army led by one of the consuls was entrapped and surrounded. In this emergency it was decided to appoint Cincinnatus dictator. The deputation sent to notify him found him engaged in plowing his little farm of a few acres across the Tiber. Leaving his humble task, he quickly organized another army, went forth and defeated the enemy, and re-entered the city in triumph—all within the space of sixteen days. His work ended, he resigned his high office and returned again to his interrupted plowing. Rome owed much of her early success to men like Cincinnatus, sturdy yeomen farmers, who tilled their own lands, lived simple, frugal lives, and in time of danger took up arms to defend their country. Although warfare might bring honor and fame, these Romans looked upon it mainly as an unwelcome interruption in their normal lives, and found in agriculture the occupation which gave them real enjoyment and satisfaction.

Another factor in Rome's success was the spirit of self-sacrifice among her citizens, and many tales are told of generals or soldiers who sacrificed their lives to save the community. Such, for example, was the 'devotion' of the consul Decius. Warned in a dream, the night before a battle, that whichever army lost its leader would win the victory, Decius spurred his horse into the midst of the enemy's ranks, and thus by his own death purchased victory for his country. Upon another occasion, when Rome was visited with pestilence and earthquake, a great chasm suddenly opened in the forum, in the very heart of the city. The priests proclaimed that this portent meant disaster for the state, unless Rome's most precious possession was cast into the chasm. A young warrior, Marcus Curtius, holding that Rome possessed nothing more precious than her own brave sons, mounted his war-horse and in full armor leaped into the yawning gulf. Immediately it closed over him, and the threatened disaster was averted.

The war with Pyrrhus throws a vivid light upon the characteristic qualities of the Romans. We have here a brilliant general with an experienced professional army, pitted against a citizen-militia without leaders of conspicuous merit, but possessed of the Roman virtues of courage and determination. How Pyrrhus admired the fighting qualities of the Romans has already been mentioned. In their deliberations and diplomacy an equal steadfastness was manifested. A Roman envoy, Fabricius, who had been sent to arrange for the release of some prisoners, was hospitably entertained by Pyrrhus, who tried to bribe him to use his influence at Rome in favor of an advantageous peace.

Cincinnatus abandons the plow to serve as dictator by Juan Anotnio Ribera, Prado Museum

Failing in this, he thought to practice on his fears by suddenly confronting him with an elephant which had been concealed close by. The Roman, who was unused to such a creature, gazed quite unmoved upon the menace of its waving trunk. Pyrrhus thereupon sought to induce him to leave Rome and become one of his court, but in vain. On another occasion Pyrrhus sent his chief minister, Cineas, to try to persuade Rome to make peace. This man, who was a practiced orator and diplomat, and whose tongue, as Pyrrhus said, 'had won for the king more battles than his own sword' had all but persuaded the Roman senate, when his efforts were brought to naught by the appearance of the senator Appius Claudius. Blind and feeble with extreme old age, he was led into the senate, and rebuking his colleagues for wavering, he had them send Cineas back to Pyrrhus with the answer that Rome would not make peace with him as long as he was in Italy. So impressed was Cineas that he reported to his master that the Roman senate was an assembly of kings.

Once before, the senate had impressively displayed its dignity. When the Gauls captured Rome those senators who were too old to fight remained in the city, and, as the invaders entered the forum, they found these aged Romans seated there in silent majesty, each on his chair of state and clad in his official robes. Awe-struck, the Gauls approached, believing them to be gods. Then one ventured to stroke the long white beard of one of the senators, who smote him with his ivory staff. Enraged, the barbarian struck him down; and, the spell thus broken, in a few moments all were slain.

Such are some of the legends which illustrate the character that the Romans loved to attribute to their forefathers, and which were quite as influential in molding their own character as if they had been historical fact.

Questions

1. How did the Romans of the early republic differ from the Attic Greeks?
2. In what things were the Romans primarily interested?
3. Describe the Roman family. That is, who were the members and what were their roles?
4. Describe the life of a typical Roman of this time.
5. How did the Roman religion and their gods differ from the Greeks? How were they similar?
6. How do we come to know about the morals and character of the Roman people?
7. In the stories of the following Romans explain what they did and what moral their story taught:
   A. Mucius
   B. The consul, Brutus
   C. Coriolanus
   D. Cincinnatus
   E. Decius

Vocabulary

tutelage
frugality
ostentation
indomitable

Chapter XXXVIII

Rome and Carthage

We have seen how Rome extended her power over the Italian peninsula and organized the territories which she had conquered. With the acquisition of southern Italy and the Greek cities of the coast, new vistas opened up. The Romans began to learn the importance of sea-power, and possibly also some interest in trade and commerce was now beginning to develop in certain quarters.

The chief rival that the Romans now had to fear was Carthage, the greatest commercial city of the time. This city, after its foundation by adventurous colonists from Phoenicia, had grown and prospered, and its Semitic people had shown themselves to be the most enterprising traders of the age. Their merchant vessels were to be seen throughout all the western Mediterranean. Then, venturing past the Straits of Gibraltar, they explored the coast of Africa far to the south, and sailed as far north as Britain, where tin could be obtained. The people had made themselves a nation of traders and middlemen, bringing home the products of the most distant regions for manufacture or for barter with other countries.

The city itself was built on a magnificent scale, with strong fortifications, sumptuous palaces belonging to the wealthy, busy manufacturing and commercial quarters, and extensive docks for its navy and merchant marine. The population numbered perhaps nearly a million. The empire over which the city ruled comprised not only all the neighboring territory on the north coast of Africa but also extensive oversea dependencies in Spain, Corsica, Sardinia, and Sicily. From these coasts and the adjacent seas all rivals in trade were jealously excluded.

The government of Carthage was a narrow oligarchy, the control of affairs being practically in the hands of the wealthy nobles. Within this oligarchy there was bitter strife between rival factions with their respective leaders, while in her rule over her subjects, Carthage showed all the despotic harshness characteristic of Asiatics. The government maintained a well-equipped and efficient navy and an army of considerable strength. The latter, however, was made up almost entirely of subjects and mercenaries, for the native Carthaginians were traders and artisans rather than soldiers. Another source of weakness lay in the fact that the party in power tended to look upon generals belonging to the opposite faction with suspicion and jealousy, fearing them as possible rivals and giving them grudging support.

In all this we see a striking contrast with the resources of Rome, whose chief strength lay in the loyalty and efficiency of her citizen army, but who as yet possessed no fleet and knew little of the science of naval warfare. For leaders she depended not on professional generals, as did the Carthaginians, but on the annually elected consuls, who were not always commanders of conspicuous merit. The consuls and their armies were, however, loyally supported by the home government, and all classes were always ready to co-operate unselfishly in the service of the state.

In any war which might arise between these two powers, the outcome would be difficult to forecast, and the Romans must have looked upon any possible conflict with misgivings. Their diplomatic relations with Carthage had hitherto been friendly, and a treaty had been made declaring on what conditions Roman ships might visit Carthage and Sicily, and Carthaginian ships enter the ports of Italy. In time, however, when the Romans had gained control of the Greek cities of southern Italy, they came to look upon themselves as the natural protectors of the Greeks of Sicily also. By this time Carthage had conquered all the island except the cities on the eastern coast, and these were in danger of further aggression. The Romans had reason to fear the possibility of Carthage getting control of the narrow straits between Italy and Sicily and closing them to Italian shipping. War between the two countries was becoming inevitable, and, as frequently happens, a comparatively insignificant disturbance resulted in the outbreak of hostilities.

The first task of the Romans was to build and equip a fleet. They were seriously handicapped by their lack of knowledge and skill, but their energy and ingenuity partially compensated for this. They realized that they were inferior in seamanship, but they hoped to be able to make use of the superior fighting qualities of their soldiers. To this end they devised an instrument to which they gave the name of *corvus* (or 'crow'). This was a narrow movable gangway, one end of which could be raised aloft and then dropped upon the deck of an enemy vessel. A sharp spike at the end of the *corvus* pierced the enemy's deck, locking the two vessels together. The Roman soldiers could then rush across the gangway and fight hand to hand, as in a land-battle.

Roman Vessels.

The Romans quickly won two naval victories, which were due partly to this new device and partly to the contemptuous carelessness of the Carthaginians. The war was carried into Sicily, and an invasion of Africa was undertaken. This, however, was badly managed, as the Romans had not yet had any experience in distant oversea campaigns. The disaster which followed has given to history the story of the heroic consul Regulus, the commander of the expedition. He was defeated and captured with a great part of his army and was later sent to Rome by the Carthaginians with an offer of peace, on the understanding that, if he did not persuade the Roman government to accept their terms, he was to return to Carthage. On his arrival at Rome, he strongly urged his countrymen to refuse the unfavorable terms offered by the Carthaginians and to continue the war, even though this would involve his own death and that of his captured soldiers. He asked for no consideration, for, having become a captive, he refused to count himself a citizen. His advice was followed, and he thereupon kept his promise by returning to Carthage, where he was put to death with cruel tortures.

The war continued with varying fortunes. New Roman fleets were constructed, only to be destroyed by storms at sea or lost in battle through bad generalship. In Sicily, most of which was now in the hands of the Romans—their forces in the west of the island—were for three years harried and defied by the brilliant Carthaginian leader, Hamilcar, the only first-rate commander who took part in this war. Had he been wholeheartedly supported by his home government, the Romans

Regulus Returning to Carthage -1791 by Cornelis Lens, 1791, Hermitage Museum.

might have been defeated, but the Carthaginians lacked the energy and the spirit of self-sacrifice that the Romans displayed. The latter, undismayed by repeated losses and failures, at last nerved themselves for a final effort. The state was at the end of its resources, but a fleet was built by voluntary contributions and with this the decisive victory was won at the Aegatian Islands. Carthage acknowledged defeat, gave up Sicily, and agreed to pay an indemnity.

Rome now assumed control of the government of Sicily. The country was not treated as the Italian peoples had been, but, with the exception of some favored communities, was placed under a Roman governor and made subject to annual tribute. It thus became the first 'province,' as the Romans called their foreign dependencies. The Romans themselves hardly realized the importance of the step which they were taking, and instead of creating new machinery for the efficient government of their oversea territory, they merely arranged for the annual election of two new praetors, one of whom was to exercise jurisdiction in Sicily, the other in Corsica and Sardinia, which were taken from the Carthaginians shortly after the close of the war. Two officials also were sent to Sicily to supervise the collection of the annual tribute. Syracuse, which had supported the Romans throughout the war, remained a free city, in alliance with Rome and not subject to tribute.

Questions

1. By whom was the city of Carthage founded? Describe this city.
2. How was Carthage ruled? What weaknesses did this create? Strengths?
3. Describe the differences between Carthage and Rome.
4. What was Rome's main weakness in facing Carthage? Its strength?
5. Over what did Carthage and Rome come into conflict?
6. How did the Romans compensate for their lack of naval skill and experience?
7. Describe the actions of Regulus in the first war with Carthage.
8. Who was Hamilcar? How did he contribute to the war? Why did he not succeed?
9. How did this first war with Carthage conclude?
10. After the war, how did Rome govern Sicily?

Vocabulary

contemptuous
harried
indemnity

Chapter XXXIX

Hannibal

The Carthaginians had been defeated, but their power was not destroyed, and one at least of their leaders was determined that the struggle should be resumed. Hamilcar henceforth devoted all his thought and energy to the task of some day defeating Rome. Realizing that Carthage could not be depended upon to furnish him with men and supplies, he decided to organize a new base of operations in Spain. This country was already within the Carthaginians' sphere of influence; they controlled its commerce and had established trading posts on its coast. The population was warlike and the country had vast resources. For years Hamilcar worked to extend Carthaginian rule, to win the allegiance of the native tribes, and to build up a military force for his war against Rome. After his death, his work was carried on by his son-in-law, Hasdrubal, and later by his eldest son, Hannibal, the most brilliant genius in a family of generals, and as a military leader to be ranked with Alexander and Napoleon.

Hannibal had come to Spain at the age of nine with his father, who had him take an oath that he would never be friends with Rome. This oath was never forgotten, and when, at the age of twenty-six, Hannibal succeeded to the command of the army, he at once set about vigorous preparations for war upon the Romans. His army was well organized and well trained. His soldiers were devoted to him; they admired his skill as a leader, and loved him because he shared their hardships and never spared himself in battle.

His plan of campaign was daring in the extreme. As the Romans now controlled the sea, he proposed to invade Italy by land, although he knew the difficulties which would have to be encountered. The route was little known, and it might be difficult to find reliable guides. The mighty Rhone and the mountain-barriers of the Alps must be crossed; storms might make mountains and rivers impassable; hostile tribes would have to be beaten off, and the Romans would probably send armies to bar his way. Hannibal, however, knew the courage and devotion of his troops and was confident that they could overcome all these difficulties. He hoped also that upon his arrival in Italy allies and reinforcements could be obtained. The Gauls who dwelt in the valley of the Po had only recently been subdued by Rome and would probably welcome him as a liberator. Moreover he hoped that

Hannibal, from the Gardens of the Tuileries, 1872.
[Photo credit: Loicwood]

the Italian and Greek communities also would revolt from Rome and join his forces.

His first step was to lay siege to Saguntum, a city in Spain which was in alliance with Rome. The Roman government, not realizing the seriousness of Hannibal's purpose, lost valuable time in sending embassies to Carthage to protest against this aggression, and Saguntum had fallen before they were ready to intervene.

War was now declared and preparations were begun at Rome. Even yet the government did not realize the gravity of the situation. While Hannibal had a force of probably about 100,000 men for the invasion of Italy, the Roman armies mustered only about 70,000, and these were divided into three separate forces. One of these was stationed in northern Italy and the others were destined for operations against Spain and Africa.

After taking Saguntum, Hannibal lost no time in setting out on his march. Hostile tribes were placated wherever possible; otherwise a passage was forced by the sword. The advance to the Pyrenees is said to have cost him 20,000 men. Yet the rapidity of his march outstripped the calculations of the Romans, who moved leisurely towards the Rhone, only to learn that Hannibal was already there. The latter succeeded in crossing the river before the armies met. Then, after a slight skirmish, he eluded his opponents and continued his march to the Alps. The Romans abandoned the pursuit and proceeded to Spain.

Meanwhile Hannibal pressed forward to cross the Alps, the last and greatest obstacle on his march. He had no certain information about the route, and was several times misled by treacherous guides. Hostile tribesmen harassed his march from higher ground and caused many losses. Winter was now approaching, and bad weather added to his difficulties. As higher levels were reached, heavy falls of snow made the way difficult. At one point an avalanche had destroyed the road and a new one had to be constructed by cutting away the rock. Nor were his difficulties over when he reached the summit, since steeper grades were met on the Italian side, making it harder than ever for men, horses, and elephants to keep their footing. At length level ground was reached, but at an immense cost; only about 26,000 men remained. The rest had been slain in skirmishes with the mountaineers or had succumbed to exposure. Only the indomitable energy and enthusiasm of Hannibal himself and the devotion of his troops had made the feat possible.

A Roman army under the consul Scipio was encamped in northern Italy, where it had been sent to quell an uprising among the Gauls. No really adequate preparations had been made to meet Hannibal, since the Romans had again miscalculated his determination and the rapidity of his movements, apparently relying too much upon the barrier of the Alps. The two armies soon met in a skirmish at

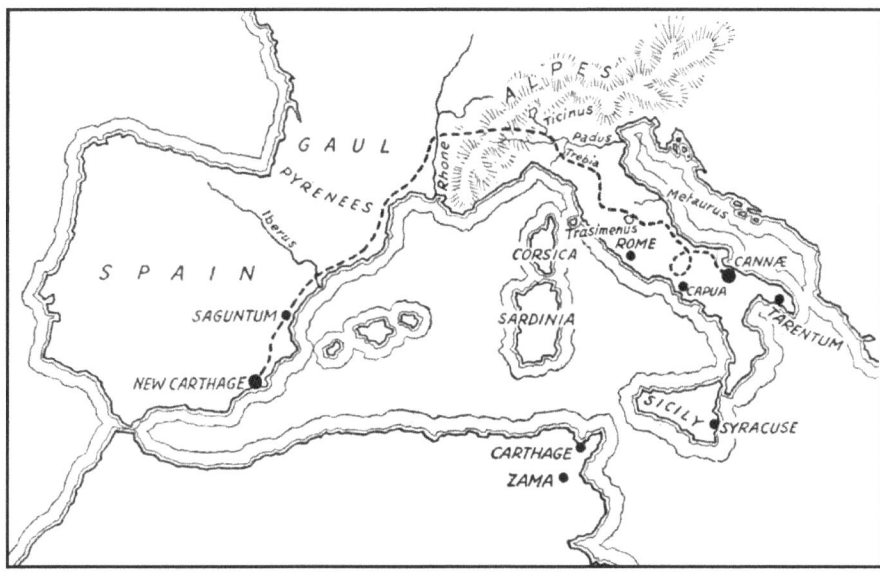
The Route of Hannibal.

the river Ticinus. Hannibal was victorious, and Scipio retreated to wait for reinforcements.

Another Roman army, which had been sent northward, soon joined that of Scipio. The united forces, now under the command of Sempronius, the other consul, were probably at least as strong as those of the Carthaginians, but the Romans possessed no general equal to Hannibal. A second battle was fought at the river Trebia, and Hannibal, with his usual sagacity, contrived that it should be fought on ground of his own choosing and under conditions most unfavorable to the Romans. The latter were enticed at dawn to wade across an icy stream and fight, chilled and hungry, on the opposite bank, where the forces of Hannibal were prepared to meet them, with some picked troops in ambush. The Romans were hopelessly outmaneuvered, and, though they fought with desperate courage, they were defeated with heavy losses and the survivors put to flight.

Hannibal had been successful, but winter was at hand and his army was in need of rest and supplies. Accordingly, he ceased his advance and went into winter-quarters in the country of the Gauls, who furnished him with supplies and reinforcements.

In the following spring he moved southwards again, and a Roman army, under the newly elected consul, Flaminius, was sent north to prevent his entering central Italy. Hannibal eluded this force by a difficult march through marshy country. The Roman commander, finding Hannibal between him and the city of Rome, also turned south, whereupon Hannibal prepared a trap for him by Lake Trasimene. Thanks to Hannibal's skillful disposition of his troops and a thick mist which aided his stratagem, the plan was completely successful. The Romans were surprised while still in marching order; their army was cut to pieces and thousands were captured. Hannibal's treatment of these prisoners is significant. The Romans were held captive, but their allies were set free without ransom. By this leniency Hannibal hoped to conciliate the Italians and induce them to revolt from Rome.

This policy serves also to explain his subsequent movements. Instead of marching upon Rome, he proceeded down the east coast into southern Italy. He probably realized that his army was not strong enough to undertake the siege of the city, and that his superiority in cavalry would be of no use to him in such an undertaking. He also hoped to cause an uprising of the Samnites and other peoples and to lead them against Rome. But in this he was disappointed. The wise policy of the Roman government in dealing liberally with the allied states and at the same time planting colonies among them had made the influence of Rome too strong to be shaken by a foreign invader.

Meanwhile, the alarm at Rome had been great, and Fabius, a trusted and cautious general, had been appointed dictator. By his direction a new policy was adopted. Hannibal was followed and watched and harassed, but Fabius resolutely refused to give him any opportunity of joining battle. There were men at Rome who scoffed at this policy, though it was undoubtedly the wisest course to follow, and nicknamed Fabius 'The Delayer' (*Cunctator*).

In the following year the people, growing impatient at the policy of Fabius, clamored for more vigorous action. As a result a powerful force was raised and sent to meet Hannibal in the field, the leaders being the two new consuls. Again the Carthaginian did not fail to make use of his superior skill in tactics. His first feat was to capture the Romans' base of supplies by an unexpected march and a surprise attack, thus forcing them to give battle or retreat. The Romans accepted the challenge, and a battle was fought near Cannae in southern Italy. The Romans are said to have had about 80,000 men opposed to Hannibal's 50,000. In drawing up his forces, Hannibal left his center comparatively weak and placed two strong columns of his well-trained infantry on either wing, the extreme flanks being held by the cavalry, which opposed the Roman horse. When the battle began, the superior numbers of the Roman infantry drove back the enemy's center, but soon found themselves assailed on the flanks by Hannibal's two columns. Meanwhile Hannibal's cavalry had routed their opponents and now closed in on the rear of the Roman infantry. The Romans were thus surrounded on all sides and the battle became a massacre. About 50,000 were slain and 20,000 taken prisoner. A mere remnant of the forces escaped to Rome.

Hannibal's success had now reached its zenith. He had won four battles and destroyed three Roman armies. As a result of Cannae, many of the southern Italians decided to throw in their lot with him, and Syracuse and some of the Greek cities followed suit. Reinforcements were expected from Carthage and Spain, and an alliance was entered into with Philip of Macedonia. But in spite of the battles he had won, Hannibal was still far from winning the war. For the Romans on their side had no thought of giving up the struggle, and set to work with characteristic tenacity to reorganize their forces, while no aid came to Hannibal from Carthage. A strong party there was bitterly opposed to him and not at all eager to see him victorious and powerful. Nor did any reinforcements come from Spain, where his brother, Hasdrubal, had been left in command. A Roman army which had been operating there under Scipio, the son of the consul who had first met Hannibal in battle, completely occupied Hasdrubal's attention. It is a striking proof of the stubbornness of the Romans and their faith in their ultimate success that this army was never recalled from Spain, but actually reinforced. Philip of Macedonia also was prevented from doing anything because of an alliance of Greek states which Roman diplomacy had succeeded in opposing to him. Even in Italy the position of Hannibal was becoming increasingly difficult. His new allies were only half-hearted, and it was necessary for him to guard them against possible attacks. His movements were constantly hampered by the unbroken chain of Roman fortresses throughout Italy; nor, with the solitary exception of Capua, did any of the important Latin or Italian cities open their gates to him.

Thus the war dragged on for several years, neither side being able to inflict any vital blow. Only once did Hannibal appear to be within sight of success. Hasdrubal finally succeeded in setting out from Spain with reinforcements. He reached northern Italy, only to be intercepted and defeated at the river Metaurus before he could join forces with Hannibal.

For the Romans the last great crisis was now past, and for Hannibal the future must have appeared hopeless. Yet for four years more he maintained himself in southern Italy, almost unmolested by the

Romans. His supreme qualities of leadership were never more manifest than in this period, when he kept his army together and maintained its discipline and devotion unshaken. His fifteen years of campaigning came to an end in 203 BC. The Romans had discovered a military genius in the youthful Scipio, who had succeeded in driving the Carthaginians out of Spain. He then carried the war into Africa and caused such alarm at Carthage that it was decided to recall Hannibal. Reluctantly he withdrew his army from Italy and returned to defend his own city.

The last battle of the war was fought at Zama, in Carthaginian territory. Hannibal played his part with skill and courage, but in Scipio he found a worthy antagonist, while the motley Carthaginian army, of which his veterans formed only a part, was inferior to the well-disciplined and homogeneous Roman force. The Carthaginians were defeated, and their government sued for peace. By the treaty which followed, Carthage was deprived of her oversea territory, and was compelled to surrender most of her warships, to pay an indemnity, and to allow her foreign relations to be directed by Rome.

One cannot but admire the genius and daring of Hannibal and his unfaltering devotion to his one great purpose; at the same time one must also be struck by the tenacity and courage of the Romans, who refused to be daunted by successive defeats and staggering losses. Scarcely any romantic stories of individual heroism are recorded in this war, nor can much be said for the military skill displayed by most of the Roman commanders; but the whole people, commons and senate alike, left a remarkable record of courage in the field and of self-sacrifice and unshaken morale at home. Furthermore, no admiration for the heroic figure of Hannibal should blind us to the fact that a victory for the Semitic Carthaginians would have meant a great disaster for western civilization. This war was but another episode in the great struggle between East and West, and Rome's victory meant that the western world was still to be free to develop in its own way.

Scipio Africanus Major, the Conqueror of Hannibal. [Shakko]

Questions

1. When Hamilcar decided to continue the struggle with Rome, where did he decide to turn for soldiers and supplies? Why did he have to go here?
2. How did his soldiers feel about Hannibal? Why did they feel this way?
3. Describe the general outline of Hannibal's plan to attack Rome and list some of the obstacles he would have to overcome for his plan to succeed.
4. How did Rome react to Hannibal's siege of Saguntum?
5. Describe Hannibal's crossing of the Alps. What effect did this crossing have on his army?
6. How did the Gauls treat Hannibal and his army during their first winter in Italy?
7. Describe the outcome of the battle at Lake Trasimine? How did Hannibal treat the prisoners taken there and why?
8. Why did Hannibal not attack Rome immediately? What was his strategy? Why was this not successful?
9. Describe the new policy implemented by the Roman leader Fabius.
10. After the replacement of Fabius, the Romans faced Hannibal at the battle of Cannae. Describe Hannibal's strategy in this battle. What were the results?
11. Why did Hannibal's brother Hasdrubal not send reinforcements from Spain?
12. Why did Hannibal finally leave Italy?
13. What were the terms of the Carthaginian surrender after the Battle of Zama?

Alternatively, write a paper in which you retell the events in this chapter.

Vocabulary

zenith
motley
sagacity

CHAPTER XL

THE CONQUEST OF THE MEDITERRANEAN WORLD

Rome had now reduced her great rival to submission. Her own resources had been strained to the utmost, and her people would have benefited by a period of peace and recuperation. But many causes combined to make this impossible. The task of reasserting authority over the Gauls of northern Italy demanded immediate attention, and much work had to be done in Spain before this newly conquered country with its warlike people could be pacified. The difficulty of the task and the size of the peninsula led to its being divided into two provinces, each governed by a praetor. The southern province rapidly adopted Roman ways and the Roman language. In order to have secure communication by land with Spain, the Romans, by arrangement with the Greek colony of Massilia, acquired control of a strip of territory along the coast of Gaul.

The Romans also soon became involved in conflicts with more than one power east of the Adriatic, which led in the end to their assuming control of the eastern as well as the western Mediterranean. It has sometimes been supposed that Rome was eager for foreign conquest and took advantage of slight pretexts to wage war and annex new territory. All the evidence, however, shows that this was not so. Rome had genuine grounds for fearing the ambitious and aggressive policy of the kings of Macedonia and Syria. Each of these was unceasing in his efforts to extend the kingdom that he had inherited; they both had dreams of conquering Rome; and Rome had no assurance that in a conflict with these unknown and ancient civilizations she would prove victorious. Moreover, the Romans were undoubtedly very reluctant to assume any responsibilities east of the Adriatic. They desired nothing so much as peace and security in that quarter, and whenever they felt themselves obliged to intervene, their policy was to leave the defeated states their independence. Rome greatly preferred having on her eastern borders a number of allied and peaceful friendly states, and only as a last resort, when it was evident that this could not be attained, did she assume the unwelcome responsibility of annexing and governing.

The first beginning of trouble in the east was due to the activities of Philip of Macedonia. This ruler had allied himself with Hannibal and had been hostile towards certain Greek states with

Antiochos III

whom Rome was on friendly terms. With Hannibal's invasion in their minds, the Romans could not but be alarmed at Philip's aggressive attitude. Philip and Antiochus, king of Syria, had also formed a compact to attack the young king of Egypt and annex part of his dominions. This might not seem to be any concern of the Romans. But because of the long warfare and the consequent devastation of Italy and Sicily, the Romans had had to look to Egypt for their grain-supply, and had thus come to conclude an alliance with the king of Egypt. The inevitable conflict came when Philip attacked Athens. War was declared, and after a brief campaign fought on Greek soil, the power of Macedonia was broken and, while the country was not annexed, Philip was forced to subject his foreign policy to the control of Rome. By this victory Rome had crippled a dangerous rival and made herself the protector of the liberties of Greece; at the Isthmian Games a proclamation was made by the Roman general that the Greek states were henceforth to be free from Macedonian control.

Shortly after, the Romans again had to intervene in eastern affairs because of the aggressiveness of Antiochus, who, not content with warring against Asiatic independent states and Egypt, finally sent an army into Greece. Apart from his own ambition, he was urged to this course by Hannibal, who had been forced to leave Carthage and had been welcomed at the court of Antiochus. A second eastern campaign was undertaken by the Romans, which ended in their crossing over into Asia Minor, where they won a decisive victory. Hannibal took refuge with the king of Bithynia, and there, finding that he was about to be delivered over to the Romans, he took poison. Antiochus was compelled to give up western Asia Minor, and this country, too, passed under Roman influence. The native kingdoms in Asia Minor as well as Rhodes were left independent, to act as 'buffer states' between Rome and the still formidable power of the Seleucid kings of Syria.

Rome's moderate policy in not annexing Macedonia did not prove successful, for Philip and his son Perseus continued to plot against her. The situation finally became intolerable, and Rome was forced to embark upon another war, which ended in still another victory for her armies. Even now Macedonia was not annexed, but was simply divided into four republics, which were forbidden to combine with one another. Twenty years later a rebellion caused Rome to take the final step of forming Macedonia into a Roman province.

Philip V of Macedon

Meanwhile the Greek states had continued to enjoy independence under Roman protection. But unfortunately they used their freedom to continue those inveterate quarrels which make the political history of Greece during the third and second centuries BC one continuous record of jealousy, aggression, internecine warfare, and a general inability to 'live and let live.' At the same time, Rome's efforts to keep the peace caused strong anti-Roman feeling in many cities. Finally, when, in spite of remonstrances, a more serious conflict than usual broke out, the Romans lost patience and sent an army into Greece to take from it the liberty which it did not know how to use. The war was over in two brief campaigns and culminated in the destruction of the great commercial city of Corinth. With a few exceptions, the Greek states were made tributary vassals of Rome; it was more than a century before they were constituted a separate province, called Achaea.

The year 146 BC also witnessed the destruction of Carthage. Even after the Hannibalic War, the city had continued to prosper, and its success was looked upon with jealousy and alarm at Rome, for both political and commercial reasons. Hence when Carthage made war upon her turbulent Numidian neighbors in order to defend herself from their incursions, she was charged with violating the treaty with Rome. A party at Rome demanded her absolute destruction, and Cato, one of the most eminent Romans of this time, is said to have concluded every speech that he made, whatever the subject, with the words *Delenda est Carthago* ('Carthage must be destroyed'). His advice was followed, and Carthage was razed to the ground after a three years' war marked by a desperate defense of the city. The Roman general who commanded in this war was the nephew and adopted son of Scipio, the conqueror of Hannibal. In memory of these victories, the name *Africanus* was given to both Scipios. In the ruthless destruction of Corinth and Carthage we find clear indication that Roman policy was now beginning to be dictated by more selfish and less defensible motives than hitherto. Trade was being found more profitable than agriculture, and a commercial and capitalist class was springing up in Rome, which found a rich field for profit in the growth of Rome's control over the wealthy older civilizations. The powerful influence of those engaged in exploiting these new opportunities for gain had an evil effect upon Roman policy; too often now the honest desire to promote peace and order is found intermixed with selfish commercial ambitions and sometimes with an unscrupulous imperialism.

Roman Soldiers. (From a spiral relief.)

Thus, a half-century largely occupied with the first two wars[30] with Carthage was followed by a half-century of conquest overseas. Immense territories had been won, including provinces in Sicily, Spain, and northern Africa, and subordinate kingdoms or republics under Roman protection in western Asia Minor, Greece, and Macedonia.

---

[30] The various wars with Carthage are often called the First, Second, and Third Punic Wars, from the Latin equivalent (Punicus) of the word Phoenician.

Questions

1. How was Rome drawn into other conflicts after the end of Punic Wars?
2. After a century of war, how was Rome changed?
3. Draw or copy a map showing the current extent of the Roman territory around 140 BC.

Vocabulary

internecine
remonstrances
inveterate

CHAPTER XLI

THE ROMAN PEOPLE DURING THE PERIOD OF CONQUEST

In the wars with Carthage and Macedonia, the Romans had passed through a long-continued period of stress. No people could undergo such an ordeal without being profoundly affected by it. In the case of Rome two powerful influences were at work: that of the wars themselves, and that of contact with the civilization of Greece and the East; and both of these resulted in great changes in Roman life which showed themselves in the first half of the second century.

During the campaigns men were taken from their farms for long periods of service with the legions. Countless thousands of these lost their lives in battle and left Italy the poorer for their death. And of those who did return, many a Roman farmer found that his land had been laid waste, his buildings destroyed, and his family scattered. In other cases his farm had been sold to pay accumulating debts and had been incorporated in one of the large estates which were springing up all over Italy. Often too the farmer was not satisfied to go back to his hard and frugal life, and preferred the excitement of army life with its opportunities for plunder; or again, when discharged from military service, he was drawn to Rome by the attractions of city life.

Farm life and family life of the simple old-fashioned type were rapidly decaying, and in their place a new and less healthy social structure was growing up. The farms abandoned or seized for debt and the immense tracts of land, especially in southern Italy, confiscated as punishment for support given to Hannibal, made it possible for men of wealth to become possessed of large estates, hitherto unknown among the Romans. On these estates great numbers of slaves were used, for slave-labor had become cheap and plentiful as a result of the successful wars and the opening up of commercial relations with the East. This cheap slave-labor made the position of the small independent farmer still more difficult, while the hard life of these plantation slaves resulted in perpetual discontent and frequent outbreaks of violence.

Large numbers of the peasant-proprietors drifted to Rome to swell the growing city mob of indigent, idle, and discontented men. To placate the populace and to win its votes, free amusements and distributions of food were arranged by the state and by candidates for office, a practice which only increased the numbers of the rabble and taught them to lead a life of idle amusement. This brought out a strain of coarseness and brutality in the Roman character, which always showed itself at its best amid conditions of hard toil and rude simplicity. The favorite forms of amusement were the gladiatorial shows, introduced from Etruria, combats with or between wild beasts, and the chariot races held in the circus (a long, narrow stadium with rows of seats surrounding a race-track).

Not only was foreign grain imported in large quantities, much of it for free distribution to the people, but new and costly delicacies were brought from all quarters of the Mediterranean world for the tables of the rich. In other ways, too, luxury and ostentation were increasing, largely as a result of contact with Greece and the Hellenized East, with which the Romans had suddenly become acquainted, unfortunately at a time when Greek taste itself had deteriorated. As a result they rapidly forsook the simplicity and frugality of the typical primitive household, and foreign fashions in dress, food and drink, furniture, and dwellings were generally adopted by the upper classes. The change in the whole standard of Roman life was too rapid and too great to be healthy.

But the influence of Greece upon Rome was by no means wholly bad, for Greek culture had much that was good to offer to those who could appreciate it. Unfortunately, the Romans were a hard-headed, practical race, to whom art and literature, science and philosophy, as a rule, meant little. There were, however, a few Romans, like the younger Scipio Africanus and a group of his friends, who became keenly interested in Greek thought and Greek art, and who were the first to form an educated class at Rome. But the number of these was as yet small, being confined to a few enlightened families. The conservative minds of many leading Romans looked with suspicion upon such novelties, and the movement was slow in gaining momentum.

Another new development was the appearance of the first Latin literary works. Rome had as yet produced practically nothing which could be called literature, but now a number of writers appeared who translated Greek poems and plays into Latin. Most of these were from the Greek cities of southern Italy; none was Roman-born. Among them was Livius Andronicus, who translated Homer's *Odyssey* into Latin verse to serve as a school-book for Roman boys. A few other writers produced original works written in Greek meters, the most notable of these being a rude but vigorous epic poem by Ennius recounting the history of Rome. Nearly all the literature of this period, however, was either translated from or modeled upon Greek originals; it was not in any sense a native growth, and it made little impression on the masses of the Roman people. The high seriousness of tragedy was never popular, as at Athens. Comedy was more to the taste of a Roman audience, and we still have several plays written at this time by Plautus and Terence, who sought to give a Roman coloring to comedies adapted from the Greek. The somewhat coarse and boisterous humor of Plautus won more popular favor than the more subtle wit and more refined style of Terence, who was better appreciated by the small literary circle in Rome.

Romans who had seen such cities as Athens, Corinth, and Alexandria, could not help admiring the splendor of their buildings and the beauty of their works of art. Large numbers of paintings and statues now began to appear in the houses of wealthy Romans, in some cases honestly purchased in Greece, but more often obtained as a result of the destruction and sacking of Corinth or of other victories in the East. At the same time, a beginning was made of the erection in Rome of temples and other public buildings constructed in imitation of Greek models, and domestic architecture also began to follow the Greek style.

These social and cultural developments were accompanied by important political changes. The long-continued wars, which had kept the Roman citizens from their farms, had also prevented them from attending the assembly. With so many of its members abroad on military service or living at a distance from the city in some Roman colony, the assembly could not be truly representative of the citizens; it was an unwieldy body for the transaction of pressing business. Thorough discussion was impossible, as only magistrates could address it, and the assembly merely voted to accept, or reject, without amendment, the proposal brought before it by the magistrate who had summoned it. On the other hand, the senate was a much smaller body, whose members were mostly resident in Rome; it was composed of men of ripe experience, and discussion of any question was always possible. During these years new problems were continually arising—problems connected with the conduct of war and the settlement of terms of peace, negotiations with foreign states, the organization and government of the new provinces. What more natural than that the custom should arise of referring these matters to the senate, even though theoretically they should have come before the assembly? The mass of the people, absorbed in the war and content with having secured constitutional protection against injustice, made no objection, and willingly entrusted the general direction of state affairs to the senate, the one body which was able to exercise continuous and efficient control of policy from the capital.

The consuls too, the chief executive magistrates, were busily engaged in administrative duties and often absent from the city leading the armies of the republic, and so were usually ready to leave the responsibility of making important decisions with the senate, a body to which they themselves always belonged. Thus the senate came to be more and more, not an advisory body which the magistrates might consult, but a directing body, whose policies the magistrates carried out. In this way war-time conditions tended to increase the power of the senate at the expense both of the people and of the annually elected magistrates. The progress of democracy was arrested, and, without any change in the theory of the constitution or any new legislation, custom and practice gradually effected such a transfer of power in the state that the republic became more than ever a narrow oligarchy, dominated by the 'noble' families who composed the senate.

The confidence reposed in the senate was not unjustified; it had rendered magnificent service, and in the stress and strain of war it had proved a powerful steadying influence. Nonetheless, this new authority of the senate, sanctioned by custom and jealously maintained, was to prove a menace to peace and good government in the century following the era of conquest.

With the addition of new territory overseas, an entirely new problem faced the Roman government, for a system of provincial administration had to be devised. This was accomplished largely by making use of the machinery of government already existing. The governor of a province was not specially selected for his task, but was either one of the praetors of the year, or a man who had already held the consulship or praetorship.[31] This governor controlled the military forces in the province and exercised a general supervision. The detailed administration of local affairs was largely left to the provincials themselves, the Roman government merely laying down general principles, fixing the total amount of taxes to be contributed, and appointing the governor. Apart from this the province was not treated as a unit, nor had its communities the same rights and privileges. The Roman government made a separate arrangement with each community, as had been done in Italy, and thus the danger of combined opposition was lessened and each community realized its direct dependence on Rome.

---

[31] With the organization of the provinces of Spain, the Romans ceased creating a new praetorship for each new province added, and instead sent out ex-magistrates with the title of pro-consul or pro-praetor.

The system was not in itself unfair or unreasonable, but it lent itself to serious abuses and provided no effective means of guarding against them. There was, for example, no way of securing redress against a governor who chose to act in a despotic way or to practice extortion. The system of taxation also was defective. It was the practice in some of the richest provinces to sell the right to collect taxes to the highest bidder, who was thus tempted to make a profit by extorting from the provincials sums far in excess of the money which was ultimately paid into the treasury at Rome. Such extortion might have been checked by the governor, but too often he allowed the tax-gatherers a free hand or even took a share of the plunder for himself. For many a Roman noble at this period, impoverished by extravagant living and the expense of free shows to win the popular vote, looked forward to the governorship of a province as a certain means of restoring his finances.

In criticizing the defects of this system, we must remember that the Romans were making a new experiment in government. The ancient eastern monarchies had provided examples of the efficient government of large empires by the agents of a despot, and some of the Greek states had had some limited experience in the control of small dependencies; but it was quite a new thing for a city-state to attempt the control of a widespread empire. In making this attempt, the Romans made many mistakes, but they were at the same time gaining valuable experience which was later to be turned to good account.[32]

That the Romans were able to profit by their experience in administrative matters is shown by the development of Roman law at this time. The growth of commerce and the influx of foreigners into Rome had already led to the appointment of two judicial praetors instead of one. Of these, one tried cases between citizens, the other between citizens and foreigners. The judgments rendered and the principles followed in these courts gradually built up an important body of Roman law. Later, the extension of Roman dominion over foreign nations which had quite different legal systems and ideas of justice led to the formation of a second body of legal principles, the *ius gentium,* or 'equity common to all nations.' This was based, not upon the letter of the Roman law, but upon what would generally be regarded everywhere as common-sense practice. This, in its turn, tended to modify the strict legalism of the formal Roman law, and, as Roman law and justice always accompanied Roman rule, the wide extension of a uniform and reasonable system of law was an important contribution to European civilization.

This period of great wars and conquests was a momentous era of transition for the Roman people. Their horizon had been widened, new influences had come into their social and political life, and new problems had arisen. In particular, three important questions called for solution: (1) How was Rome to organize a just and efficient system of provincial government? (2) Could Rome profit from her contact with Hellenistic culture without being corrupted by the evil influences of Greece and the East? (3) What remedy could be found for the social and economic evils caused by the decay of agriculture and the growth of the city populace?

---

[32] We may compare the great change which the nineteenth century witnessed in Great Britain's dealings with her colonies, as the earlier mistakes came to be realized.

Questions

1. Why did soldiers returning from war turn to city life (give three reasons) and what problems were created by this?
2. What were the good and bad influences of the East on the life of Rome?
3. What was the effect of slave labor on the farming of Rome?
4. How did the Senate gradually gain more control over the government of Rome?

Vocabulary

extortion
oligarch
impoverished

CHAPTER XLII

THE GRACCHI AND THE BEGINNING OF THE REVOLUTION

Among the Roman families who had come under the influence of Greek culture was that of the Gracchi. One of the notable members of this house was Cornelia, the daughter of Scipio (the conqueror of Hannibal), and the mother of Tiberius and Caius Gracchus, the great reformers. Her husband having died while the children were still young, she had attended to their training herself and had taught them all that was best in the old Roman ways of life and in the new culture which had been brought from Greece. She was herself a woman of refinement and of liberal and patriotic ideas, and she taught her sons to be cultured and public-spirited men. A well-known story tells that when some friends were boasting of their wealth and fine possessions, Cornelia pointed to her children and said, 'These are my treasures.'

Tiberius, the elder of the two brothers, was the first to enter public life. As a youth he had been quiet and retiring, and in happier times might have become a scholar and thinker rather than a man of action. But when he saw the distress of so many of his countrymen, caused by the decay of agriculture and the growth of large estates tilled by slave-labor, he was roused to action, and got himself elected tribune. With passionate eloquence he called upon the people to support him in the work of reform. 'The wild beasts of Italy,' said he, 'have their dens and sleeping-places; but the men who risk their lives in battle for Italy have nothing in it of their own but the air and the sunlight; houseless and homeless they wander from place to place with their wives and children.'

His aim was to provide farms for men who had become landless, and thus to restore the class of peasant-proprietors who had once been the backbone of Rome's military strength. The provision of the Licinian Laws restricting the amount of land that any one man could hold had been disregarded, and Tiberius simply proposed that it should again be enforced with some slight modifications. All public land illegally held by the rich was to be reclaimed by the state and distributed in allotments to the poor. Despite opposition, the proposal was carried by the assembly, and a commission was appointed to supervise the redistribution. While these measures were both reasonable and legal, the wealthy classes were violently opposed to them, and, unfortunately, the senate identified itself with the opposition and used its influence to thwart the proposals of Tiberius. The latter was thereupon driven to question the senate's

Cornelia, Mother of the Gracchi by Kauffmann.

right of interference and to assert that the people in their assembly should be supreme. The senators induced another tribune to veto his further measures, and Tiberius retaliated by persuading the people to depose this tribune, contrary to established usage. Violent disturbances followed, and Tiberius was slain in a riot by some of the more violent senators. This was the first bloodshed in Rome in civil turmoil. The law stood, however, and for a time the number of small landholders was considerably increased.

Ten years later the struggle was renewed by his brother Caius, who also held the office of tribune. Like Tiberius, he was a man of high idealism and passionate enthusiasm. With these he united a great capacity for work and an aptitude for practical politics. As a result his program was broader than that of Tiberius had been. Its aim was twofold: to complete the redistribution of land, and to take away from the senate the undue influence which it had come to exert. The latter was a preliminary step necessary in order to remove the great obstacle that had prevented the success of Tiberius. He not only revived the land-laws and added to them a scheme for assisted oversea colonization to relieve poverty among the citizens, but he also brought forward a series of measures designed to win the support of various parties who might help him in his opposition to the senate. Thus a law providing for the state sale of grain at a low price confirmed the loyalty of the populace. He also sought to enlist the support of the growing commercial aristocracy, the financiers and capitalists of Rome, who had joined with the senators in opposing Tiberius. They were possessed of great wealth acquired in the commercial enterprises made possible by the recent development of Rome's power, but they were excluded from the magistracies and the senate because they were not of 'noble' descent. These *equites* or 'knights' [33] Caius planned to detach from the senate by transferring to them from the senate the control of the courts which dealt with charges of extortion in the provinces by Roman officials and governors. This measure had more significance than appears on the surface; it gave the *equites* a definite status in the constitution, and the political importance thus acquired was a considerable factor in the controversies of the next century.

Having got these measures adopted by the assembly, he then brought forward a proposal, to confer the full franchise on the Latin citizens and the so-called 'Latin franchise' on the Italian cities.[34] The Italians had fought bravely in Rome's wars, and Italy had become more and more unified in feeling and culture, so that the proposal was reasonable and statesmanlike, and its acceptance would have saved years of turmoil and war. But the Roman populace was as bitterly opposed to this generous measure as was the senate, and Caius' opponents took advantage of his loss of popularity to proclaim martial law in the city. In the rioting which followed, Caius, like his brother, met his death with hundreds of his supporters.

The proposals of Caius Gracchus were a singular mixture of wise and unwise measures, and there has always been a doubt how far he was actuated by concern for the welfare of the people, and how far by the ambition to become a great leader of a Roman democratic state, like Pericles in Athens.

The laws of the Gracchi accomplished little in the solving of the land problem, but their indirect results were of the greatest importance. A breach had been made between the senate and the people, and between the rich commercial class and the senatorial aristocracy. Moreover, they had shown what a single leader with a strong party at his back might accomplish. While the Gracchi themselves may not have aspired to a kingdom or a tyranny, as some of their opponents charged, their careers had suggested that one-man rule was not beyond the bounds of practical politics and might prove the best way of putting an end to intolerable conditions. This attempt at reform by the two brothers ushered in a century of civil strife and gradual revolution, in which they themselves had unconsciously and unintentionally taken the first steps.

---

[33] These financiers were called *equites* from the ancient Servian military organization, in which the cavalry *(equiles)* of the state had been composed of the richest citizens. By this time the cavalry actually used in war was furnished by Rome's allies, and was inferior to the legionaries composed of Roman citizens; but the term *equiles* was still preserved as the official designation of the citizens rated as possessing the greatest wealth.

[34] The citizens of the Latin towns differed from the other Italians in that, while neither class had the full rights of Roman citizens, the former could acquire them on meeting certain conditions.

Questions

1. What reforms did each of the Gracchi brothers try to accomplish?
2. Why did the reforms meet with resistance?
3. What were the results of the attempts to reform?

Vocabulary

actuated
extortion
franchise

Chapter XLIII

Marius and Sulla

The failure of the Gracchi had shown that popular leaders could not succeed by relying solely upon the votes of the people in the assembly. The troubled state of the times and the bitterness of party feeling placed a premium upon violence, so that a leader who was to succeed must depend upon either a mob of armed followers or an organized army. It is not surprising then that the next popular leader was, above all things, a military man.

Caius Marius, the son of a day-laborer in the hill-country, was a rough, untutored soldier who had served in the ranks and by his ability and ambition had risen to a position of command. His genius was purely military, and he was as much out of place in politics as in the aristocratic society of Rome. Yet after he had attained military success, the circumstances of his times and his own ambition led him to attempt the role of statesman.

He first attained prominence during a war with Jugurtha, the king of Numidia in Africa. The campaign had been so scandalously mismanaged by the leaders sent out by the senate that the people cried out for a change of command, and, taking the matter into their own hands, appointed Marius as general. After some hard fighting, he was able to win a decisive victory. Jugurtha was captured, and Marius returned to Rome to celebrate a triumph.

Meanwhile, a serious situation had developed on the northern frontier, where two warlike German tribes, the Cimbri and Teutons, had for some time threatened an invasion of Italy. The Cimbri, after making their way southward in search of new homes, had passed through the modern Switzerland into Gaul, where the southern part of the Rhone valley had not long before been made into a Roman province. For some years they hovered about the borders of the province, plundering and terrorizing as they went, and several times they came into conflict with Roman armies, which in every case they defeated. On the last occasion at Arausio (Orange) in the center of the province, two armies which had been combined were overwhelmed with a loss eclipsing that at Cannae. There was nothing to prevent an invasion of Italy, and the utmost alarm prevailed; but luckily the Cimbri turned in the other direction, and it was some years before they again threatened the province. By this time they had been joined by the Teutons, a kindred tribe of equal strength. Their plan

Cauis Marius Amid the Ruins of Carthage by John Vanderlyn, 1807, Fine Arts Museum, San Francisco.

was for the Teutons to enter Italy from the west, while the Cimbri were to come in from the north, and the two tribes were to join forces in Cisalpine Gaul. The interval had enabled Marius to make careful preparations for stemming the invasion, and when he met the Teutons at Aquae Sextiae (Aix), near Massilia, his masterly tactics gave him an overwhelming victory. Next year, when the Cimbri entered Italy, he was ready to meet them, and again was victorious. The two tribes were annihilated, and it was 500 years before barbarian invaders again set foot in Italy. This was Marius' greatest service to his country, and few generals have ever rendered a greater.

The army which had won these victories had been reorganized by Marius and transformed into a fighting force very different from the citizen-militia of the early republic. As a result of his own experience in the ranks, Marius had an unusual knowledge of the needs of the common soldier and was able to make many improvements in his training and equipment. An even more important change was made in the method of recruiting. The army in its origin was simply the citizen-body called out to defend its territory, with each man providing his own weapons. Hitherto, therefore, only landholders had been called upon to serve; but these felt increasing reluctance to leave their farms for army service, now that wars were being waged in distant provinces and might entail a prolonged absence. Marius disregarded this restriction; he accepted men of all classes who were willing to serve, and largely substituted voluntary enlistment for the former compulsory levy. He thus created virtually a professional army of long-service volunteers. This in turn made possible a more intensive training. He divided the legion into ten cohorts, each capable of acting independently, and thus gave the legion a degree of flexibility which made it far superior to the Greek phalanx. The characteristic weapons of the legionary soldier were the javelin, which he threw when nearing the enemy to cause confusion in their ranks, and the deadly short sword with which he rushed in and smote the enemy. Marius gave his soldiers prolonged and individual training in the use of these weapons and also fostered their *esprit de corps* by giving each cohort an ensign and each legion a standard in the form of an eagle. The Roman legions with which Julius Caesar later conquered Gaul were the result of Marius' reorganization.

There was, however, a serious disadvantage in the new system. Soldiers in such an army were apt to lose touch with all home-ties in Italy, to forget that they were soldiers of the state, and to regard themselves simply as the followers of the general, who looked after their interests, led them to victory, and gave them a share in the spoil. Indeed, according to the Roman custom, it was to his commander, and not to the state, that the soldier swore obedience and loyalty. The political consequences of this simple change were tremendous. It has been said with a certain justification that Marius robbed the state of its army. The military commander with his army becomes henceforth the dominating figure in Roman history. Marius' military reform paved the way for the downfall of the republic and the establishment of the empire.

Marius had held the consulship five times while leading Rome's armies, and on his return to Rome he was elected to the office for the sixth time. Although such frequent tenure of the chief magistracy was quite legal, it was at the same time a violation of the spirit of republican government, which is generally opposed to long tenure of office. Marius now entered the political field, a sphere for which he soon showed himself to be quite unfitted. Like many other successful generals, he could not adapt his rough-and-ready ways to the tasks of statecraft. He failed to keep the peace between the two rival parties in Rome, and, disgusted with the position in which he found himself, he withdrew for some years into private life.

The political troubles of this period were aggravated by the question of the enfranchisement of the Italian allies. These had fought in ever-increasing numbers in the armies of Rome and had shared her dangers, but they were still debarred from voting and the other rights and privileges reserved for Roman citizens. Many of the more liberal men in Rome, like Caius Gracchus, recognized the injustice of this and favored more liberal treatment of the Italians. But the selfishness of both the commons and the governing classes at Rome barred the way. The senate feared that a multitude of new voters would imperil their control, and the common people were averse to having the material benefits of citizenship, such as the distribution of lands and booty and of cheap grain, shared by any but themselves. Finally the Italians were driven to resort to arms, and what was virtually a civil war broke out, with the forces on either side about equally matched. A new government was set up by the Italians, and a capital was chosen, to which the name Italica was given. This Social War (or war with the allies, *socii*) lasted for three years, and although Marius and other able generals took the field, it was ended not so much by Roman victories as by the belated granting of full Roman citizenship to practically all free inhabitants of Italy south of the Po.

Roman Legionary

This great extension of the franchise made the assembly at Rome less than ever representative of the whole body of citizens, and still further lowered its prestige. Yet there was no remodeling of the traditional city-state government to suit the altered conditions. No one had yet thought

Asia Minor at the time of the First Mithridatical War from the Historical Atlas by William R Shepherd, original image University of Texas.

of the modern system of representative government, by which an assembly is made up of elected representatives of all sections of the citizen-body, however distant from the capital.

Marius was still the most popular general with the people, but his reputation was now being challenged by Sulla, a brilliant military leader who belonged to the senatorial party. As a lieutenant of Marius he had fought in the war with Jugurtha and had actually provoked the jealousy of his chief by his skillful work as commander of the cavalry. In the battles with the Cimbri and Teutons he had again played a subordinate part with distinction, and in the Social War he had held an independent command and had won more conspicuous success than Marius. The two men resembled each other in little else than their military genius. Sulla was a thorough aristocrat, a man of cultivated tastes and brilliant social gifts, endowed with a mind of unusual keenness. The great defect in his character was a vein of cynicism, which made him cold-blooded and indifferent to the feelings of others. He ascribed his own success to Fortune and looked upon life as a game and himself as a lucky player.

The rivalry between Marius and Sulla soon led to a political crisis. A war had broken out in Asia Minor which threatened to overthrow Roman rule in the East. Sulla was chosen commander, but Marius and the popular party made an attempt to supersede him. Sulla thereupon settled the question in a drastic and unconstitutional manner. He marched upon Rome with his army and made himself master of the situation by force of arms. Marius was outlawed, but managed to make his escape to Africa. Sulla's action might well have proved a death-blow to constitutional and republican government. For the present, however, he was more concerned with the danger in the East than with political questions. Mithradates, the ambitious and able king of Pontus in eastern Asia Minor, a region never conquered either by Persia or by Alexander, had taken advantage of the Roman government's absorption in the Social War to make himself master of all Asia Minor. On one day 80,000 Roman residents of Asia were massacred by Mithradates' orders, zealously carried out by a population which had grown to hate the tax-collectors and other agents of the Roman capitalists and commercial exploiters. Then, with his fleet controlling the Aegean, Mithradates sent his armies into Greece, and soon this peninsula also was lost to Rome. Besides the military danger and the blow to Rome's prestige, great distress was caused by the enormous financial losses and by the closing of all the East to trade and the movement of grain. Sulla left Rome and spent three years mainly in Greece, from which, after winning several victories, he was able to cross over into Asia and compel Mithradates to abandon all his conquests and make peace.

During Sulla's absence the Marian party had regained power in Rome after much rioting, in which thousands of lives were lost. Marius returned from Africa, and in a passion of anger took his revenge by a wholesale slaughter of his opponents in the senatorial party. Soon after, he died, and for a few years the city was under the control of the leaders of the Marian faction, who carried their party bitterness so far as to seek to thwart Sulla in his campaign against Mithradates. On Sulla's return with his veterans, the conflict broke out afresh; after two years of bitter fighting, Sulla entered Rome victorious, and then in his turn took vengeance on his opponents by putting many thousands of them to death and confiscating their property.

At no time in all her history did Rome experience such a period of bloody and ruthless civil war as in this decade of strife between Marius and Sulla and their partisans. Forgetful of the old patriotism and self-restraint, both sides alike were unscrupulous in their self-seeking and ungovernable in their fierce passions. Yet, in spite of the bitterness of the political strife of this period, there were still many who remained devoted to the best ideals of Roman character and government. Rome might yet be saved from chaos and ruin by the appearance of the right kind of leader, a man of moderate views and more disinterested aims than Sulla or Marius—one who could compose the strife of parties and reawaken in the people and the army their old loyalty to the state.

Having made himself master of Rome, Sulla had himself appointed dictator, and set about restoring and re-establishing senatorial government. The reforms which he introduced were quite in keeping with his character. His shrewdness and common sense suggested to him many useful administrative improvements, notably a reform of the law-courts. But, apart from this, his work was illiberal and reactionary. His cynical contempt for the commons made him disregard their claim to an effective voice in the government. All real authority was centered in the senate, which was to supervise and control both the assembly and the magistrates chosen by the people. The sanction of the senate was required before any proposal could be brought before the plebeian assembly, while the veto of the tribunes was restricted to its original function of protecting the commons against injustice. The tribunate was further weakened by a measure forbidding ex-tribunes to hold any other office. Thus in various ways Sulla sought to prevent men like the Gracchi and Marius from gaining too much power, his whole object being to put the senate in control of affairs and to throttle the opposition. It would not have been difficult for Sulla to make himself 'tyrant' of Rome; but for that role he had no ambition. After two years of office, he resigned his dictatorship, to the surprise of all and the relief of many, and retired into private life.

Looking back over the troubled times of Marius and Sulla, we can see a marked development in the direction of one man exercising autocratic power in the state. The senatorial and popular parties continued their strife, but it was becoming more and more evident that the real power in Roman politics was not the political party or the political 'boss,' but the successful general with an army at his back. Rome was moving rapidly towards a monarchy or a military dictatorship.

Questions

1. What was the cause of the civil war between the factions of Marius and Sulla?
2. What contributions did each man make to the army and the government?
3. How did these supposed improvements subsequently cause more trouble to Rome?

Vocabulary

tenure
phalanx
cohort

Chapter XLIV

Pompey and Cicero

Among the lieutenants of Sulla was a young commander of great promise, who was looked upon as the most likely successor to the leadership of the senatorial party. This was Pompey, who had already been given the name of Magnus ('The Great') by Sulla and who was now sent as general to Spain to deal with a remnant of the Marian party which had established itself there. This was no easy task, for in Sertorius the Marians had an able leader and organizer, whose uprightness had won the confidence of the Spaniards. The fighting lasted several years, and only when Sertorius was assassinated by some of his own officers was Pompey able to gain the victory. During his absence, a serious outbreak had occurred in Italy. Thousands of slaves and gladiators had risen in revolt and formed an army which was strong enough to meet the forces of the state in the field. The revolt had finally been checked by Crassus, one of the wealthiest men in Rome, who was seeking further distinction in war and politics. After the defeat of the rebels in battle, Pompey, while returning from Spain, happened to fall in with the remnant of their army and annihilated it.

Thus Pompey was able to claim credit for having finished two wars. He returned to Rome flushed with victory, and his future success might well seem to be assured. But, in spite of his military skill and his great ambition, he lacked some of the qualities that make for success. In politics he was without definite aims and positive convictions, and was lacking in judgment and decision. He desired honor and deference, and when he failed to obtain these, which he thought his rightful due, he more than once showed his resentment by a change of policy and allegiance. On the other hand, he was honorable and upright to a degree not always found in the political leaders of that age.

When Pompey now demanded a triumph and a grant of land for his veterans, the senate refused, being jealous of the rapid rise to eminence of a possibly dangerous army leader. His answer was to break with the senate and ally himself with the popular party and with Crassus, the representative of the moneyed classes. Pompey and Crassus were elected to the consulship, and to reward the popular party for its support the political changes which Sulla had made were now largely annulled; in particular, the tribunes had their former powers restored. Pompey himself had no political program, and was content to wait for another opportunity of winning distinction in war.

Cicero Denouncing Catiline by Cesare Maccari, 1888, exhibited at the Palazzo Madama in Rome.

This was not long in coming. The Mediterranean had for some time been infested by pirates, who had now become so bold that even the shores of Italy were not safe, and Rome, always dependent on imported grain, was threatened with a shortage of food-supplies. The situation called for drastic measures, and a law was passed by the assembly giving to Pompey control of all the Mediterranean coasts and a large armament with which to put down the pirates. In facing a problem of this sort, Pompey could display great energy and organizing skill. His success was rapid and complete, the seas being cleared within three months of his appointment.

In the following year an even more important command in the East was given to him. Mithradates, having spent several years in repairing his losses and reorganizing his forces, had again invaded the adjacent districts of Asia Minor. The Roman general sent against him had met with considerable success and had forced him to take refuge in Armenia, but the army, disliking hard service in so wild and remote a country, had mutinied, and Mithradates was able to recover his kingdom of Pontus. In this serious situation a further law was passed giving Pompey the command in this war, together with the control, for an unspecified period, of all Asia Minor. The powers conferred upon Pompey by these two laws, passed in spite of the senate's opposition, were more extensive than had ever been exercised by any magistrate of the Roman republic, and it would not have been difficult for him to use them to make himself monarch. He did not do so, but the very possession of such power by one man was a fresh indication that Rome was drifting in the direction of a military monarchy.

During Pompey's absence in the East, events at Rome brought other leaders to the fore. Notable among these was Cicero, orator, writer, and statesman. Coming to Rome from a small Italian town, he had quickly made a name for himself by his remarkable gift of eloquence, which was exhibited first in the law-courts and afterwards in politics also. As a representative of the great Italian middle class, he hoped to be able to mediate between the extreme claims of the senatorial and popular factions and to bring about a union of all classes for the good of Rome and Italy. As a moderate conservative, he took as his ideal the Rome of former times, when all parties had worked harmoniously under the guidance of the senate and when the senate had been a body which commanded the respect and support of all citizens. Such an ideal would be difficult, perhaps impossible, to attain, but Cicero was prepared to devote himself to its realization. He hoped also to secure the cooperation of Pompey, who enjoyed the confidence of the populace and was also by birth and natural sympathies well fitted to lead the senatorial party.

For a time circumstances brought him a large measure of success. Catiline, a bankrupt and dissolute noble, offered himself as a candidate for the consulship, and enlisted the support of all the lawless element in the state, who hoped to profit by opportunities for plunder and by the cancellation of debts. He was opposed by Cicero, who was supported not only by the moderates but also by the senatorial party and the wealthy class. By their votes Cicero was elected. Catiline thereupon turned to violent measures and formed a plot to overthrow the government by force. The conspirators were denounced by Cicero, and again all the upholders of law and order rallied to his support. The conspiracy was soon suppressed and the leaders put to death or killed in battle. Cicero was now at the zenith of his career. He had put down what appeared to be a dangerous conspiracy and was acclaimed as the savior of his country. Above all he had brought about at least a temporary alliance of men of different parties. It remained to be seen whether this alliance could be held together when the danger was past.

Shortly after this Pompey returned from the East, where he had achieved a brilliant success. Mithradates had been overcome, a fabulous amount of treasure had been captured, Roman armies had penetrated to the Euphrates and the Caspian, and the eastern frontier had been established virtually where it was to remain for centuries. Pompey had brought to an end the kingdom of the Seleucids and had made Syria into a province, to which Judaea was annexed; the provinces of Asia Minor had been reorganized and new cities founded; and treaties had been made with the vassal kings on the borders of the provinces, who acknowledged the suzerainty of Rome. This settlement of the East was a notable piece of work and stood the test of time. All now depended upon the course which Pompey took. Would he use his army to make himself master of Rome, as the senate feared he would, or would he fall in with Cicero's plans and work in harmony with the senate?

He soon declared himself by disbanding his army as soon as he reached Italy. While he wished for power, he was not ready to achieve it by the unconstitutional use of force, as had Marius and Sulla. It was a mistake, however, to disband his army before he had secured the necessary legal ratification by the senate of the thorough reorganization he had effected in the East. And the senate, jealous and fearful and incredibly stupid, made the mistake of refusing its sanction and failing to assign lands to his veterans as he had promised. Pompey, feeling insulted and humiliated, then turned elsewhere for support and allied himself with Crassus and Julius Caesar, the rising leader of the popular party. This coalition was known as the First Triumvirate. Although it was entirely unofficial, its power was such that the three leaders now had complete control of the situation. Cicero's dream of a regenerated republic was fated never to be realized. The political situation was more than ever under the dominance of ambitious individuals, and it merely remained to be seen what use the three would make of their power.

Questions

1. List the successes and accomplishments of Pompey.
2. Why did Pompey disband his army before returning to Rome?
3. What were Cicero's hopes for Rome?
4. Why were his hopes not realized?

Vocabulary

suzerainty
dissolute
triumvirate

Chapter XLV

Greco-Roman Culture

The greatest contribution made by Cicero to his country and to civilization was not in the field of politics. It was Cicero who first showed that the Latin language could be the vehicle of noble thought, not unworthy of being ranked with Greek, and with a stately movement and a sonorous music all its own. Moreover, many of his writings were treasured by later ages and were among the chief influences that molded education and literary culture in western Europe.

The circle of educated men in Rome and Italy had been steadily widening since the first introduction of Greek in the days of the younger Scipio Africanus. Intercourse with Greece and Asia Minor, to say nothing of southern Italy (Magna Graecia) and Sicily, had made the Greek language familiar to thousands; and, with increasing acquaintance, even the hard, practical Roman began to feel the beauty and charm of Greek art and literature. This brought about a revolution in the education of the Roman and Italian youths of the upper classes. No longer were they content with the very elementary instruction, given mostly at home, which had sufficed for a simpler age, even though to this practical training had been added, of late, the reading of the first crude beginnings of a Latin literature. The knowledge of Greek opened up to them the vastly richer stores of Greek literature, and many a Roman youth conceived the ideal of becoming not merely a capable man of affairs but also an enlightened and cultured man, with a mind awake to a wider world of interests and better trained withal for practical life.

There were plenty of Greeks available to act as teachers. These were not always free Greek citizens; many were educated slaves attached to some rich family. Where wealth and ambition were present, this education was often supplemented by young men going for a time to visit Athens, Rhodes, and Asia Minor, where famous schools of philosophy and oratory were to be found, as well as the artistic treasures of Greek sculpture and architecture.

The chief subjects of this new education were literature, rhetoric or oratory, and philosophy. The Roman still retained his practical bent. The pursuits of war, politics, and law were regarded as the only ones befitting a Roman noble. As the Athenian youths flocked to the sophists' lectures (page 157), so a Roman youth studied the rules of rhetoric and practiced oratory, because this would

Cicero finding the tomb of Archimedes by Martin Knoller. 1775, private collection.

directly serve his ambition and tend to eminence in public life. But he did not study literature to become a poet or historian, or philosophy to make himself a philosopher; all that was aimed at was a general education that would train the mind and form the character for the life of a Roman citizen of the upper classes. Philosophy was valued because it afforded abundant practice in discussion and declamation, as well as presenting admirable ideals of conduct.

To these three main subjects were added arithmetic, geometry, astronomy, and music. These made up the 'seven liberal arts' which formed the staple of education all through the Middle Ages. The Roman took these additional subjects simply because they were usually taught in the Greek schools. But he had neither the Greek intellect nor the Greek taste, and a very little mathematics sufficed him and probably even less music. It is significant that of the seven subjects, literature and oratory are the only ones that acquired Latin names: the other five, always more superficially studied, retained always their Greek names. For the training of the body in the athletic exercises of the Greek gymnasium the Romans had rather a contempt, probably because they despised the Greeks of their day as they saw them on the battlefield.

Eminent Romans had begun to publish their speeches on state-affairs, partly as political pamphlets, but also as worth preserving for their literary value. In time speeches delivered in the law-courts were also published. These played an important part in the training for the bar and for political life; and a large part of Cicero's fame as a writer rested upon his published speeches and his various works on the art of speaking. His own magnificent style became the standard of prose Latin, and his writings were studied as models of diction and arrangement. He wrote also many philosophical works, in which he sought to give a worthy Latin expression to the views of the Greek philosophical schools which flourished in his day. The world for long centuries knew Greek philosophy mainly through Cicero's writings. His remaining great, contribution to Latin literature is a vast collection of letters written by him to his friends, or in some cases received from them. These give so intimate a picture of men and events in Rome during the last years of the republic that no period in history, until recent centuries, is so well known.

We are told that, as an orator, Julius Caesar was no mean rival of Cicero; but the writings he has left are historical—the story of the conquest of Gaul and an account of the civil war with Pompey. He, too, like Cicero, aimed at purifying the Latin style of archaic or vulgar or foreign words; and these two, Caesar and Cicero, have always been regarded as the highest authorities on what constitutes the purest and best Latin prose style.

This age contributed to literature two other writers of high merit—the poets Lucretius and Catullus. The latter wrote lyric poems and other 'occasional' verse, suggested often by Greek originals, but displaying a warmth of feeling and a keen delight in the beauty of nature that show he was no mere imitator. Lucretius wrote a long poem setting forth the Epicurean doctrine of the atomic system as the one salvation from superstitious fears and the dread of death. This unpromising theme he treats with a passion, a power of description, and a high poetic imagination that have made his work, in our opinion, the finest didactic poem, not merely in Latin, but in any language. Latin poetry had not yet reached its highest perfection, but these two poets had made an immense advance on anything hitherto attained.

Let us live, my Lesbia, let us love,
and all the words of the old, and so moral,
may they be worth less than nothing to us!
Suns may set, and suns may rise again:
but when our brief light has set,
night is one long everlasting sleep.
Give me a thousand kisses, a hundred more,
another thousand, and another hundred,
and, when we've counted up the many thousands,
confuse them so as not to know them all,
so that no enemy may cast an evil eye,
by knowing that there were so many kisses.
                    Catullus

Questions

1. What was the education of Roman boys like and how was it different in intention if not content then that of the Greeks?
2. What are the seven liberal arts?
3. How did the work of Cicero, Julius Caesar, and the poets contribute to the culture of Ancient Rome?

Vocabulary

declamation
ditactic
vulgar

Chapter XLVI

Julius Caesar

At the time when the followers of Marius were being hunted down by Sulla's party, Julius Caesar, the nephew of Marius, though of ancient patrician descent, was one of those whose lives were in danger. Sulla spared him, but made the significant remark, 'In that young man there are many Mariuses.' Caesar's career was then but beginning; before its end Sulla's estimate of his character had been abundantly justified.

Up to the time of the First Triumvirate, Caesar's work had not been so spectacular as that of Pompey, but he had been slowly and surely laying the foundations of his future greatness. While holding only comparatively minor offices and commands, he had worked with thoroughness and determination both at Rome and in the provinces. At the same time he had won the favor of the people and secured for himself the leadership of the popular party.

It was not until the organization of the triumvirate that he found scope for his genius; he soon overshadowed both Pompey and Crassus, in spite of the military fame of the former and the wealth of the latter. The plans of the triumvirs were simple. The combined influence of the three was to be used to secure for each what he chiefly desired. Pompey received land for his veterans, and his arrangements in the East were ratified. Crassus secured better terms for the wealthy tax-gatherers than the senate had been willing to grant. Caesar received the consulship for 59 BC and afterwards the command of the province of Gaul for a period of five years.

The territory thus entrusted to Caesar included the northern part of Italy with its Gallic population, and also the small province on the other side of the Alps, which had been organized in order to protect the coast road to Spain. The rest of the territory of Gaul was inhabited by warlike Celtic tribes, as yet quite independent. Of late the coming into Gaul of large numbers of Germans, under their king Ariovistus, had caused much uneasiness among the southern tribes, and now an impending westward movement of the Helvetians, a Celtic tribe living in what is now Switzerland, threatened the peace of the districts bordering on the province. Nothing could have happened more opportunely for Caesar, and he was far too clear-sighted a man not to perceive his opportunity. The events of the last few decades had shown that for success and mastery in Roman politics

Bust of Gaius Julius Caesar in the National Archaeological Museum of Naples. [Photo Andreas Wahra].

one must have a strong army at his back; and also that a prolonged governorship of a province where military operations were in progress was the surest way to acquire such an army.

Caesar threw himself into the tasks that awaited him with amazing energy and soon showed himself to be a military genius of the highest rank, a brilliant tactician, a skillful organizer, and a born leader of men. The story of his conquest of Gaul has been preserved in his 'Commentaries,' an unpretentious but masterly narrative which he found time to write while engaged in the work of campaigning. In this we can read how the invading Germans were driven back across the Rhine, how the various tribes were subdued one by one, how two expeditions were made to the distant island of Britain, and how finally a great concerted revolt of central Gaul was crushed. Caesar spent nearly ten years in Gaul, his original term having been extended for another five years. When he left, the whole country had been conquered and organized and its resources and man-power were henceforth an important element in Rome's empire. The addition of this great territory extended the boundaries of Roman civilization and removed all danger of invasion from that quarter, so that, as one Roman said, the Alps might now sink; they were no longer needed to protect Italy from the barbarians. As Pompey had fixed for centuries the eastern limits of the Roman world, so in the west Caesar fixed the frontier of Roman civilization at the Rhine.

At Rome, meanwhile, the old quarrels between the parties continued, and only too often led to outbreaks of disorder, there being no one competent to cope with the situation. The most important political event of the period was the conference of Luca, at which the triumvirs met and renewed their compact: Caesar's command in Gaul was to be prolonged for a second period of five years, while Pompey and Crassus were to receive similar appointments in Spain and Syria respectively, after holding the consulship for the following year (55 BC). Crassus went to his province when the time came and met his death not long afterwards while leading an ill-advised expedition against the warlike Parthians. Pompey ruled Spain by deputies and himself remained at Rome to watch the course of events.

The senatorial opposition to the triumvirs' disregard of constitutional forms and usages was becoming stronger, and the growth of Caesar's power was causing even greater alarm. But the relations between Caesar and Pompey continued friendly, whatever secret misgivings the latter may have had. The alliance between them had been cemented by the marriage of Caesar's daughter, Julia, to Pompey. She was dearly loved both by her father and by her husband, and her death at this juncture, closely followed by that of Crassus, severed some of the links which held the two together. Pompey, growing increasingly distrustful and jealous of Caesar, now turned to the senatorial party, to which, when it did not thwart his wishes, his sympathies naturally inclined him; and the senate gladly accepted him as their champion against the danger that threatened them from Caesar, who now had nine veteran legions (some 50,000 men) under his command, probably the most efficient army the Roman world had ever known.

When the time came for Caesar to give up the governorship of Gaul and, according to the agreement at Luca, to become consul for the following year, certain difficulties arose on constitutional points as to the procedure to be followed. Both the senate and Caesar sought to put the other technically in the wrong, though it was obvious that the real question was simply who was to be master of Rome. Finally, when Caesar offered to resign his military command if Pompey would simultaneously resign his, the senate passed a decree requiring Caesar to disband his legions, while allowing Pompey to retain his. This, and subsequent measures by the senate, determined Caesar to act. Leaving the main army to follow him, he set out with one legion, although he knew that to leave his province and enter Italy with an armed force was equivalent to declaring war. 'The die is cast,' he exclaimed, as he crossed the little stream of the Rubicon, which marked the boundary between Italy and Cisalpine Gaul.

The rapidity of his movements took Pompey and the senatorial party by surprise. Realizing that they could not immediately gather a sufficient force to meet Caesar, they hastily abandoned Italy and crossed with several legions to Greece. There they intended to gather an army from the Roman veterans settled in the East, where Pompey's influence was strongest, and with it to return to Italy and crush Caesar. Pompey also controlled Spain and had command of the sea.

Caesar first secured his position in Italy, and by his moderation and clemency won over many people who, remembering Marius and Sulla, had feared that his victory would be followed by confiscations and slaughter. His next problem was to secure the food-supply of Italy, and to effect this he dispatched one of his lieutenants to Sicily, while he himself set out for Spain. His plan was ultimately to follow Pompey eastward, but it would be highly dangerous to leave in his rear the strong Pompeian forces in Spain. Here he routed his opponents after a short and severe struggle, and then returned to Rome. Sicily also had been wrested from the Pompeians, and all the western part of the Roman dominions except Africa was now in Caesar's hands, so that ample supplies of food could be brought to Rome.

Caesar was now ready to deal with his rival's main force. Pompey, who had never known defeat, had been taking his time with his preparations; he felt certain of ultimate victory and failed wholly to reckon with the rapidity and effectiveness of Caesar's campaign. It was Caesar and not Pompey who now took the aggressive. He succeeded in conveying his army to Greece. Although it was only half as large as Pompey's, and although Pompey's skill in maneuvering and his command of the sea created grave difficulties for Caesar, when the armies met in battle at Pharsalus in Thessaly, Pompey's motley legions, many of them newly levied from the eastern provinces, were no match for the trained and devoted veterans from the virile new peoples of the West.

Pompey fled to Egypt, but, as he was landing, he was treacherously murdered. Caesar followed close after and found Egypt full of turmoil because of a dispute between the young Ptolemy and his sister Cleopatra regarding the succession to the throne. Caesar intervened on behalf of Cleopatra, and, after barely escaping with his life in a rising of Ptolemy's supporters, he reduced the country to order and then proceeded to Asia Minor. Here he crushed an attempt of Pharnaces, the son of Mithradates, to regain the kingdom of Pontus. It was to this success that the famous words refer: *Veni, vidi, vici* ('I came, I saw, I conquered'). After a short stay in Rome, he crossed over to Africa, where the remnant of the Pompeian leaders had gathered a formidable army and allied themselves with the native king of Numidia. This force was overwhelmingly defeated by Caesar, and Numidia became a Roman province. A few months later, he went to Spain, where Pompey's sons had been able to raise an army which Caesar had more difficulty in defeating than any other he had met.

This final victory of Munda put an end to all open attempts at resistance. Caesar was now made dictator and commander-in-chief for life, as well as consul for ten years. These and other offices and powers conferred upon him made him, if not in name yet in reality, absolute ruler. He had hitherto been able to spend but brief periods at Rome, between the various campaigns; now he was at last free to devote himself to the task of giving the Roman world an orderly and stable government.

The work of Caesar as a statesman is notable first because of his moderation. His victories were never followed by executions or promiscuous slaughter, such as had been only too common in the time of Marius and Sulla. Instead of this, the followers of his opponent were freely pardoned and allowed to retain their citizenship. There was no vindictiveness in Caesar's nature. When he celebrated his fourfold triumph in 46 BC over Gaul, Egypt, Pontus, and Numidia, no Roman prisoner marched behind his car, nor was any reference made to the purely civil war with Pompey and his followers. More than this, he showed himself to be a great organizer, a statesman with an instinct for order, who saw the needs of his time far more clearly than any of his contemporaries. He realized that the republican machinery of government, which had sufficed when Rome was but a small state, had broken down under the strain of controlling a great empire. The senate was not capable of checking either civil discord at home or misrule in the provinces, and the annually changing magistrates could not give the necessary stability and continuity. What was apparently needed was the control of some central and permanent authority. A firm and wise dictatorship seemed the only remedy for anarchy and misrule. Caesar did not abolish the republican magistrates and senate, but they played a quite subordinate part under his supervision. All officials, in Rome and in the provinces, were made responsible to Caesar, who demanded from them just and efficient administration. He gave the citizenship to the people of Gaul between the Alps and the Po, and enlarged the Roman senate by including members of other classes than the old exclusive nobility, and even some provincials from Gaul and Spain.

Caesar's system was far from democratic; its justification was that it promised to give the Roman world good government and prosperity after a century of violent disorder and civil dissension. A scheme of land settlement was introduced, trade and agriculture were fostered in various ways, and colonies were founded overseas. The colonies greatly lessened the number of idle citizens at Rome dependent on the 'dole' and also became centers of Roman civilization in distant lands. Many important public works were undertaken throughout Italy, and the city of Rome was adorned with new buildings. An imperial coinage was introduced, and the finances of the empire were for the first time reduced to something like a budget system. Among his many other achievements, Caesar carried out a reform of the calendar, by introducing the Julian system, which, with a slight modification, is in use today.[35]

---

[35] The fact that the solar year (of nearly 365 ¼ days) does not contain an exact number either of days or of lunar months caused much trouble in keeping the calendar accurate. Before Caesar's time the method adopted was to reckon twelve lunar months (of 29 1/2 days) to the year, and from time to time to insert an additional or thirteenth month to balance things. Through negligence, however, the official calendar was now two or three months ahead of the sun, so that the spring equinox came in June. Caesar introduced the custom of regulating the year by the sun, not by the moon, and gave to each year 365 days, with an additional day inserted every fourth year. He also shifted the official beginning

Assassination of Julius Caesar by Jean-Léon Gérôme - Walters Art Museum.

We do not know what permanent form Caesar intended to give to his government; whether he would in time have made himself king or emperor and founded a dynasty, or whether he would have devised some more democratic form of government. Before he had time to carry out his many plans of reform, his work was cut short. Within six months of his return to Rome from Spain, on the 'Ides of March,' he was assassinated by a group of misguided patriots who thought that they could restore the republic. The Roman republic, as administered during the last hundred years, did not deserve restoration. And yet the believer in democracy and free institutions can easily conceive how men who had lived under a republic and wielded influence in it would resent the change to Caesar's absolute authority. Caesar was generous in his clemency, but he took no pains to soothe the susceptibilities of those about him, who found themselves becoming puppets in his hands and who believed also that they saw indications that he thought of taking the hated title of 'king.' The assumption of the perpetual dictatorship was especially obnoxious; it was a glaring violation of all constitutional government; and it is noteworthy that none of Caesar's successors assumed the title. The foremost of the conspirators was Junius Brutus, a close friend of Caesar. He was a scholar and a theorist rather than a man of affairs, and yielded to the repeated appeals of baser men that he should prove himself a worthy descendant of that Brutus who had led in the expulsion of the Tarquins.

The death of Caesar removed a man who towered like a giant above his contemporaries. His genius was many-sided, for he had been a great general, an author of distinction, and an energetic and business-like administrator. More than this, he possessed the rare gifts of scientific insight and creative genius—the gifts which enable the true statesman to perceive what his country needs and to work out practicable and permanent reforms.

of the year to January from March, where previous custom had placed it. In his honor the month of his birthday, hitherto called *Quintilis*, was renamed *Julius* (July). Similarly, the next month, *Sextilis,* was later renamed after his successor, the emperor Augustus.

Questions

1. Why was a leader like Julius Caesar not only inevitable but needed?
2. Although he assumed control, how did this help Rome?
3. What admirable qualities did Caesar possess?
4. What does his treatment of the followers of Pompey show about him?

Vocabulary

unpretentious
clemency
formidable

Chapter XLVII

Octavian and Antony

The assassins of Caesar had hoped to restore the republic, but in the existing state of affairs the only alternatives were anarchy or the rule of some new military leader.

Of the aspirants to Caesar's power, the two most important were Mark Antony (Marcus Antonius), his colleague in the consulship and one of his most trusted officers, and Caius Octavius, his grand-nephew, whom he had adopted as his son and heir and who was therefore renamed Caesar Octavianus. The latter was but a youth of eighteen, and Antony was consequently inclined to treat him with contempt. Octavian, however, soon showed by his shrewdness and determination that he was worthy to be the heir of his great-uncle. Finally Antony was glad to join forces with him, and the two associated with them Lepidus, the governor of Gaul and Spain. The three thus formed the Second Triumvirate and had themselves appointed as a commission to administer the government and restore order.

The formation of this triumvirate was unhappily followed by the execution of a number of republican sympathizers, prominent among whom was Cicero. Since the First Triumvirate had been formed, he had had little influence in politics and had found that his eloquence and his political ideals carried little weight in an age of generals. After Caesar's death, however, he had emerged from his retirement to denounce Antony, whom he disliked and distrusted, in a series of bitter speeches which he called *Philippics.* Antony took his revenge by insisting that Cicero's name be included in the list of those who were doomed to death by the triumvirs.

One of the first tasks of the triumvirs was to dispose of a republican army which had been raised by Brutus and Cassius, two of the leaders in the conspiracy to kill Caesar. A battle was fought at Philippi in Macedonia and the triumvirs were victorious. Brutus and Cassius thereupon put an end to their lives.

Antony and Octavian then proceeded to divide the Roman world between them, Antony receiving the East, and Octavian Italy and the West. Lepidus, who had counted for little from the first, was given merely the province of Africa, and even this was later taken from him. Octavian devoted himself to the task of restoring order and establishing his government in the territory allotted to him.

Bust of Octavian, from Capitoline Museum, Rome. [Rosemania]

His hardest task was to destroy the power of Sextus Pompeius, who had a strong army in Spain and with his fleet had again seized Sicily and seriously interfered with the Roman food supply. This was finally accomplished by Octavian's great lieutenant, Agrippa. In marked contrast to Octavian's activity was the conduct of Antony, who proceeded to spend his time in extravagant and riotous living at the court of Cleopatra, queen of Egypt, of whom he had become enamored. The difference between the tastes of the two men was so great that lasting friendship between them was impossible. Finally, when it became apparent that Antony's infatuation and frivolity were weakening Rome's prestige in the East, Octavian and the senate determined to make war upon him. It was commonly believed that Antony intended to set up an independent monarchy of the oriental type with Cleopatra as his queen, and perhaps eventually to absorb the West and transfer the government from Rome to Alexandria. The rival fleets met at Actium on the west coast of Greece. Antony was defeated, fled to Egypt and, finding that further resistance was hopeless, took his own life. Cleopatra also killed herself to escape being taken to Rome to figure in Octavian's triumphal procession. Actium reunited the empire, which for nine years had been parted between two masters. That momentous battle saved the unity of Rome for five hundred years and secured the interval for the development of Roman law and government. Had Antony conquered, the ideas and government of the Greco-Roman world might have been submerged in a flood of Orientalism before they had sown their seed in the nations of modern Europe.

The Meeting of Antony and Cleopatra by Sir Lawrence Alma-Tadema.

Octavian was now the sole master of the Roman world. His victory brought to an end a century of civil war and may also be said to have marked the final stage in the development of one-man rule. The transition from the republic to the empire was not a sudden change, but a long and gradual process. The primary cause was not that ambitious men sought power for themselves, but that the Roman people had conquered the other nations of the Mediterranean, and that for so vast an empire a radical readjustment of the form of government was inevitable. The strife between the senate and the people, which had begun in the time of the Gracchi, had gradually developed into a series of contests between rival party-leaders. The dominant figure in politics came to be the successful general with an army of his own, seeking political power. Marius, Sulla, Pompey, and Caesar had all played a part in the development of personal rule, while the career of Cicero had shown the powerlessness of a civilian statesman. It now remained for Octavian to reap where his predecessors had sown and to prove whether the undisputed rule of one strong man was the solution of the problems which had troubled the world so long.

Questions

1. Who were the members of the second triumvirate?
2. What did they do after taking power?
3. How did Octavian become the sole master of Rome?
4. What is the reason given for the gradual change from republic to empire?

Vocabulary

riotous
infatuation
oriental

Chapter XLVIII

Augustus and the Principate

The assassination of Julius Caesar has been called 'the greatest blunder in history.' At last a man had appeared who was strong enough to enforce peace upon a world long vexed by civil wars, and who also had the will and the ability to effect such reforms as would bring order out of chaos. His death, it may be urged, meant simply thirteen years more of devastating civil war, and in the end the substitution of an inexperienced youth for the ablest Roman that ever lived.

And yet there is much to be said on the other side of this question. Octavian succeeded where Julius had failed; he was able to secure the loyal cooperation of the most eminent men in public life, where Julius had excited jealousy and hostility; and he organized an empire that endured for centuries and that brought to the Mediterranean world a peace and a prosperity that large portions of it have scarcely known since that empire passed away. When the arguments are summed up *pro* and *con*, it is not so certain that the world did not gain by having the politic Octavian rather than the masterful Julius superintend its rebuilding.

He had, to be sure, two things in his favor: in 31 BC the Roman world was even more weary of war and more ready to welcome peace than it had been in 45 BC; and few, if any, were now left of the strong men of republican Rome whose criticism or whose opposition he had to fear. But the chief reason for the marvelous and enduring success of the work done by Octavian must be found in his wise tactfulness, his cautious sagacity, and his patient self-restraint. Julius was the more brilliant genius, but Octavian proved the better statesman.

The main features of the organization he effected may be treated under four heads: his own position in the state; the provinces; internal reform; and the frontiers of the empire.

1. He sought to co-operate with the senate, and to avoid offending republican sentiment as Julius had done. After the victory at Actium, having settled the eastern provinces, he returned to Rome, undisputed master of the Roman world. But instead of assuming any title that would suggest an absolute ruler, he resigned his offices and gave back to the senate and the Roman people their ancient authority, including the right of appointing the old republican magistrates and of passing legislation. His own words are, 'I transferred the republic from my own authority to the control of the Roman

Fountain of Juturna in the Roman Forum.

senate and people.' The grateful senate conferred on him the title of Augustus (about equivalent to *His Majesty*), and by this Octavian has ever since been known. This abdication of power was, however, more seeming than real. The interests of peace required that the army should be under one man's control, lest civil war should break out again; and Augustus therefore retained his title of commander-in-chief *(imperator)* of the armies in the provinces. But the master of the Roman legions was the real master of the Roman state, and the title Imperator now began to acquire a new meaning (Emperor). Technically at Rome Augustus might be merely the *Princeps*— the first citizen; but his wishes were scrupulously consulted, and he exercised more real authority by this shrewd pretence of a return to the old republican constitution than if he had had himself openly proclaimed dictator or king.

2. The government of the provinces was put upon a new basis. The more peaceful provinces were still left to the senate to administer, but there was henceforth much less mismanagement and rapacity, thanks to the restraining influence of Augustus. It was the more distant provinces that had suffered most from the old system of misgovernment, and these Augustus arranged should be placed under his own control, on the ground that they still required military garrisons for the protection of the frontiers or the suppression of rebellion. These provinces Augustus governed through his own nominees, responsible directly and solely to him. In this way a permanent body of officials was built up, a sort of civil service, and able men were led to enter upon such work as a career, where

Virgil Reading the Aeneid to Augustus and Octavia by Jean-Joseph Taillasson, 1787, The National Gallery

efficiency and zeal would be rewarded by promotion. An end was promptly put to the former practice by which a rapidly changing succession of senatorial governors with their attendant tax-gatherers, usurers, and greedy hangers-on had exploited the provinces. The financial and judicial administration was now under the direct supervision of Augustus through his deputies and administrators, and efficiency, justice, and stability marked their work. The result of these sound business methods was not merely a rapid increase in the wealth and prosperity of the provinces, but also a settled contentment with their dependent position in the empire, especially as the provincials were left considerable freedom in the management of their local affairs. Augustus' whole system of government was so well conceived and so firmly established that it survived unchanged for 300 years, and remained scarcely shaken even when the imperial throne was occupied by weak or vicious rulers.

3. Having thus laid the foundations of the Roman empire, Augustus turned his attention to affairs in Italy. Agriculture had suffered from the long civil wars and the economic evils of the past. Augustus sought to restore it to its old dignity and importance and to recolonize the depopulated areas. He saw with alarm the laxity of morals, the disregard for family and marriage ties, and the lessening of the birth-rate. By various legislative measures he strove, with less success than in most things, to discourage celibacy, to restore the moral tone of the people, to renew their faith in the old religion, and to revive the old virtues that had made Rome great. He improved the great system of roads that ran throughout Italy and linked it with the remotest provinces, and he established an effective postal organization along these roads. In Rome itself he made great improvements in the supply of water and of grain, in the policing of the city and its protection from riots and from fire; he restored the temples of the gods and added many new and splendid public buildings to the city; so that his boast was fully justified that he had found it of brick and had left it of marble.

In these and many other schemes of reform, Augustus had the good fortune in the first place to live long enough to ensure the carrying out of his projects (he held power for 45 years after Actium); and in the second place to have for his chief advisers and ministers such men as Agrippa, eminent equally as general and as engineer, and Maecenas, the diplomatist and patron of literature. It was through Maecenas that the cordial support of Rome's two greatest poets, Virgil and Horace, was enlisted for the policy of Augustus. Their writings emphasize the same ideals of life that Augustus sought to realize in Italy and contain many eulogies, quite evidently sincere, of the man who had given to the world orderly peace and settled government.

4. The consolidation of the empire and the maintenance of peace within its borders depended upon the stability of its frontiers. Throughout republican times Rome had been continuously extending her borders and misgoverning the new provinces that were added; under Augustus the policy of extension ceased, and his efforts were directed to securing efficient government for the Roman world. We find now the beginning of the idea that there were natural boundaries for a Mediterranean empire, beyond which no attempt to advance should be made. Roughly, these were the Rhine and the Danube on the north, and the Euphrates on the east; on the west and south natural limits were set by the Atlantic Ocean and the African desert. Henceforth consolidation rather than conquest was to be the policy of Rome. A strong permanent force guarded the frontiers behind which men could carry on the activities of peace in complete security. It was to Augustus chiefly that the new policy was due. He had himself little taste for military affairs, and rightly judged that men desired peace above all things.

Only at one point was an attempt made in his reign to extend the frontiers. On the north the Elbe offered an alternative boundary instead of the Rhine. This would include a considerable portion of German territory within the empire, and would keep at a further distance the danger of incursions from the barbarian tribes that for hundreds of years came ceaselessly swarming down from northern Europe. Several expeditions were made and some success had been achieved when at last the Roman general Varus met with a disastrous defeat. Under the leadership of Arminius (Hermann), the Germans succeeded in decoying Varus with three legions into the heart of one of their forests and there destroyed his whole force. Augustus, heart-broken at so unparalleled a disaster, abandoned any further attempts at conquest, and the Rhine was henceforth for centuries the boundary of the empire and of civilization.

Two results of this defeat of Varus deserve to be noticed. Had western Germany been incorporated in the empire, it would doubtless have become as settled and as civilized a country as Gaul or Spain, and it is scarcely conceivable that the invasion of Britain by the Angles and Saxons in the fifth century would have taken place or that the English nation would ever have existed. Again, the fact that Germany was never part of the Roman empire and developed an alien civilization to that which the rest of western Europe received, has deeply affected the whole history of Europe. The differences in tradition, customs, and outlook between Germany and her western neighbors are in large measure due ultimately to this fact. It was not by accident nor without historical significance that, in World War I, Germany was confronted by France, Belgium, Britain, and Italy, the descendants and heirs of that Roman empire to which Germany never belonged.

When Augustus died at the age of seventy-seven, he had outlived all the trusted advisers of his early years with the exception of his devoted wife, Livia. It was in her arms that he died, and his last words were, 'Livia, never forget our married life.' He had a few moments before asked those present whether he had not played the farce of life well. Possibly he had in mind that all life is a stage on which each man plays his part; more probably he was referring to the way in which, under the guise of the first *citizen* in a republic, he had really been an absolute monarch. The 'Principate,' as his government was called, was undoubtedly a compromise and a temporary expedient; but it is doubtful if any other course would have succeeded half so well, and few systems of government in the world's history have endured and been effective on so great a scale for so many centuries.

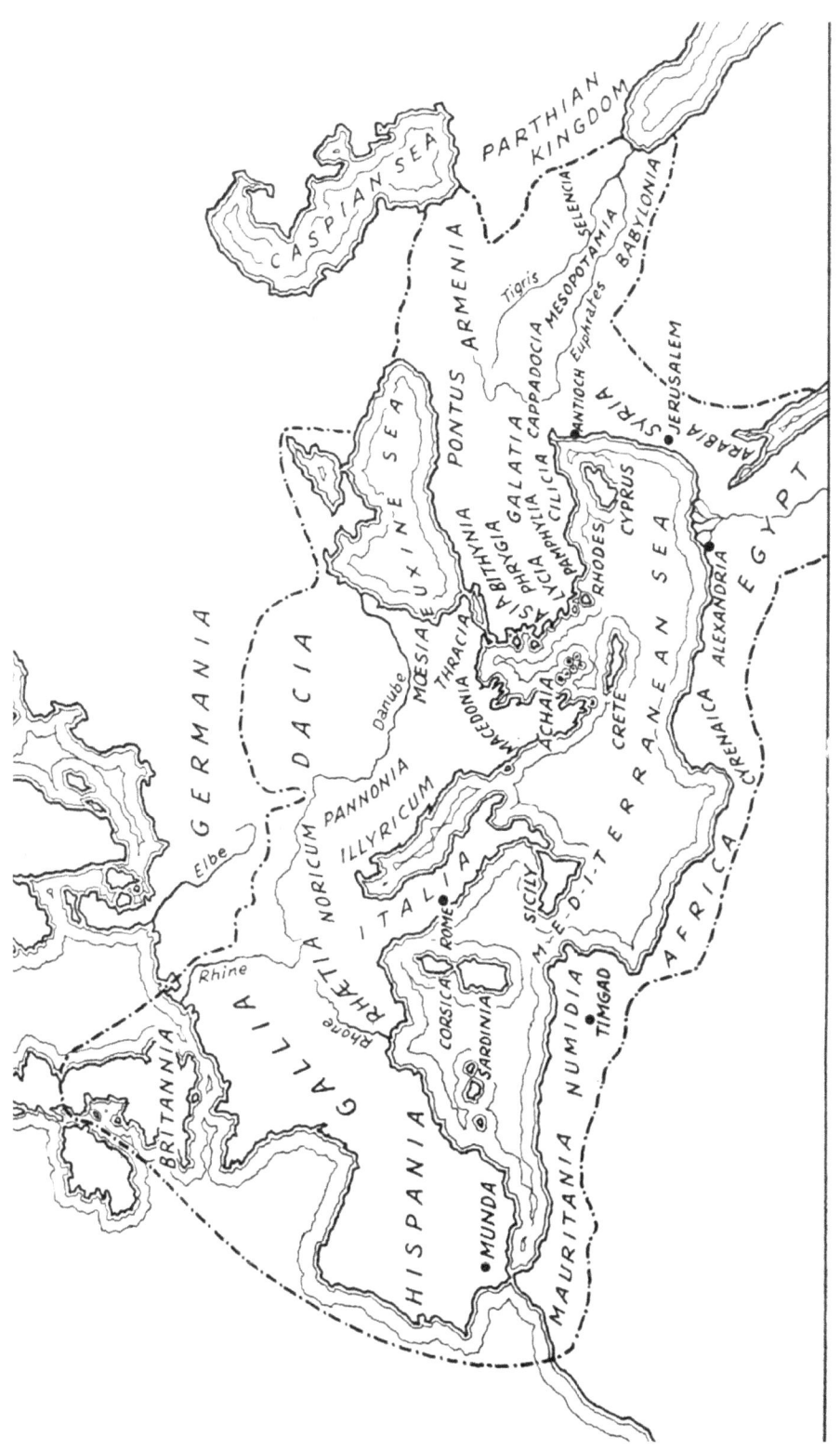

Map XI. — Roman Empire at its greatest extent.

Questions

1. How did Octavian endear himself to the Senate and win their cooperation?
2. Name and describe the four main features of the organization he effected. Which of these do you consider to be the most important to the stability of the empire?
3. What were considered to be the boundaries of the empire at that time?
4. What were the results of the defeat of Varus on the northern frontier?

Vocabulary

principate
scrupulously
rapacity

Chapter XLIX

The Successors of Augustus

1. The Julio-Claudian Emperors

Augustus had no son, and his two grandsons, Gaius and Lucius, the children of his only daughter, Julia, had died in early manhood. For the last ten years of his life his stepson Tiberius, the son of Livia by her first husband, Claudius Nero, had been designated by Augustus as his heir, and at the age of 56, Tiberius was proclaimed by the senate the successor of Augustus. Tiberius was a careful and successful administrator, but his aloofness and moroseness made him unpopular with the people. Thus it was not difficult for enemies to blacken his reputation, so that, until historians within recent years have cleared his memory, he has been regarded as a tyrant and a moral degenerate. He was followed by Caligula, a great-grandson of Augustus, an insane monster, whose travesty of a reign was fortunately brief.

Claudius, the next emperor, was a nephew of Tiberius. He was a timid, undignified, pedantic man, in many ways not unlike James I of England, and little was expected of him. Nevertheless he exhibited some ability and taste for governing, and had he been a man of stronger will or had better advisers, he might have accomplished much. Two events of this reign are of more than passing interest. Claudius revived Julius Caesar's idea of invading Britain, and succeeded in adding the southern part of the island as a new province to the Roman empire. Claudius, furthermore, was broad-minded enough to advocate the extension of the privileges of Roman citizenship beyond the Italian peninsula. Augustus had been content with working for the unification of Italy, which he always believed should be predominant over all the other parts of the empire. The speech of Claudius advocating the admission of eminent Gauls to the Roman senate itself contains these words: 'What else brought ruin to Sparta and Athens, in spite of all their military prowess, but this, that they spurned as aliens those whom they conquered? But our founder Romulus showed his wisdom when he treated as fellow-citizens those whom that same day he had fought as enemies.'

Nero, the last of this line of emperors, was the nephew of Caligula, and had been a youth of great promise. He had a sincere liking for art and literature, and under the guidance of good advisers his reign had a happy beginning. But after a time the evil side of his nature prevailed, and the last years of his reign were filled with a series of wild extravagances and odious crimes. He met his death by suicide to escape assassination, and his name has become a byword for tyranny. To this his persecution of the Christians contributed greatly. A disastrous fire had destroyed a large part of the city, and Nero's character was such that the rumor that he had ordered the fire was generally believed. To get rid of the report and to divert the anger of the people, he incited them against the Christians, alleging that the guilt was theirs, and he himself caused the most hideous tortures to be inflicted upon them.

The Arch of Titus.

2. The Flavian Emperors

After a brief period of confusion and civil war, caused by the disputes of rival generals for the succession, the imperial power passed into the hands of Vespasian and his two sons, Titus and Domitian, who succeeded him. Vespasian was a rough and untutored soldier, of Sabine descent, who gave the empire wise and vigorous government. At the time of his election as emperor he was prosecuting a campaign in Palestine against the Jews. These alone of the peoples included in the empire continued to resent the rule of Rome, and at last they broke out into open rebellion. Titus was left by his father to carry on the war, and Jerusalem was finally captured after a five months' siege marked by the most desperate fighting. The spoils of the temple were carried off to Rome and the temple itself was burned, never to be rebuilt.

Interior of a Roman house.

Then followed the all too brief reign of Titus, whose saying has come down to us that a day passed without doing some good deed is a day lost. The most memorable event of his reign was an eruption of Vesuvius, which buried the cities of Pompeii and Herculaneum under a rain of ashes and volcanic mud. This, while destroying much, also preserved a great part of the buildings and their contents for the time when the modern excavator should bring them to light, and thus enable men to form a vivid and accurate conception of the life of an Italian town in the first century AD.

His brother Domitian proved a very different ruler, and when his tyrannical reign was ended the world breathed with relief. Roman senators and eminent nobles as well as humble Christians had been victims of his jealous and cruel persecution. One bright spot in this reign was the administration of Britain by the Roman general Agricola, who not only extended the province far beyond the Scottish boundary, but by his good government reconciled the Britons to accepting Roman civilization.

3. *The Antonine Emperors*

The period that now followed was one of the most notable, most happy, and most prosperous in the whole history of the Mediterranean world. This was due in no small measure to the rulers themselves, who are known as the 'five good emperors.' It is worthy of note that four of the five belonged to families of Roman descent but resident in the provinces of Spain and Gaul—an indication of the growing unity of the empire. Nerva, the first of these rulers, was a kindly, aged senator, of whose reign a Roman writer, who had lived under Domitian, has well said that 'he blended things once

The Ruins of Pompeii, view from the Forum looking towards the Temple of Jupiter showing Mount Vesuvius. [Kim Traynor]

The Interior of a House in Pompeii at the Brooklyn Museum Archives, Goodyear Archival Collection. [Photo William Henry Goodyear]

irreconcilable, sovereignty and freedom.'

Nerva was followed by the Spaniard Trajan, the most aggressive and successful soldier who had held the imperial position. In order to make the northern frontiers more secure, he undertook to subdue the turbulent regions beyond the Danube. After several years' warfare his campaign against the Dacians was successful, and a new province was added to the empire. Dacia corresponds nearly to the present kingdom of Romania, a name which itself indicates that the country was once under the influence of Roman culture. The Romanian language, too, is akin to those other modern tongues, such as French and Spanish, which are derived from Latin and are therefore termed the Romance languages. Trajan also sought to extend the eastern frontier far beyond the upper Euphrates, but his conquest of Parthia was far from complete when he died while on this eastern campaign.

His more cautious successor, Hadrian, found it advisable to abandon these eastern conquests and to withdraw across the Euphrates again. Hadrian was a statesman rather than a general, and a great builder rather than a great soldier. He devoted himself to the work of directing and perfecting the government of the provinces, and gave particular attention to the legal system of the empire and the administration of justice. He was an untiring worker, and travelled immense distances, spending in fact the greater part of his long reign in journeys through Britain, Syria, and Spain, as well as the nearer provinces. In these journeys he gained first-hand acquaintance with every part of the empire and left innumerable memorials of his zeal for building.

Under Antoninus Pius, the Roman world continued to enjoy peace and prosperity. His reign was singularly uneventful, and this in itself indicates that the people of the Roman world were satisfied with the beneficent and efficient government which they received in this century.

Marcus Aurelius, the last of the five good emperors, was one of the most remarkable rulers of all time. A scholar, a philosopher, and almost a saint, he was the author of some of the noblest writings that have come down to us from the ancient world. Without doubt he would have preferred to devote himself to reflection and study, but his sense of duty impelled him to give his whole-hearted attention to the work of governing. He proved himself a wise administrator, and, when compelled to take the field to defend the empire from invasion threatened by the German tribes beyond the Alps and the upper Danube, he showed himself also a capable general.

Hadrian's wall at Milecastle 39. [Photograph by Adam Cuerden]

Questions

1. Describe the Julio-Claudian Emperors and their accomplishments or notoriety.
2. Describe the Flavian Emperors and their accomplishments or notoriety.
3. Describe the Antonine Emperors (the five good emperors) and their accomplishments or notoriety.

Vocabulary

morose
pedantic
odious

Chapter L

Arts and Letters Under the Empire

The settled conditions of the times were favorable to the production of works of literature and art, and in both spheres a well-marked imperial style was developed. The architecture of the empire reveals both the practical bent of the Roman and his love of grandeur and magnificence. The structures built were mainly for the public service or for the glorification of the state. Such were the imperial palaces, the basilicas for the conduct of public business, the memorial columns and triumphal arches to commemorate great events, the amphitheaters and circuses built for public spectacles, and the vast public baths which served also as community halls and public libraries. The development of the arch, with the closely related vault and dome, is one of the outstanding achievements of this period. The Romans did not discover the principle of the arch, which, though unused by the Greeks, was known already to Asia and Etruria; but it was left for the Romans to reveal its possibilities. The erection of these secular buildings on a colossal scale was made possible by the discovery that the volcanic earth which abounded near Rome and Naples would make cement and concrete of wonderful strength. Many of the most impressive buildings were built of concrete, faced with brick or marble, or, like the vast dome of the Pantheon, lined with bronze.

The Roman of the empire loved elaborate and florid ornamentation, and the exteriors of his buildings displayed little of the severe simplicity which Greek taste preferred. The Roman was, in fact, more engineer than artist, and massive solidity rather than graceful symmetry marked his productions. Some of his most characteristic work was the building of permanent roads, aqueducts, and bridges, many of which have lasted to this day and are still in use.

In the adornment of the exterior of buildings the Romans made great use of rows of columns surmounted by arches. These were often arranged in tiers one above another, with different orders (Doric, Ionic, and Corinthian) in the successive stories. They also found new uses for groups of figures carved in relief. These were often placed as panels on triumphal arches, or were arranged in a long spiral on memorial columns. The scenes are treated more realistically than the Greek reliefs in the frieze of the Parthenon, and are apt to be crowded with detail. Other features of imperial art are the mosaic floors which are found in all parts of the empire, and the frescoes painted on the walls

The Colosseum, Rome.

of private dwellings, of which those found at Pompeii are examples, though of an inferior, popular variety.

An enormous quantity of richly colored foreign marble was brought to Rome from quarries in various countries, to be used both for lining the walls built of concrete, and for the innumerable columns with which their buildings were adorned. This is the source of the magnificent marble columns and marble-lined walls of so many of the great churches in modern Rome.

One of the most notable branches of Roman art is the portrait-bust. Doubtless, as with most Roman art, the execution was by Greeks, but the taste for realistic portraiture, instead of the Greek idealized types, was thoroughly Roman. Great numbers of these busts exist, giving apparently most faithful and lifelike representations of both men and women, from late republican times on. Unfortunately in most cases the identity of the person represented is quite uncertain.

The age of Augustus and the preceding age of Cicero together constitute the so-called Golden Age of Latin literature. As the earlier period saw the greatest writers of Latin prose, so the later produced, in Virgil and Horace, the greatest of all Latin poets. It was an age of hope, when the world seemed to be born again to new life and vigor, now that the long agony of the civil wars was past; and in both poets one hears repeatedly the note of gratitude to the great prince who had restored peace and order to the world, and under whom Rome might now hope to fulfill her high destiny. Both poets, but more especially Virgil, succeeded in bringing out of the sonorous Latin tongue all the music of which it is capable, and half of the haunting charm of their lines is due to the subtle appeal of their cadences and sound-effects to the ear.

Virgil's most important poem, the *Aeneid,* is an epic recounting the story of the coming of Aeneas from captured Troy to Italy, where, after long wanderings, he at last found a new home, from which, in the course of time, Rome was destined to arise. Not merely did the old legends make Romulus a descendant of Aeneas, but the Julian family also, to which the Caesars belonged, traced

The Meeting of Dido and Aeneas by Sir Nathaniel Dance-Holland. [Photo: Tate, London, 2011]

their lineage back to him. The *Aeneid* is a great national epic; while telling of the divinely guided origin of the Roman state, it also suggests throughout that its present greatness, culminating in the reign of peace under Augustus, had been from the first the cherished purpose of high heaven, which had destined Rome to endless dominion. Few poems have been so widely and so continuously read as this. The Romans not only welcomed its patriotic note, but also recognized at once its literary merits. Every young Roman read and studied it, and ever since it has been an important factor in the culture of the western world.

If the *Aeneid* may be called 'the glorification of Rome,' Virgil's other writings, the *Eclogues* and the *Georgics,* may be called 'the glorification of country life.' Their origin is due in part to Virgil's own love of the country and his sense of the dignity of farm-labor, and in part to his desire to further Augustus' policy of bringing about a revival of agriculture.

The poems of Horace include his lyric Odes and his more didactic and familiar *Epistles* and '*Conversations,*' as he called them. In all these he reveals himself a genial man of the world, full of shrewd but kindly criticism, tolerant, yet never flippant or cynical in his attitude to life. Many of his personal odes dwell on the value and charm of friendship, others on the need for prudent moderation ('the golden mean') in all things. Many also are patriotic odes, combining eulogy of the worthies of Roman history and recognition of the great achievement of Augustus with a call to his countrymen to turn from the civic hatreds and private vices which had brought ruin in the past.

With less passion and fervor than Catullus, he far surpasses him in the finished perfection of his style and in his mastery of melodious verse. In these, as in his subsequent fame, he is Virgil's only rival among the Latin poets.

Of the other Augustan poets, Ovid is the most notable. He had a much less finished style and less of true inspiration than Virgil or Horace, but he had the gift of telling a story with consummate skill in an easy, fluent style. A long series of poems in which he retold many of the Greek myths was immensely popular in later centuries. The only important prose-writer of this age is the historian Livy, who undertook to write a detailed history of Rome from its foundation. The thirty-five books which remain are but a quarter of the whole work; they include the story of Rome under the kings and the early republic and of the war with Hannibal. The old legends come to life again under the touch of Livy's eloquence, and it is due to him more than to all other writers that we can appreciate the pride which the Romans felt in the stirring and glorious records of their past. If he was careless of verifying his statements by consulting documentary evidence, so that his history has scarcely more authority than an historical novel, most readers willingly forget this in the enjoyment of his vivid and dramatic stories.

It is worthy of note, as illustrating the degree to which Italy had attained cultural unity, that none of these four writers was Roman-born. All were of Italian middle-class parentage, Virgil and Livy coming (like Catullus) from Cisalpine Gaul, Ovid (like Cicero) from central Italy, and Horace from the extreme south.

Tacitus

The post-Augustan period was on the whole one of deterioration in literature. Writers were numerous, and many of them wrote profusely, without producing much of real value. The term 'Silver Age' applied to this period marks its inferiority. Without genuine inspiration, writers tended to make up for the lack of noble thought by cultivating affected or pedantic forms of expression and by a parade of cleverness and learning. It was an age of rhetoric, of over-ornamentation, of striving after effect, of exaggeration and bad taste. Only when the death of

Domitian and the accession of Nerva and Trajan brought again to the Roman world the sense of a new era dawning, do we have any literature produced that has high merit and permanent value.

Of all the writers of the Silver Age three stand out conspicuously, all flourishing in the early years of the second century. Tacitus, who is in many ways the ablest historian that Rome produced, wrote the history of the emperors from the death of Augustus to that of Domitian. Juvenal, the greatest satirist of the ancient world, in his bitter attacks upon the vices and follies of Rome, painted a picture much too black to be wholly true to life. Pliny, a kindly, high-minded, cultivated gentleman, eminent in public life as well as in literature, published a series of letters which give a much more favorable view of the Roman world. Doubtless good and evil were commingled. Juvenal and Tacitus fix our attention chiefly on the evil side of political and social life; the life revealed by Pliny's letters shows that much that was wholly admirable co-existed with moral degeneration.

Under the empire the Roman youth continued to be educated according to the tradition inherited from the last century of the republic. Their chief studies were still literature and rhetoric, and the object proposed was to make them efficient in public oratory. But with the loss of political freedom there was little room for real oratory or debate on questions of public moment. Instead of vigorous discussion of live political issues, we find a showy and artificial type of declamation growing up. The subjects chosen were commonplace themes or fictitious problems suggested by literature or history; and instead of seeking to develop a style of argument that would carry conviction in a public assembly or a court of law, the speaker's aim was to win applause from his invited audience of friends by his ingenuity in coining smart, striking phrases whose chief merit was their glitter and their novelty.

Another modification was the decreased importance of Greek in education. In part this was due to the growth of Latin literature. Having Cicero, Virgil, and Horace, the teacher no longer needed to go to the Greeks for models of style or for interesting subject-matter. A second reason for the disuse of Greek was the extension of the empire over the western provinces. This greatly increased the number of those who sought a liberal education, but who had no contact with Greek civilization and found in the language and literature of the Romans all the elements necessary for their culture. Thus, while the 'liberal arts' inherited from Greek theory and practice still provided the main subjects of education in the schools of the empire, yet the Latin language was now the medium of instruction and the works of Latin poets and orators were the text-books employed.

More and more under the empire the custom spread of education being supported by the state or by municipal grants or by endowments given by private benefactors. Government support soon brought government control, and Roman education, which began by being wholly a matter for the individual father of a family, ended in both schools and teachers being under the absolute authority of the state.

Questions

1. What were the differences between Greek and Roman architecture?
2. What is the importance of the *Aeneid* to Roman culture?
3. Who were the three most important writers of the 'Silver Age' and why was each one important?

Vocabulary

sonorous
eulogy
consummate

Chapter LI

Life in the Roman World

The Mediterranean world had now for two centuries enjoyed an unbroken peace and security such as it had never known before and has never known since. The whole empire was benefited by the settled conditions and orderly government brought by the *pax Romana* (the Roman peace). Now that producers were free from the disastrous interruptions of wars and political upheavals, agriculture and industry flourished everywhere. New lands were cultivated, new mines opened, new wares manufactured, exports sent into regions formerly closed or unknown. It was a time of great economic expansion; there was an immense increase in production, and the agricultural and industrial products of the various lands were carried to the ends of the Roman world.

The provinces, to be sure, paid a considerable tribute to Rome, but their taxes were reasonable and equitable; and probably less was exacted than under the former system of many independent states, often at war, and seldom justly or wisely governed. Moreover, a large part of the taxes collected from the provincials was spent on local government, and also on the improvement of local conditions, by building permanent roads and bridges and aqueducts, for instance. There remained, however, a large amount of tribute which annually went to Rome to be expended by the imperial government. Thus Italy was enriched not only by sharing in the universal prosperity, but also by the expenditure of all this tribute received from the provinces, by being the distributing center for the world's commerce, and by being itself free from the land-taxes required from the rest of the empire.

1. Italy and Rome

As a result Italy seemed to be enjoying the greatest prosperity. In Rome itself emperor vied with emperor in erecting stately palaces, temples, and places for amusement or public business. Practically all the magnificent structures which, even in their ruins, amaze the visitor in Rome today were built during the first two centuries of the empire. The other cities of Italy reflected in their various degrees the prosperity and magnificence of the capital; while from end to end of the peninsula were to be seen the country estates and luxurious villas of the wealthy. These were especially numerous

Ruined tombs on the Appian Way. [Photo credit: Anderson]

in the hill country near Rome, round the shores of the Italian lakes, and along the seashore in the neighborhood of the Bay of Naples.

There were well-established trade-routes during the summer-sailing season from the Black Sea, Spain, Northern Africa, and Alexandria, and the bulkier imports to Italy, such as grain, wool, and hides, were brought by sea. But there was also an immense traffic carried by land over the well-kept Roman roads, the arteries, as it were, of the empire's life. There were no railways then, of course, but travel was at least as safe and as rapid as it was in England or America a century ago. Today on our great highways one hour's traffic is very like another's; a swiftly passing procession of people and vehicles all looking much alike and seldom disclosing anything novel or arresting. But the Roman roads, especially near the great cities, must have presented an aspect of amazing variety and interest. With people of all countries and all ranks and callings, with a bewildering variety of costume, travelling singly or attended by trains of slaves, with pack-animals laden with every kind of local produce or foreign ware or with conveniences for the travellers' comfort; companies of acrobats or gladiators; troops of cavalry or marching legionaries; officials and members of the court with their glittering equipages; nobles and their ladies, some in litters, others in luxurious carriages, taking an outing or setting out for the country villa or for foreign travel; with all this variety and show the Roman roads must have been as absorbing a spectacle as the streets of an Oriental capital today. No wonder that the Roman who, with little belief in immortality, yet felt the natural craving of the human heart for remembrance after death and looked with horror on a lonely and forgotten grave. So he built the monuments for his dead beside the great roads leading out from the city-gates, where many an inscription has been found begging the passing stranger to pause for a moment to read and think of the departed and then with his blessing to resume his journey.

But there was in Italy and Rome a reverse side to all this show of magnificence and prosperity. The influx of wealth and the increased luxury and ease of living were fatal to the old Roman virtues

A Mosaic Pavement. [British Museum, London]

of simplicity, hardiness, frugality, and self-restraint. The craving for amusement and sensation, the love of luxurious ease and self-indulgence made all discipline and moderation distasteful. There is much color in history for the belief that the increase of worldly wealth and material comfort which, at the time, is hailed as progress, is apt to be found, later on, to have corrupted the character and sapped the morale of a people.

Wealth too, then as now, was very unequally distributed. There were millionaires and a pauper proletariate, with the evils and problems such a state of affairs always entails, mitigated only by the mild climate of Italy which makes life for the impoverished easier there than in a northern country. On the hills of Rome were the spacious palaces of the wealthy, sumptuously furnished with imported luxuries; while below in the narrow streets of the crowded valleys were the teeming tenements of the poor, noisy, bare, dilapidated, and veritable death-traps in case of fire. So too throughout the country were to be found in close proximity the senator's lordly villa and the cottager's wretched hovel.

All large cities seem to contain thousands of worthless idlers and shiftless poor, attracted by the gregarious and changing life of the city-streets and the chances of amusement and excitement. Of this sort ancient Rome had far more than its share. It had long been the policy of the authorities to keep the city rabble quiet by providing them with free food and free amusements. The dole of free food was regularly distributed in Rome to more than 200,000 'citizens.' Not all of these were mere idlers; some were but temporarily out of employment, and others were workers whose meager earnings barely sufficed to keep them alive. But it is easy to see how a custom like this would draw to Rome thousands of undesirables, and, being perpetuated generation after generation, would breed a populace devoid of the self-respect that honest labor, however humble, will give and incapable of any good.

Finally, to complete this darker side of the picture, the amusements so freely provided at Rome were such as tended to degrade and brutalize the spectators. Unlike the Greek, the Roman cared little for athletic exercises or the theatre, but never grew tired of the exciting spectacles of the circus and the Amphitheatre. The Circus Maximus was an oblong racecourse with many tiers of seats holding 300,000 persons, and in it the favorite spectacle was the chariot-race. In the Colosseum, which held some 85,000 persons, contests between gladiators or between men and wild beasts were held. The 66 days annually given up to such spectacles under Augustus grew to 135 under Marcus Aurelius, and there were often additional exhibitions on special occasions. In the vast Amphitheatre the audience itself was an impressive part of the spectacle. The emperor with his court occupied the seats of honor, and in the other front seats were senators and their ladies, high officials, and the Vestal Virgins, while behind them, tier upon tier, sat the rest of the populace according to rank. It is hard for us to understand the passionate love for the scenes of cruel and inhuman slaughter in the arena which was felt by high and low among the citizens of Rome.

Circus Maximus from an engraving from 1580.

But while these evil aspects of Roman life and character cannot be ignored, we must not make the mistake of assuming that there is no other and better aspect. The Rome of this period, as it is often depicted in books, conjures up the same sort of image as Paris or New York does to many—that of a city given over to frivolity and immorality, to extravagant luxury and the mad pursuit of pleasure. But we all know that in the most wicked and

Ruins of the Roman Forum.

profligate of modern cities there are countless people living blameless and normal lives which furnish no material to a sensation-loving reading public. So it was in Rome. The wits and satirists of the period give us highly colored pictures of the scandals and intrigues of the court, the vices, follies, and fashions of the smart set, and the vulgar display of the newly rich. But from other sources, less piquant and exciting to read, but certainly not less truthful, we learn of families, both humble and noble, which maintained the old Roman traditions of uprightness and devotion to duty, of women worthy of being ranked with the most honorable matrons of republican times, of men who used their wealth in the service of their fellow-men, of parents who trained their children according to wholesome ideals of simple and clean living, and of numberless people in the common walks of life with honest, homely ideals and virtuous family affection, proud of their industries and sustaining one another by help and kindness. We learn from many sources of the frequent endowment of educational and charitable foundations, of orphanages and other private benefactions to relieve want and suffering. The quiet country districts of Italy especially remained, as they had always been, the home of an unspoiled and frugal race, kindly, industrious, and self-respecting, content with the common round of useful labor and simple pleasures. It says much for the character of the Romans that so many of them loved to escape from the noise and excitement and frivolities of the city to the simplicities of Italian country life.

2. The Provinces

On the eastern part of the empire, including Greece, Asia, and Egypt, Roman manners and Roman customs made little impression. It was rather the luxuries and sensualities of the East that were invading Rome, along with the superstitions and the impressive rites of eastern religions, such as the worship of Isis and of Mithras. As we have seen, this whole eastern world had been Hellenized before the Roman came; the Greek language, the Greek influence and culture were everywhere to be found side by side with the native tongue and culture. In these long-settled lands the Roman was content to keep the peace, supervise the administration of justice, and collect the taxes. In other respects each district and city was left to live its own life and retain its own traditions, usages, and institutions. Greece itself had declined in many respects under Alexander and the Romans. Athens still retained some fame as a seat of learning, but Alexandria with its immense libraries and vigorous life was really the intellectual as well as the commercial capital of the East. Hadrian, however, had done much to reinstate Athens, by building on a lavish scale structures that were often more imposing and elaborate than in harmony with the best Greek taste. If Alexandria was the second city in the empire, Antioch in Syria ranked next. This city, like Rhodes, Ephesus, and Smyrna, was well planned and adorned with many magnificent and beautiful buildings, while all through Asia Minor and Syria were hundreds of flourishing communities, enjoying a prosperity that is in striking contrast with the desolation since wrought in those lands by the unprogressive Turk.

It was in the western half of the empire that the greatest transformation took place during these two centuries. When Caesar came to Gaul, the south-eastern portion, called the 'Province' since its conquest some sixty years before, had already a long-established civilization with its center in the old Greek colony of Massilia (Marseilles). In such a community Caesar found what he rightly called culture and refinement; in the rest of Gaul he found a brave but undisciplined people, not yet fully civilized, divided into numberless tribes engaged in constant strife, and possessing few large settlements except their hill-strongholds. To these, in time of war, or to the forests that covered a large part of the country, they fled for refuge from their open hamlets of thatched wooden huts.

The coming of the Romans in the first place put an end to the tribal wars, with their constant drain of men and resources, and brought settled conditions which fostered agriculture and industry.

Ancient Roman bridge near Dolen, Bulgaria over the river Bistrica. [Photo credit: Reneman]

It was discovered before long that Gaul was an extremely fertile country and that its people possessed great manual skill combined with ingenuity and good taste. As a result, before the end of the first century Gaul ranked with Egypt as the richest of the imperial provinces. Although its population had enormously increased, it was the only European province able to export grain; and it had a reputation all over the empire for its manufacture of woollen and linen goods and for skillful metal work.

In the second place the Romans, while leaving undisturbed the tribal divisions, encouraged the building of towns that should serve as a local center for the outlying villages and farms of the tribe. This is the reason why so many cities of France bear the names of the tribes of Caesar's day. Rheims, for example, is the town which grew up as the municipal center of the *Remi,* Amiens of the *Ambiani,* Tours of the *Turones.* Other towns developed from Roman military settlements at important strategic points, as Cologne *(Colonia)* and Lyons *(Lugdunum).* In so wealthy a province, the villas of the rich came to be as extensive and as sumptuous as any in the empire, and the towns as well equipped with baths, aqueducts, libraries, temples, amphitheaters, and the other adornments and conveniences of Roman cities. Nowhere perhaps today are there such impressive remains of Roman architecture as in the lower Rhone valley; for while they are less extensive and massive than the buildings to be found in Rome, they have suffered less severely from the vicissitudes of the Middle Ages and they are not so dwarfed by the huge structures of a great modern city.

And in the third place these towns became the natural centers of Roman influence, through which the whole country soon became completely Romanized in language, dress, and customs. If the provincials imitated some of the less admirable features of the life of Rome—the shows and

Roman Baths, Bath, England; By Photochrom Print Collection - Library of Congress

excitements of the amphitheater, the aping of social gradations and municipal titles, and the love of luxurious living—they also adopted or emulated some of the best things, such as the expenditure of private wealth on the adornment of one's native town or on charitable benefactions and the Roman system of education. Thus Augustodunum (now Autun) and Burdigala (now Bordeaux) became famous for their schools of rhetoric and oratory.

The Roman conquest of Spain was earlier than that of Gaul, and by the time of Augustus her people, except for some turbulent hill-tribes in the extreme north-west, had become completely Romanized. As early as the time of Julius Caesar, Gades (Cadiz) was deemed worthy of a special charter as a Roman town whose inhabitants had the right to call themselves Roman citizens. The country was rich in mineral wealth, and in the south and the west (the present Portugal) was very fertile. One striking evidence of its complete Romanization is the fact that in the first century half of the leading writers of Latin literature were not only of Spanish descent but also educated in Spain. Such were the poets Martial and Lucan, the poet and philosopher Seneca, and Quintilian, the great authority on rhetoric and education.

How Rome civilized her subject provinces is strikingly shown in northern Africa. Ever since the invasion by the Arabs in the seventh century, the condition of Tunis, Algeria, and Morocco has been so backward and benighted that it is difficult to realize that during the first centuries of our era these lands were in the forefront of Roman civilization. Where now are desert solitudes were

A Hypocaust. The baths in southern countries and living rooms in Britain were warmed by fires built beneath a concrete floor, resting on short piers and often covered by a mosaic pavement. The hot air passed by flues into the walls. This one is located at Bignor Villa, UK.

once fertile fields from which Rome drew no small part of her grain supply. The district was full of well-built cities, connected by a network of the incomparable Roman roads, abundantly supplied with water by aqueducts where necessary, and possessing forums, temples, theatres, and triumphal arches as substantial and as beautiful as could be found in any town in Europe. In the third and fourth centuries Roman Africa was one of the strongholds of the Christian faith, and among its sons were Tertullian the earliest, and Augustine the most illustrious, of the Latin theologians of the church.

In recent years the amazing ruins of many of these towns have been unearthed from the sands that have buried them for more than a thousand years. Of one of them, Timgad, often called 'the African Pompei,' a recent visitor writes: 'It is difficult to believe that in any of the real essentials of a full and reasonable life we are today one step advanced upon the Timgad of seventeen centuries ago. The public buildings of the city were all vastly finer than any existing in any town of like dimension or importance in the world today. The public baths, immense as cathedrals some of them, were great centers of social enjoyment, where lectures were given, entertainments were held, and the pleasures of friendship and cultivated human interaction experienced to the full. The public markets were as practical as any in modern Europe or America, and incomparably more artistic, while the sanitation was far ahead of anything that even cultured France could boast a generation or two back.' And all this was a score of leagues south of the Mediterranean, on the borders of the Sahara.

A few miles away was Lambessa, which for two centuries was the headquarters of the Third Legion. It was not the Roman custom to shift the frontier garrisons from place to place. Whether stationed in Britain, on the Rhine, or in Africa, a legion might remain for generations.[36] The wives and families of the soldiers lived near the permanent camp; the sons, as they grew up, joined the legion; the time-expired veteran settled down where he had served. The permanent legion thus became almost a hereditary caste, and was an established part of the district where it was stationed.

---

[36] Thus the Twentieth Legion was quartered at Chester, England, for over three hundred years.

A paved street in Timgad. (The arch at the end of the street commemorates the founding of the city by Trajan.)

Theatre at Timgad in Northern Africa. (The stone benches would seat 3500 spectators.)

Timgad was originally a place built for the veterans of the Third Legion of Lambessa. As a rule these frontier legions had little fighting, particularly in the second century; and they were employed on great engineering works (roads, aqueducts, bridges) in their district, or in erecting permanent buildings for military or other public purposes. In this way the military headquarters of such a legion might become the center of an increasing circle of important, well-built towns in which the Roman civilization was established and perpetuated.

It is what Rome had accomplished in such provinces as Gaul and Africa that inspired the enthusiastic eulogy of Aristides, a Greek writer who died in the same year as Marcus Aurelius. 'Regions, once desert solitudes, are thickly dotted with flourishing cities. The world has laid the sword aside, and keeps universal festival, with all pomp and gladness. All other feuds and rivalries are gone, and cities now vie with one another only in their splendor and their pleasures. Every space is crowded with porticoes, gymnasia, fountains, temples, with studios and schools. Sandy wastes, trackless mountains, broad rivers present no barriers to the traveller, who finds his home and country everywhere. The earth has become a vast pleasure-garden.'

It has been said that 'the greatest glory of the imperial administration was the skillful and politic tolerance with which it reconciled a central despotism with a remarkable range of local liberty.' It might with equal truth be said that Rome's greatest glory was her success in building everywhere strong municipal centers whose people were full of local pride and patriotism and yet equally proud of their common status as Roman citizens; provincial towns infinitely diversified, yet all filled with the consciousness of the unity of the empire. In a later century this success of Rome was attested by the poet Claudian: 'This is she who alone has taken the conquered to her bosom and has cherished all mankind alike, as mother not as queen, and has bound them to her afar by bonds of love. To her rule of peace we owe it that the stranger is at home in every land, that men may dwell in every clime, that we are all one people.'

Thus it came about that Gauls, Spaniards, Africans, Asiatics alike regarded themselves as Roman citizens first. The whole world, even including the barbarians, was profoundly impressed with the idea of a universal and eternal empire. The results of this have affected the whole history of western Europe. Even when the empire was dissolved into the nations of mediaeval Europe, the idea of a universal Roman empire never entirely disappeared. The empire instituted by Charlemagne and the visible unity of the organized Christian church served to keep the conception alive for a thousand years. And although the vigorous growth of national feeling in Europe has in recent centuries almost obliterated the tradition, it may not be wholly fanciful to conceive of the League of Nations as reviving that idea of an organized unity of civilization which was once realized under the Roman empire.

A Building Crane. [Anderson]

Questions

1. Compare and contrast the life in Italy and Rome to that in the Provinces.
2. Describe the influence of Rome on the people and culture of the provinces. Describe any influence that these provinces had on Rome.
3. Why is it that Gauls, Spaniards, Asiatics, Africans all considered themselves Roman citizens?

Vocabulary

proletariate
mitigated
profligate
benighted

Chapter LII

Confusion and Reconstruction

The death of Marcus Aurelius in AD 180 closes the first two centuries of the empire, the period of its greatest prosperity, most unbroken peace, and best government. There followed a century of turmoil and confusion. This in part was due to problems that arose in connection with the succession to the imperial throne.

The authority of the emperor was in no sense hereditary, although an emperor often virtually named his successor by making him his heir and associating him in the government. It was by the voice of the senate that the emperor was proclaimed; but in the last analysis it was the support of the army that really decided who was to succeed. The prestige of Julius Caesar and Augustus determined the choice of the first few emperors. When their line died out, Vespasian was one of four rival generals who, with the support of their respective armies, contended for the throne, each of the other three in turn holding it for a few brief weeks or months until overthrown and slain by a stronger rival. (AD 69 is known as the year of the four emperors.) On the death of Vespasian's son Domitian, the happy choice of Nerva seems to have been the act of the senate, approved by the people and the army. Nerva made Trajan, already an eminent and successful general, his son by adoption and named him his heir, and this was the method followed down to Marcus Aurelius. Hence the 'five good emperors' are also known as the 'adoptive emperors.'

This haphazard system had not prevented the empire from receiving good government during the greater part of the first two centuries after its foundation. But from the death of Marcus Aurelius the good fortune of the Roman empire seemed, save in rare instances, to have deserted it. In the next century there was a succession of military nominees, 'barrack emperors,' as they are termed. Few of them were capable rulers; their reigns were usually brief; and in nearly every case they met violent deaths, being supplanted by rivals.

One of the most notable events in this third century AD was the extension of the Roman citizenship to all free provincials. This was decreed when Caracalla was emperor. His object was probably to facilitate the collection of taxes; but the measure was in itself a proper recognition of the unity of the empire, and was but the logical completion of the partial extension under Claudius, or rather

The Roman Theatre of Verulamium. Built in about 140AD it is the only example of its kind in Britain, being a theater with a stage rather than an Amphitheater. Initially, the arena would have been used for anything from religious processions and dancing, to wrestling, armed combat and wild beast shows. From about 180AD the stage came into greater use and the auditorium extended. By about 300AD, after some redevelopment work, the Theatre could seat 2000 spectators. [Source: Wikimedia Commons; Photo credit:Carole Raddato]

indeed the culmination of the wise policy of incorporation of conquered subjects pursued by Rome from the earliest times.

But the Roman state, for all its imposing splendor, had within it the seeds of decay, which in the end were to bring about the dissolution of the imperial system. The sources of this weakness were both internal and external.

1. It was not rebellion or disaffection that sapped the strength of the empire; the causes at work were more subtle and more deadly. In the first place there was no true freedom in the empire. The fiction of a return to republican usage and the pretense of cooperation between emperor, senate, and people had gradually been abandoned. The authority of the emperor was now frankly recognized as practically absolute. There were no constitutional ways by which the oppression of a tyrannical emperor could be restrained or opposed. As was said of the late Russian Czardom, the Roman empire had become 'a despotism tempered by assassination.' Men might be satisfied with their loss of freedom because of the assured peace, the material comfort, and even splendor of life, and the absence of all responsibility for the government of the state; but the very fact that they were satisfied is itself evidence that the spirit of freedom had fled. Despotism, however paternally beneficent, and

bureaucracy, however efficient, are incompatible with the vigorous life of a free and enlightened people.

Moreover, it was also now becoming evident that economic stability and material happiness were not being secured; the price for which freedom had been bartered was not being paid. Italy itself had long been declining in population and productiveness. This process had begun in republican times, and Augustus had early striven, but ineffectually, to undo the evil that the long civil wars had aggravated. The attraction of city life with its amusements and free doles of food was drawing the rural population into Rome. The abundance of slaves provided so much cheap labor of every degree of skill that life for the free artisan became difficult; and the small farmer could not compete with the rich holder of vast estates worked by slaves, even apart from the enormous importation of cheap foreign grain to feed the city multitudes. The growing distaste for the obligations of married life and the increase of luxurious and vicious tastes cooperated with these economic causes to bring about a steady decline in the birthrate.

These evils were manifest chiefly in Italy; in the provinces, and more particularly in the western provinces, life was much more wholesome and vigorous. But all the empire suffered from the ever-increasing burden of taxation. The cities and towns everywhere had been enriched with innumerable vast and splendid structures, through the munificence of emperors or by local pride and enterprise; but all these imposing evidences of advancing civilization had in the long run to be paid for by the taxes levied on the people. Added to this was the expense of maintaining the armies garrisoning the far-flung frontiers, and the cost of the frequent little border wars.

2. At the same time that these evils were increasing within the state, the danger from Rome's external enemies was becoming more and more threatening. There had always been a vast population of barbarians to the north of Roman territory, who at various times had threatened the civilized countries to the south. Rome had never forgotten the invasions of 390 and 102 BC and there was always the danger of fresh incursions, if famine or the pressure of other tribes behind them drove the barbarians to seek new homes in the attractive rich lands of Gaul or Italy.

In the reign of Marcus Aurelius a Teutonic tribe overran the frontiers of the upper Danube in such strength that the empire was seriously threatened. The emperor and his armies were able to stem the tide, but Rome's power was distinctly shaken and her resources weakened. Further, Rome had now adopted a new policy which was itself a confession of growing weakness. Great numbers of barbarians with their families were allowed to settle within the frontiers of the empire. Not unnaturally the legions on the Rhine and the Danube came more and more to be recruited from these partially Romanized Teutonic immigrants, so that in time this alien element became the largest and most efficient part of the frontier armies. All this meant an extension of Roman culture to immensely larger numbers, but at the same time it weakened the lines of defense and broke up the solidarity of the army.

In the century of confusion following the reign of Marcus Aurelius both the hostile invasions and this peaceful penetration of the barbarians increased enormously, and there were times when there seemed to be danger of Roman rule being overwhelmed by these restless warlike tribes. Towards the end of the century, for example, we find that the Emperor Aurelian was compelled to abandon the province of Dacia and to withdraw behind the Danube, and also—an ominous sign—that he set about building huge defensive walls about Rome itself. Moreover, the frequent changes in the succession were a further menace to the stability of the empire (there were 29 emperors in the 103

Porta Nigra in Trier (known as Treves in the time of the Empire), Capitol of the Prefecture of the Gauls under Diocletian. [Photo credit Berthold Werner]

years following the death of Marcus Aurelius); and the wars which so often attended the struggle for power weakened the resources of the state and increased the danger of invasion. The breaking-up of the empire seemed imminent unless some ruler of exceptional ability could arrest the decay.

Such an emperor finally appeared in the person of Diocletian, who restored order, kept the frontiers intact, and devised a reorganization of the empire which, varied and modified by later emperors, postponed its fall for two centuries more. In order to reduce the burden of empire, which had become too great for one man to bear, and also to lessen the dangers arising from disputed succession, he divided the empire into an eastern and a western half, and associated with him a second emperor. Each emperor was to bear the name of Augustus, and each to hold sway over half the Roman world, though the two were regarded as colleagues and all decrees were to be issued in their joint name. With each was associated a junior prince, to be called Caesar, with subordinate authority. These four were to rule in four separate capitals, with all the pomp of oriental potentates. All pretense of following republican usage was now cast aside; the emperor's person was deemed sacred, and a host of courtiers and officials hedged the sovereign about from contact with his subjects. For purposes of administration the empire was divided into nearly a hundred provinces, each with a multitude of officials, both civil and military. Whatever gain arose from the increased efficiency of administration was counterbalanced by the increased burden of the taxation needed to maintain the four imperial courts and the enormously increased bureaucracy.

The arrangements of Diocletian were too elaborate and complicated to work smoothly after his own reign of 21 years was ended. In the next year, when Constantine became one of the four

A Roman Aqueduct at Segovia in Spain. [Photo credit Felver Alfonso]

imperial colleagues, there began a period of intrigue and warfare between the heads of the state, which lasted for nearly twenty years. In the end, Constantine emerged as the sole and absolute ruler of the Roman world. Soon afterwards he took the momentous step of transferring the capital of the empire to Byzantium on the Bosphorus. This city, which for many centuries was called Constantinople (modern day Istanbul, Turkey), was so situated as to become a great commercial center; it occupied a position of almost impregnable strength; and it was more suitable than Rome as an imperial headquarters from which to direct military operations in the north and east, the two-directions from which danger chiefly threatened. Even before this removal, Italy had lost its pre-eminence and had become merely one of the provinces. In fact, in the reorganization of Diocletian, Rome was not even one of the four capitals. The name of Rome retained its ancient prestige, but the city itself was no longer the strategic center of the Roman world. A second event of far-reaching importance in the reign of Constantine was his official recognition of the Christian religion.

Questions

1. Why are the five good emperors known as adoptive emperors? What does this say about the empire?
2. What were the sources of weakness in the imperial system (internal and external)?
3. How did Diocletian attempt to improve the administration of the Empire? What were the pros and cons of this system?

Vocabulary

despotism
munificence
potentates

Chapter LIII

The Dissolution of the Empire

Although for a time Diocletian's plan of partition was abandoned, the idea was not forgotten; and within a short time after the death of Constantine the Roman world was again divided into an eastern (Greek) and a western (Roman) empire. Constantine's establishment of a new capital in the East doubtless facilitated this separation of East and West. The division this time was more complete, and the two governments were never reunited.

The strong, vigorous rule of Diocletian and Constantine had kept the Roman empire practically intact until nearly the end of the fourth century. Now the pressure on the frontiers was becoming too strong to resist. First at one point and then at another the Teutonic tribes made their way in increasing numbers into the Roman provinces; their purpose was not to make brief raids and then retire with their booty; rather they intended to occupy the land for themselves, and in many cases they formed permanent settlements and kingdoms within the borders of the empire. They came not to destroy Roman civilization, but to appropriate and enjoy it for themselves.

These tribes were no longer so uncivilized as when the Romans had first come in contact with them centuries before. They still retained their warlike temper and their strong love of freedom; they still lived in simple fashion in villages rather than ordered cities; and it was still easy for them to move with women and children and all their worldly goods from one settlement to another. But some knowledge of the Roman ways had spread among them through the centuries of contact with the Roman civilization at the frontiers, through their intercourse with kinsmen settled in the neighboring province, through the visits of traders with their stories and their wares, and doubtless also through the reports brought back by such of their number as had seen with their own eyes what the Roman lands contained. And thus when the final movement came, and the Teutonic tribes slowly established themselves through the provinces, they entered not as savage strangers, but as settlers knowing something of the system into which they came, and not unwilling to be considered its members; despising the degenerate provincials who struck no blow in their own defense, but full of respect for the majestic power which had for so many centuries confronted and instructed them.

The massive ruins of one of the rooms in the Baths of Caracalla in Rome. [Photo credit Felver Alfonso]

The most spectacular of the Teutonic invasions were those of the Goths and the Vandals, both by way of the Danube. Each of these tribes at some stage of its wanderings sacked the city of Rome. In the case of the Goths, under Alaric, the resort to pillaging was due very largely to the short-sighted mismanagement of the situation by the emperor Honorius. These Goths, who settled for a time in Aquitania, ultimately removed to Spain and there founded a kingdom which endured until the conquest of Spain by the Moors in the eighth century.

Other Teutonic tribes came across the Rhine into Gaul, the Burgundians settling in the valley of the Rhone, and the Franks in northern Gaul. These latter in a short time laid the foundations of the kingdom of France. The coming of the Jutes, Angles, and Saxons to Britain was part of the same Teutonic movement, as was also the settlement of the Lombards in Italy in the sixth century. The Vandals, who crossed over to northern Africa and created much havoc in that province, alone of these invading tribes founded no permanent settlement.

The cause of these great movements was only in part the native restlessness of the Teutonic people and the attractiveness and weakness of the Roman provinces. These tribes were themselves being driven forward by the pressure of the dreaded Huns, a savage, alien race originally from Asia. The Huns were wild horsemen of the plains, whom the Romans considered ugly and dwarf-like, with flat, yellow, Mongolian faces and broad nostrils. They were fierce pagans, who under their leader Attila, 'the Scourge of God,' finally made their way westward from the steppes of southern

Russia until they crossed the Roman frontiers into Italy and Gaul. Unlike the Teuton leaders, Attila's object was the destruction of Roman civilization. It is worthy of note that in repelling the Huns from Gaul, the Roman armies had the whole-hearted and efficient support of the very Goths who only forty years before had besieged and sacked Rome. The great victory over Attila at Chalons saved for the western world not only Roman civilization but also Christianity. For by the time the Teutonic movement began, Christianity had become firmly established throughout the Roman world, and nearly all the Teutonic tribes that made settlements within the empire embraced Christianity as an integral part of the Roman culture, while the pagan Attila was as bent on destroying the Christian religion as he was on crushing the Roman power.

This victory at Chalons was the last great effort made by the Roman empire in the West. Gaul, Spain, northern Africa, and Britain were virtually no longer under the control of the western emperors, and their power in Italy rapidly declined, until the last of the line, Romulus Augustulus, abdicated the throne in 476 AD and formally transferred the insignia of his vanished authority to the eastern emperor. In the East the Roman (or Byzantine) empire survived, with varying fortunes for another thousand years, and played a great part in the history of eastern Europe until the capture of Constantinople by the rising power of the Turks.

While the year 476 is that commonly assigned to the Fall of the Roman Empire, the real breaking-up of the empire had begun long before, as early as AD 300, and the process of disintegration went on for nearly another century. There was no sudden collapse, but a slow transformation which

Ampitheatre at Arles in France. [Photo credit Karelj]

Temple ruins at Baalbek in Syria. [Photo credit Justin Ames]

no one detected or realized at the time, a transformation from the unity of the centralized empire of AD 300 to the various new kingdoms that before AD 600 were being established all over the western provinces, and that were destined to develop into the nations of modern Europe.

Only in this sense of a gradual political change can we speak of the fall of the Roman empire. There was no destruction of its civilization; its arts and industries, its education, its literature, and above all its law and its religion remained, and profoundly impressed the new masters of the western provinces. It must be remembered that relative to the total population in the conquered provinces, the number of the newcomers was small. Their leaders took the conduct of affairs in their territory into their own hands, but they were glad to have the advice and guidance of Roman officials and Christian bishops.

They gave up their own Teuton speech and learned the Roman language of the provincials. As usually happens when a conquered country possesses a civilization superior to that of its conquerors, as had happened before when 'vanquished Greece took captive its fierce conqueror,' Rome, so now the Teutons sought to make the culture of their new subjects their own.

In the process doubtless much was lost. Only a few minds would be impressed with the finer elements of Roman civilization. In the turmoil of the times the noblest treasures of literature and learning were not appreciated, and so were neglected and for a time forgotten. The new communities, isolated from one another and from the great centers of the world, often showed narrowness, ignorance, and prejudice; and the world in many ways presented a less orderly appearance than in the palmy days of the empire. But over against all possible regrets for the passing away of an imposing system of government must be set certain gains. New blood was brought into the empire, which had long exhibited little of the hardihood and tenacity of the early Romans. Western civilization

Roman roads in Britain.

in the end was all the better for the union of Teutonic vigor and love of freedom with the Roman respect for law and order. Again, men were set free from the deadening effects of a too rigidly paternal oversight. The majesty of Rome's sway and the massiveness of her machinery of government should not make us forgetful of the truth that the character both of individuals and of communities suffers when deprived of responsible initiative and freedom of self-direction.

Rome's last great legacy to the world was the code of civil law promulgated by the eastern emperor, Justinian, in the sixth century. The Roman genius for law and order shows itself nowhere so strikingly as in its success in evolving that system of Roman law which is the basis of the legal systems of much of the civilized world today. Justinian's great work was the final, most complete, and most authoritative statement of Roman law, and both directly in the law-courts and indirectly through its influence on the law and institutions of the Roman church, it has been of such far-reaching importance that Justinian has been called 'the Lawgiver of Civilization.' The permanence and value of Roman law are due to two factors:

(1) The Roman's practical instinct for organizing and governing was applied to the task of executing justice and protecting life and property over all his extensive domains. The result was a body of laws so just, so practical, and so comprehensive that they commanded the respect and obedience of even the barbarian invaders of the empire. (2) A succession of great lawyers and jurists had worked for centuries at the task of formulating those principles of universal right and justice on which a system of world-wide law should rest. Thus Roman jurisprudence came to unite in one the two great excellences of being eminently practical and of being founded on universal principles; it was the union of long experience and sound theory.

The mission of Rome was now accomplished. Her work had been to organize and unify the ancient world; to preserve under the Roman peace all the rich inheritance from earlier ages and especially the Greek contribution to civilization; to hold the Mediterranean world together in her firm grasp until the Greco-Roman culture and the Christian religion were everywhere so firmly established, that, after the breaking up of her power, they remained a permanent and potent influence in the world. Rome founded a universal empire, in which all earlier history loses itself and out of which all later history grew. And now the new nations in the western half of Europe were to begin building up a new world that by degrees was to assume the form of our modern western civilization, a civilization in which the elements derived from Greece and Rome were reinterpreted and given a new spirit, by the principles of the new religion derived from Palestine.

Questions

1. What happened to the Roman civilization when the barbarian tribes settled there?
2. Explain the two factors that led to the permanence and value of Roman law.

Vocabulary

jurisprudence
provincials
abdicated
palmy

Nativity by Bernardino Fasolo

CHAPTER LIV

CHRISTIANITY AND THE ROMAN EMPIRE

The founder of Christianity was born in Bethlehem not many years after the Roman empire was first established, when 'there went out a decree from Caesar Augustus that all the world should be enrolled.' His preaching and crucifixion were in the reign of Tiberius.

The Christian church began as a small and obscure sect in one of the less important provinces. Its advance was from the first surprisingly rapid. Its members were at first recruited largely from the lower classes, for it was to the poor and downtrodden that it made its greatest appeal. Before long, Christian communities, organized on very simple lines, were springing up in all parts of the empire, especially in the East.

Three circumstances, apart from its own merits, favored the rapid spread of Christianity.

(1) Under the universal dominion of Rome and the worldwide Roman peace, the barriers between nations were broken down, while the great commercial and military roads of the empire made travel and communication between important centers very easy. It was in the great cities on these roads that the missionaries of the new religion planted their first churches, thus securing strategic points from which the further spread of their message was made easier. It took a longer time for Christianity to penetrate into the outlying country districts, so that the term *pagani* (dwellers in the country districts or *pagi*) became synonymous with non-Christians.

(2) The Jews, to whom the Christian missionaries naturally made their first appeal, were widely scattered over the cities of the empire. This dispersal was due in part to the settlement by Alexander the Great of large numbers of Jews in his new city of Alexandria; and in part it was due to the ease of travel and the opportunities of gain which the Roman peace afforded. In the first century more than half of the four or five million Jews in the empire were living in Egypt, Asia Minor, Greece, and Rome. These Jews of the Dispersal carried everywhere their institution of the synagogue—the meeting-place for worship, instruction, and discussion; and these synagogues had large numbers of adherents drawn from the more religious-minded of the Gentiles of the neighborhood. Everywhere, therefore, the missionary had more or less ready for him on his arrival a meeting-place and an audience.

(3) Over all the cities of the empire east of the Adriatic—the region of Alexander's empire-—as well as in many important centers in the West, where Greek colonies had been planted, the Greek language was freely spoken. Moreover, Greek was the language in common use among all these scattered Jews, and the scriptures read in their synagogues were in the Greek version called the Septuagint. Naturally, therefore, Christian missionaries like Paul and others who spoke and wrote Greek, the language of the New Testament, found easy access to the people in any large center that they visited with their gospel.

The Roman policy was, as a rule, extremely tolerant of local institutions, customs, and religions, and for the greater part of the time there was little, or no interference with the Christians. But even when there was no deliberate, open persecution there was often suspicion and an atmosphere of hostility. The chief reasons for this were political. An important part of the Roman state-religion was the worship of Rome and the emperor, and, in case of suspected disloyalty, participation in this worship was made a test. The Christians felt that such worship was idolatry and therefore inconsistent with their faith. The Romans could not understand this view; to them this act of worship meant much the same as saluting the flag or singing the national anthem means today; and they interpreted the refusal to do this homage to the emperor as an evidence of disloyalty. Furthermore, the government was suspicious of secret associations of every sort, since they had been known to develop into seditious organizations and to disturb the peace. Since many of the meetings of the Christians, such as their love-feasts or communions, were held in private, they were suspected of plotting treason. Not a little hostility was due also to malicious slander. Most Romans knew little about Christianity, having heard of it only as an ignorant foreign superstition adopted by some of the lowest classes. Hence even educated men readily believed those who accused the Christians of evil practices.

Few of the emperors who succeeded Nero were openly hostile to the Christians. Trajan, for example, when one of his governors in Asia Minor consulted him as to the course he should adopt in dealing with the Christians, advised him not to search out such persons, nor to pay attention to anonymous accusations; but if any case were brought before him, he must let the law take its course.

In the reign of Marcus Aurelius occurred the second great persecution, due to the emperor's fear that Christianity was threatening to undermine the loyalty of the citizens. The emperor Decius also in his short reign systematically persecuted the Christians, with the idea of reviving the ancient Roman religion. Diocletian was responsible for one of the last and greatest of the wholesale persecutions. Determined to break down all opposition to his autocratic rule, he persecuted with the utmost rigor the Christian church which recognized an authority that did not derive from him. Christianity, however, had by this time grown too strong to be put down even by this powerful ruler, and the next emperor, Constantine, gave it official recognition and was himself baptized.

By the time of the dissolution of the empire the church was so firmly established and so well organized that it occupied a commanding position in the new nations that began to spring up. Many men of eminent ability were attracted into its service and wielded great influence in their several communities. Furthermore, in the times of confusion that followed the dissolution of the empire, the church did more than any other agency to preserve Roman culture. Under the primacy of the bishops of Rome it was rapidly acquiring the strength that comes from a great unified and centralized administration. Thus the church as an institution was able to survive the empire, whose place indeed it took for centuries to come as the great unifying influence in western Europe.

Questions

1. Explain/describe the three factors that favored rapid spread of Christianity. Which of these do you think was the most important? Explain why.
2. What was the attitude in the Empire toward Christianity?
3. How did Christianity survive the Empire?

Vocabulary

adherent
seditious
autocratic

Time-Chart of Greek History

Main Divisions	Century	Year B.C.	Chief Events
Dominance of Cnossus	16	1600	Cretan power at its zenith. 'Shaft-grave' dynasty in Mycenae.
	15	1500	'Beehive tomb' dynasty in Mycenae.
Dominance of Mycenae	14	1400	Cnossus attacked and burned.
	13	1300	The Achaeans in the Peloponnesus. Age of the Greek 'Heroes.'
The coming of the Dorians	12	1184	Traditional date of the Fall of Troy.
	11	1100	Mycenae destroyed.
Establishment of City-States in the Aegean Area	10	1000	Colonization of Asia Minor.
	9	900	Age of Homer.

Main Divisions	Century	Year B.C.	Chief Events
Period of Expansion and Colonization	8	776	Traditional date of first Olympic Games. Rise of Aristocracies. Colonizing of Mediterranean and Euxine. Miletus the chief Greek city.
	7	650 625 621	Rise of Tyrants in Greece and Asia Minor. Messenian Revolt against Sparta. Draco's Legislation.
Period of Internal Growth and Highest Achievement	6	594 585 546 540 510	Archonship of Solon. Thales flourished. Capture of Sardis by Cyrus. Pisistratus tyrant in Athens. Democracy restored in Athens.
	5	490–479 477 461–429 431–404	Persian Wars. Delian League formed. The Age of Pericles. The Peloponnesian War.
Extension of Greek Influence over the Eastern World	4	399 338 334–323	Death of Socrates. Chaeronea and loss of Greek independence. Conquests of Alexander. Rise of Kingdoms of Syria, Egypt, and Macedonia.
	3	295 215	Pyrrhus king of Epirus. Philip of Macedonia makes a treaty with Hannibal.
Rise of Greco-Roman Culture	2	197 189 146	Defeat of Philip by the Romans. Defeat of Antiochus in Asia Minor. Destruction of Corinth. Greece incorporated with Macedonia.
	1	27	Greece made a separate Roman province (Achaea).

Time-Chart of Roman History

Main Divisions	Century	Year B.C.	Chief Events
Rome under the Kings	8	753	Foundation of Rome by Romulus.
	7	616	Tarquin, the first Etruscan king of Rome.
	6	510	Expulsion of kings; creation of consuls.
Strife between Patricians and Plebeians and conquest of Central Italy	5	494	Secession of Plebs and establishment of tribunes.
		446	Wars with Aequi and Volsci begin (lasting till 302).
		427	War with Veii (taken 396).
	4	390	Rome captured by the Gauls.
		367	Licinian laws passed.
		343–290	Samnite wars.
		338–308	Subjugation of Latium and Etruria.
Conquest of all Italy and Sicily	3	287	Hortensian Law.
		281–271	Pyrrhus in Italy and conquest of southern Italy.
		264–241	First war with Carthage.
		222	Conquest of Cisalpine Gaul.
Conquest of the Mediterranean World and Contact with the East		218–201	Hannibal in Italy; Zama.
	2	200–146	Conquest of Macedonia, Greece, and Asia Minor.
		146	Destruction of Carthage.
		133–121	Agitation of the Gracchi.
		106–101	Rise of Marius; Defeat of Cimbri and Teutons.
The Century of Civil Wars	1	82	Sulla becomes dictator.
		60	First Triumvirate.
		49	Civil war: Caesar and Pompey.
		44	Assassination of Caesar.
		43	Second Triumvirate.
		31	Actium and end of the Republic.

Main Divisions	Century	Year A.D.	Chief Events
The Empire at the Height of its Power and Prosperity	1	9 14 43 64 70 98	Defeat of Varus. Death of Augustus. Claudius invades Britain. Nero persecutes the Christians. Capture of Jerusalem. Trajan succeeds Nerva.
	2	117 138 161–180	Hadrian. Antoninus Pius. Marcus Aurelius, last of the five 'good emperors.'
Turmoil and Decay	3	180– 283 274	The century of the 'barrack emperors.' Aurelian rebuilds the walls of Rome.
Reorganization attempted	4	284 326 330	Diocletian reorganizes the empire. Constantine sole emperor. Constantinople becomes the capital.
Gradual dissolution of Central Authority.		364	Final separation of Eastern and Western empires.
	5	410 447 451 476	Sack of Rome by Alaric. The Saxons enter Britain. Attila defeated at Chalons. Romulus Augustulus, last emperor of the West, abdicates.

INDEX

A

Achaeans 21, 35
Achilles 28, 40
Acropolis 142
Actium 276
adoptive emperors 309
aediles 212
Aegatian Islands 232
Aegean civilization 11, 17
Aegospotami 167
Aeneas 203, 292
Aeneid 292
Aequi 215
Aeschylus 109, 121, 151
Africa, province of 304
Agamemnon 26, 28, 40
agrarian troubles and legislation 73–74, 77, 210, 211, 245–247, 251–253
Agrippa 276, 281
Alaric 316
Alcibiades 163, 173
Alexander 181
Alexandria 184, 191, 302
alphabet 9
Antioch 193
Antiochus 192, 242
Antoninus Pius 289
Antony 275
Aphrodite 33
Apollo 33
Appius Claudius 226
Aquae Sextiae 256
Arbela 185
Archimedes 192
architecture 89, 142, 147, 291
archons 70, 113
Areopagus 138
Ares 33
Argonauts 25
Ariadne 11
Aristides 112, 121, 134
aristocracy 59–61, 70, 137, 168, 212
Aristophanes 151, 153
Aristotle 186, 187, 192
art
   Egyptian and Babylonian 6
   Greek 147
   Minoan 14–15
   Roman 291
Artaphernes 103
Artemis 33
Artemisium 115, 117
Asia Minor 35, 45, 95–96, 99–100, 133, 166, 177, 193, 242, 258, 262, 271
assembly
   Athenian 78, 83, 139
   Roman 211, 247
astronomy 7, 8, 191, 192
Athena 33, 142
Athens 69–70, 99, 105, 131, 137, 157, 159, 167, 178, 180, 193
athletics, Greek 54, 86
Athos 103
Attila 316
Augustus 279

B

Babylonia 6–8
barbarian invasions of Italy 215, 255, 311, 316
barbarians and Greeks 45
barrack emperors 309
Boule 83
Brasidas 161
Britain 270, 285, 289, 316
Bronze Age 35–39, 43
Brutus (first consul) 224
Brutus (republican) 273, 275
Burgundians 316
Byzantine empire 317
Byzantium 48, 313

C

Caesar 269
calendar 272
Caligula 285
Callimachus 104
Cannae 238
Caracalla 309
Carthage 229, 242
Catiline 263
Cato 242
Catullus 267, 294
centuries 210

331

Chaeronea 181, 189
Chalons 317
character of Greeks 45–47, 90, 111, 128, 175, 180, 242
character of Romans 200, 205, 210, 221, 222, 239, 246, 297–298
Christianity 286, 313, 317, 320, 323
Cicero 262, 265, 275, 292
Cimbri 255
Cimon 134, 137
Cincinnatus 224
circus 300
citizenship
   Athenian 69, 78, 132
   Roman 203, 209, 217, 253, 256, 272, 309
City-State 51
Claudius 285
Cleisthenes 83
Cleon 161
Cleopatra 191, 271, 276
clients 221
Cloelia 224
Cnossus 12, 21
Codrus 70
colonies
   Greek 48
   Roman 217
Colosseum 300
Conon 167, 177
Constantine 313, 315, 324
Constantinople 48, 313, 317
consuls 209, 211
Corcyra 89, 159, 161
Corinth 17, 138, 159, 167, 242
Coriolanus 224
council
   Athenian 83, 140
Crassus 261, 269, 270
Crete 11
Croesus 95
culture
   Athenian 82, 141, 157
   Greco-Roman 246, 295
Culture, Greco-Roman 265
Curtius 225
Cyrus, the Great 96, 174
Cyrus, the Younger 97, 167, 174

D

Dacia 289, 311
Darius 97, 99, 103, 111
Dark Age 36
Datis 103
Decelea 165

Decius 225
Delian league 134
Delium 161
Delos 134
Delphi 54, 56
Delphic oracle 54, 57
Demeter 33, 91
democracy 59, 71, 78, 83, 113, 138, 168, 172, 212, 273, 280
Demosthenes, the general 161
Demosthenes, the orator 180
dialects and tribes of Greece 36, 46, 189
Diana 222
dictator 211, 212
Diocletian 312, 313
Dodona 56
Domitian 287
Dorians 35
Draco 73, 211
drama 82, 151, 152, 246

E

East and West, conflict of 26, 127, 175, 183–186, 189, 239, 275, 301
education 43, 155, 157, 222, 265, 293
Egypt 6–10, 190, 191, 242, 271
Eleusinian mysteries 91
emperors 280, 309
empire
   Athenian 134
   Roman, rise and fall 277, 310
Epaminondas 178
ephors 65
Epicurean 194
equites 253
Eretria 99, 104
Etruscans 204, 206
Euripides 151
Eurymedon 134

F

Fabius 238
Fabricius 225
festivals
   Greek 54, 82, 141
Flaminius 237
Franks 316

G

games
   Greek athletic 54
Gaul 241, 255, 269, 302
Gauls, in northern Italy 205, 215, 235, 236, 241

generals, at Athens 113, 140
geography, influence of 45, 199, 204
    51–53
geometry 8, 154
Germany and Germans 255, 270, 282, 311, 315
gladiators 246, 261, 300
Gods of Greeks 31
Gods of Romans 222
Golden Age of Latin literature 292
Goths 316
government
    Athenian 71, 83, 113, 139
    Roman 205, 246–248
Gracchi 251
Granicus 183

H

Hadrian 289, 302
Hamilcar 231, 235
Hannibal 235
Hasdrubal 235, 238, 239
Hector 28, 41
Heliaea 78
Hellas, Hellenes 46
Helots 63
Hephaestus 33
Hermes 33, 165
Herodotus 128, 151, 153
Hestia 33
Himera 127
Hippias 82, 103
Homer 39, 43, 82
Homeric age, life in 85
Horace 282, 292, 293
Horatius 223
Hortensian law 212
humanism 195
Huns 316

I

Iliad 39
Indo-European languages and races 23, 96, 204
Ionia 36, 45
Ionian revolt 99
Issus 184
Italy, races of 204, 215

J

Jerusalem 287
Jews 191, 287, 323
Jugurtha 255
Juno 33, 222
Jupiter 33, 222

Justinian 320
Juvenal 295

K

Knights. *See* Equites

L

Lambessa 305
Latins 204, 205, 215, 216
Laurium 112
law and law-courts 73, 78, 139, 211, 248, 320
Legends
    of Greek heroes 39–41
Legends, of Greek heroes 25–31
legends, Roman 203, 222
Leonidas 115, 116
Lepidus 275
Leuctra 178
Licinian laws 211, 251
literature
    Greek 39, 43, 93, 148, 150, 173, 180, 186, 194
    Latin 246, 265, 291
Livius Andronicus 246
Livy 294
Long Walls 132, 160, 167, 177
lot, at Athens 140, 172
Luca 270
Lucretius 267
Lycurgus 66
Lydia 46, 75, 95, 96
Lysander 167, 168

M

Macedonia 179, 193, 241
Maecenas 281
Magna Graecia 215
Mantinea 179
Marathon 81, 105
Marcus Aurelius 289, 309, 324
Mardonius 103, 123
Marius 255
Mars 33, 222
Marseilles (Massillia) 48
Massilia (Marseilles) 241, 302
mathematics 8–9, 154, 192
medicine 155, 191
Messenians 64, 179
Metaurus 239
Miletus 93, 99
Miltiades 104
Minerva 33, 222
Minoan civilization 11
Minos 11

Minotaur 11, 15
mission of Rome 320
Mithradates 258, 262, 263
Mitylene 161
monarchy 282
  in Greece 59, 190
  in Rome 205, 273, 277, 310
money, first coined 75
Mucius Scaevola 223
Munda 272
Mycale 127
Mycenae 17, 26, 36, 125

N

Naples 48
Nero 285, 286
Nerva 288
Nicias 161, 163

O

Octavianus 275
Odysseus 28, 42, 43
Odyssey 39, 42
Olympia 54, 55
Olympic games 54, 55
Olympus 31
oratory
  Greek 140, 180, 193
  Roman 265, 295
Orphic rites 91

P

Palestine 6
Parthenon 142
Parthians 192, 270
parties in Athens 71, 81, 112, 137, 168
patricians 209
Pausanias 125
Pelopidas 178
Peloponnesian War 159
Peloponnesus 23
Pericles 137
Perioeci 63, 64
Persephone 33
Perseus 242
Persia 96, 166, 181, 183
Pharsalus 271
Phidias 142, 148
Philip (I) 179, 180, 181
Philippics 275
Philip V 193, 238, 241
Philosophers
  Greek 171

philosophers, Greek 186, 194
Phoenicians 6, 45
Pindar 151, 183
Piraeus 112, 132
pirates 13, 193, 262
Pisistratus 81
Plataea 105, 126, 161
Plato 173, 174
Plautus 246
plebeians 209
Pliny 295
Pluto 32, 33
Polemarch 71
Pompeii 287
Pompey 261, 270
Poseidon 32
praetors 212, 232
Priam 26, 41
principate 282
provinces and provincial government 232, 247, 279, 297, 301–304
Ptolemy 191
Punic Wars 243
Pyrrhus 193, 217, 225

R

Regulus 231
religion 31, 89, 195, 222, 323
Rhodes 193
romance languages 289
Rome, and her subjects 216, 232, 248, 253, 257, 285, 297, 301–304
Rome, position and foundation of 200, 203–205
Romulus 203, 292
Romulus Augustulus 317

S

Sabines 204
Saguntum 236
Salamis 119, 119–121
Samnites 204, 216
Sappho 86, 93
Schliemann 18
science, Greek 92, 154, 186, 192
  Greek 8–9, 172
Scipio Africanus the Younger 243, 246
Scipio, P. Cornelius (Africanus) 238, 239
Scipio, P Cornelius the Elder 237
scriptures in Greek 191, 324
sculpture 143, 147–149, 291, 292
seafaring, in Greece 45, 52, 89
secession of plebeians 210
Seleucids 192, 242, 263

Sempronius 237
senate, Roman 205, 209, 212, 247, 251, 259, 261, 271, 277, 309
Sentinum 216
Septuagint 191, 324
Sertorius 261
ships, Greek 89
Sicily 54, 127, 157, 163, 200, 231, 232
slaves, in Greece 85
slaves, in Rome 221, 245, 261
Social War 257
Socrates 171
Solon 77, 82, 83, 97
sophists 157, 171, 265
Sophocles 151
Spain 229, 235, 238, 239, 241, 261, 272, 304, 316
Sparta
  foundation of 36, 63
Spartan character 65, 160
Spartan discipline 64
Spartan government 65
Sphacteria 161
Stoics 194
Sulla 258, 259
Syracuse 48, 127, 163, 192, 232
Syria 184, 192, 241, 242, 263

T

Tacitus 295
Tarentum 217
Tarquin 206
temples 89, 90, 142, 147, 222
Terence 246
Teutons 255, 311, 315, 318
Thales 92, 93, 154
Thebes 126, 177, 179, 183
Themistocles 112, 113, 115, 120, 121, 132
Thermopylae 115, 119
Theseus 11–12, 15, 69
Thucydides 151, 153
Tiberius 285
Ticinus 237
Timgad 305
Tiryns 21, 36, 125
Titus 287
Trajan 289, 324
Trasimene 237
tribunes 211, 252, 259
Triumvirate, First 263, 269
Triumvirate, Second 275
Trojan War 26, 39
Troy 26, 28
Twelve Tables 211

tyranny 60

U

Umbrians 204, 215
unity of Greeks 51, 57, 95, 111, 125, 137, 159, 177, 178, 181, 189, 200

V

Vandals 316
Varus 282
Veii 215
Venus 222
Vespasian 287, 309
Vesta 222
Virgil 282, 292, 295
Volsci 215

W

warfare, and army organization 28, 88, 105, 141, 178, 180, 230, 256, 305, 311
women, status of 43, 85, 86, 138, 221, 224

X

Xenophon 173, 174, 175
Xerxes 111, 115, 119, 121

Z

Zama 239
Zeus 32, 148

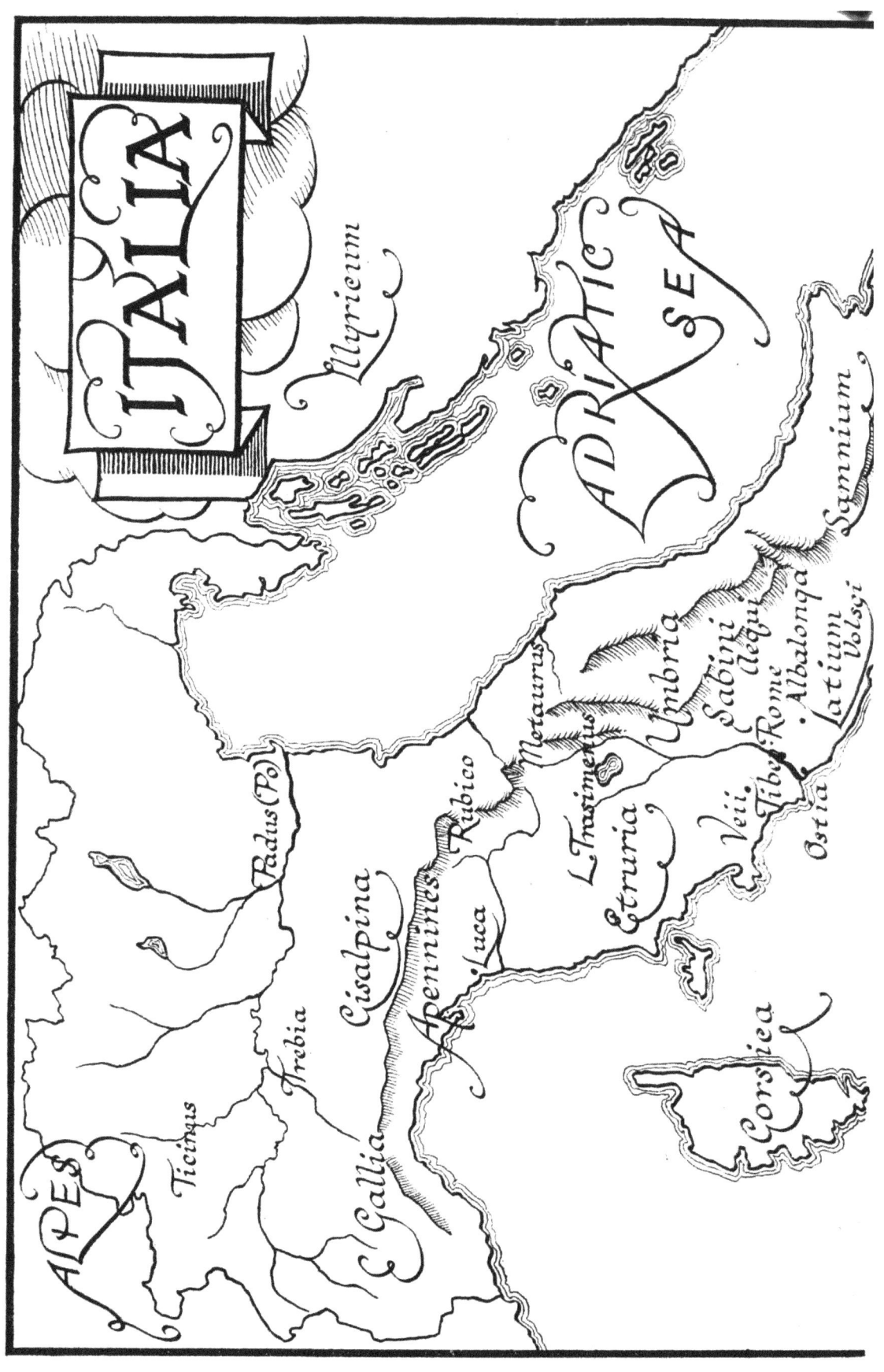

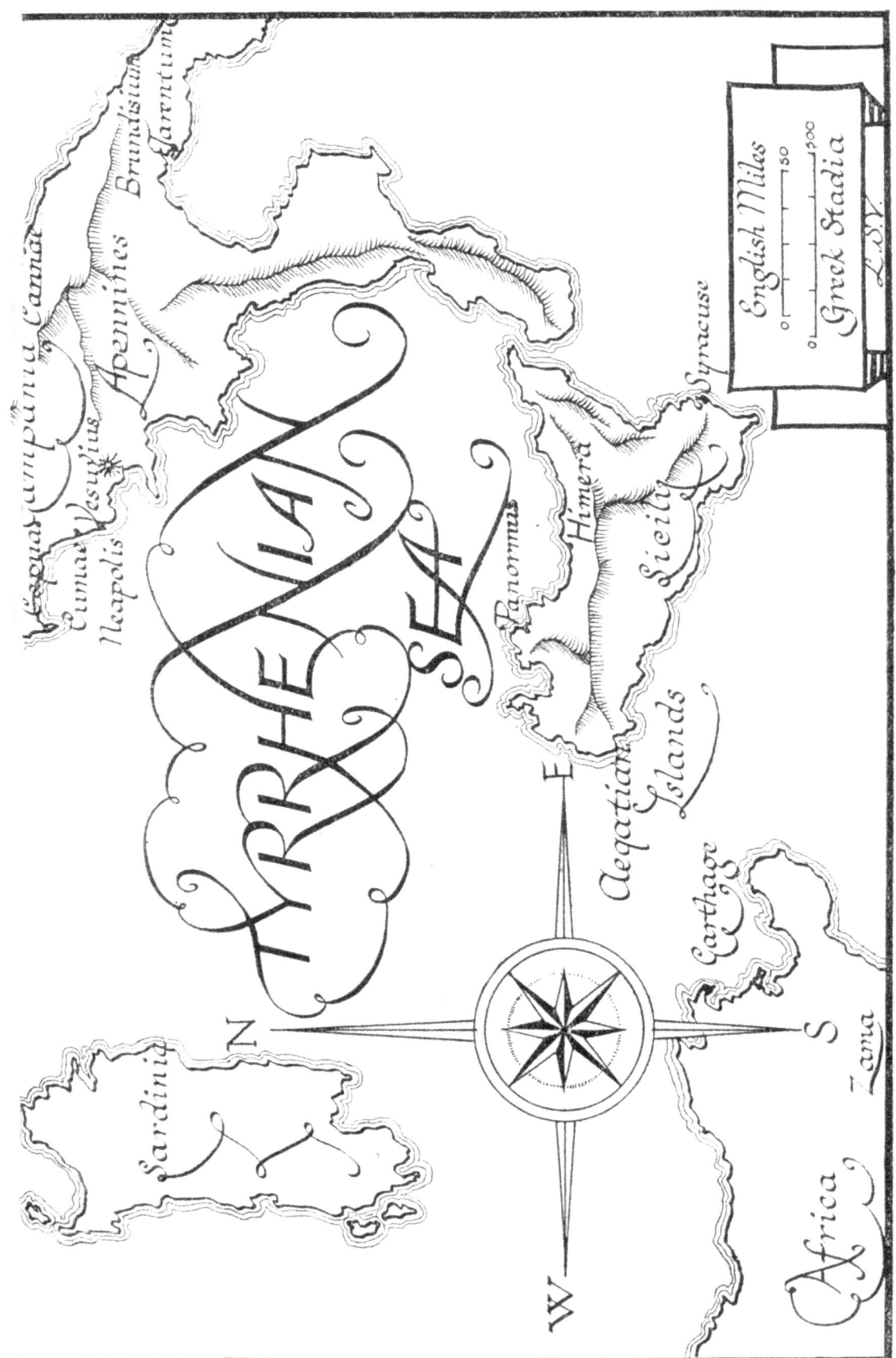

www.ingramcontent.com/pod-product-compliance
Lightning Source LLC
Chambersburg PA
CBHW041409300426
44114CB00028B/2965